RUNNING ON EMPTY

Bush, Congress, and the
Politics of a Bankrupt Government

LAWRENCE J. HAAS

BUSINESS ONE IRWIN
HOMEWOOD, IL 60430

Project editor: Jean Roberts
Production manager: Ann Cassady
Jacket designer: Renée Klyczek-Nordstrom
Compositor: Publication Services, Inc.
Typeface: 11/13 Century Schoolbook
Printer: The Book Press, Inc.

Library of Congress Cataloging-in-Publication Data

Haas, Lawrence J.
    Running on empty : Bush, Congress, and the politics of a bankrupt
government / Lawrence J. Haas
        p.   cm.
    ISBN 1–55623–227–6
    1. Budget deficits—Political aspects—United States.   2. United
States—Politics and government—1989–   I. Title.
HJ2052.H37   1990
339.5'23'0973—dc20   90–3224
                                                                              CIP

Printed in the United States of America
1 2 3 4 5 6 7 8 9 0   BP   7 6 5 4 3 2 1 0

**To my parents
with love**

CONTENTS

FOREWORD

by STUART E. EIZENSTAT

Larry Haas, in *Running on Empty*, has done brilliantly what scholarly tomes and endless articles on the budget deficit over the past ten years have failed to do: expose the deficit as primarily a political issue, not an economic one. In the process, he has written a book that explains in lively, interesting prose how policy in Washington is made and sets forth the limitations of our unique democratic system of government in dealing with a long-term problem by painful short-term actions such as raising taxes and cutting popular spending programs.

Running on Empty is full of delicious anecdotes that bring to life the key actors in Washington—from the cautious President Bush and his precocious and enigmatic budget director Dick Darman to the key Democratic leaders in Congress. Here we get behind the scenes to learn of previously unreported meetings between the giants of our nation's Capital in intimate detail, from the dramatic breakfast in Speaker Foley's office in an attempt to break the budget impasse, to the secret collaborative efforts by Bush and Ways and Means Chairman Dan Rostenkowski to work out a plan Republicans and Democrats could support, to OMB

Mr. Eizenstat is a partner in the Washington office of the law firm of Powell, Goldstein, Frazer & Murphy. From 1977 to 1981, he was Assistant to the President for Domestic Affairs and Policy and Executive Director of the White House Domestic Policy Staff. He is also an Adjunct Lecturer at the Kennedy School of Government at Harvard University.

Director Darman's unsuccessful effort to craft the Big Deal to break the back of the deficit with a combination of tax increases, domestic entitlement reductions, and defense cuts.

Mr. Haas has convincingly demonstrated that the budget deficit and how to deal with it—or to avoid dealing with it— has become the overarching public policy issue of the past decade and has cast a cloud over substantive policy-making. Top officials in the executive branch and in Congress bemoan the degree to which policy is driven by budget numbers when numbers should be driven by policy decisions on what is best for the nation. Of course, policy decisions have always had to be made with an eye to their cost and budget impact. But a rapidly growing post–World War II economy and the impact of inflation pushing taxpayers into higher tax brackets provided the luxury of additional revenues to meet the new spending programs. However, sluggish economic growth in the 1970s, the indexation of taxes to prevent bracket creep in the 1981 tax bill, and the catastrophic Reagan deficits in the 1980s put an end to this luxury.

Running on Empty underscores some critically important points about the U.S. government and the way it operates.

First, the budget deficit has been highly politicized and has changed politics in the country profoundly, leading to a historic role reversal for our political parties. For most of the 20th century the Democratic Party became the predominant party by passing popular spending programs to expand health care and income security to the elderly, educational benefits to young adults seeking a college education, housing subsidies to encourage home ownership, urban mass transportation for city dwellers, price supports for farmers, and much more. It fell to the Republican Party to be the naysayers, arguing for balanced budgets and against new spending programs. This as much as anything locked the GOP into its seemingly permanent minority status, as voters preferred to receive new services and never viewed the resulting modest deficits as a problem. Yet by the 1980s Democrats were the born-again budget balancers, and a Republican president disregarded the red ink.

Something vitally important was happening in the country, and Democrats were slow to grasp it. As Haas cogently points out, Americans have always been suspicious of taxes, even though we are one of the lowest taxed major nations in the world. After all, the American Revolution was born out of a tax revolt, albeit from a government over which the people felt they had no control. In our era Proposition 13, a 1978 California referendum passed by the voters in our country's most populous state, crystallized a growing antitax mood in the nation. Proposition 13 did more than roll back property taxes in California. Its effects spread like a prairie fire across the country, leading to similar actions in states as far away and as politically different as Massachusetts, and hit Washington with an enormous impact when I was in the White House.

Beginning even earlier, at the end of the Johnson administration, a massive public disillusionment with government set in, fed in part by the overly expansive promise of President Johnson's Great Society to end all poverty. In fact, the Great Society and the War on Poverty were remarkably successful in a short period of time. Hunger was virtually ended. The fear of medical bankruptcy for the elderly was diminished. The poverty rate dropped by about 50 percent. But to many Americans, urban riots were the lasting symbol of the era. As economic growth vastly expanded the American middle class, more and more Americans saw themselves not as consumers of the government services that had helped them reach their new status, but as taxpayers paying taxes for others—who seemed not to appreciate it.

Jimmy Carter, whom I served in the White House, recognized from the outset of his presidency that the image of Democrats as profligate spenders was, as he frequently referred to it in meetings with the Democratic leadership on Capitol Hill, an albatross around the party's neck. It is clear that in the conservative mood of the 1970s only a moderate Democrat like Carter stood a prayer of being elected. It is not coincidental that, with the exception of George Wallace, Carter was the most conservative of the Democrats seeking the nomination in 1976.

The antitax and antigovernment mood of the public coalesced in the 1980 election. Former Republican Congressman, now HUD Secretary, Jack Kemp, and later Ronald Reagan, sensed this new mood. They also realized that if the Republican Party was going to be competitive with Democrats, it had to shed its Scrooge-like image of belt-tightening and budget austerity. So was born, with intellectual support from Arthur Laffer, Jude Wanniski, and others, supply-side economics. Whatever we think of supply-side economics—and I think little of it—it had profound political implications. In effect, on its fiscal side, it proposed to substitute politically popular tax cuts, which primarily benefited upper-middle- and upper-income Americans, for Democratic spending programs, which primarily benefited middle-income, working-class, and low-income Americans. And it promised—a promise long since broken—that tax cuts would actually increase revenue and lower the budget deficit, not cause it to hemorrhage. This began the historic transformation of the two great political parties. It was a Democratic president, Carter, who urged austerity to fight the stagflation in the 1980 election and who looked askance at tax cuts at a time of growing budget deficits. And it was the Republican presidential nominee, Reagan, who was the "swinger," offering tax cuts as the answer to grow our way out of the deficit.

Reaganomics—that combination of across-the-board tax cuts, huge defense increases, and domestic reductions passed by Congress in 1981 in the full flush of President Reagan's popularity—created massive triple-digit budget deficits beyond anything ever witnessed in the United States. Democrats were now the ones arguing for restraint and for tax increases to stanch the budget hemorrhage.

Whether or not Reagan in some Machiavellian way consciously proposed policies that would lead to a deficit massive enough to deter Democrats from creating new, popular domestic social initiatives—something I doubt, given the risks that the deficit would juice up interest rates and abort the economic recovery central to the political survival of the Reagan presidency—it is certain that the budget deficit was at most a secondary concern for him. Conservative populism had replaced fiscal austerity as the centerpiece of Republican domestic philosophy. And, remarkably, budget balancing replaced social spending as the backbone of Democratic concerns.

This political shift was dramatized by the 1984 presidential election. Democratic nominee Walter Mondale made deficit reduction, to be achieved in part by higher taxes, a centerpiece in his general election campaign, rejecting the counsel of many of his advisors to concentrate instead on tax reform, as proposed by Senator Bill Bradley and Congressman Dick Gephardt. Reagan, on the other hand, gave short shrift to the record deficits over which he presided, embraced tax reform, and blasted Mondale's proposed tax increases.

Reagan's favorite refrain against the Democrats throughout his presidency was "tax and spend." This reinforced the public's suspicion that the additional taxes it was being asked to cough up would go not for deficit reduction, but for new social spending. Ironically, as Haas points out, Reagan signed "more than a dozen tax increases into law during his presidency, including sizable ones in 1982 and 1984 to cut the deficit and a big one in 1983 to help rescue Social Security." By contrast, Carter signed no income tax increases into law. Nevertheless, Reagan was adroit enough to shift the blame for tax rises to the congressional Democrats. As Haas notes, "However many he signed, though, nobody doubted his antipathy toward them."

George Bush further made taxes the basic division between the two parties in his 1988 presidential campaign. His dramatic statement, "Read My Lips, No New Taxes," was one of the defining events in the race. Remarkably, the deficit was barely an issue. Democratic nominee Governor Michael Dukakis, recognizing the beating Mr. Mondale had taken four years earlier, refused to urge new taxes to close the deficit, relying instead on collecting the billions of dollars in unpaid taxes.

With social issues such as abortion becoming less potent for Republicans and anti-Communism waning as an issue with the revolutionary developments in Eastern Europe, opposition to tax increases has become the principal glue holding the Bush Republican coalition together—the deficit be damned! As Haas cogently notes, any attempt by the Bush administration to reach a deficit reduction deal with the Democrats including new taxes is resisted by conservative young House Republicans who act as the "conscience" for the president on taxes.

There is no better evidence of the complete polarization caused by the budget deficit than the fate of the bipartisan commission, which was created by Congress in late 1987 following the stock market crash to develop a bipartisan plan to tackle the deficit. The distinguished Democrats and Republicans appointed by congressional leaders treaded water until the presidential election, following which President-elect Bush appointed members committed to follow his no-new-taxes policy. The commission passed into oblivion.

In 1983 a similar commission was established under the chairmanship of Alan Greenspan to deal with the funding crisis of the Social Security system. There, because of Americans' interest in a stable Social Security system for their own retirements, a solution was found that combined benefit reductions and tax increases. But the intense politicization of the deficit prevented a similar compromise on that problem.

Haas recounts with great care and attention to detail, in Chapters 6 to 9 of *Running on Empty*, the political maneuvering to get the Big Deal on the deficit. He demonstrates that the key budgeteers, Darman, Senator Jim Sasser, and Congressman Leon Panetta, despite their genuine desire to cut the Gordian knot on the deficit, were limited by the political maneuvering of White House leaders and others who would rather avoid the tough decisions and stake out political positions. Here we learn of the behind-the-scenes efforts to reach the Big Deal, which, like the brass ring, seems always to be tantalizingly just beyond the grasp of the key administration and congressional leaders.

A second lesson drawn by *Running on Empty* is the enormous difficulty the American political system has in exacting short-term sacrifices from the public to achieve long-term gains—the inability to face up to problems that seem to present no immediate, short-term crisis. I confronted this reality with Carter's 1977 energy program, a bold and comprehensive effort to put into place a long-term plan to reduce our dependence on foreign oil, but proposed at a time of declining real energy prices and adequate supplies of energy. Without a crisis, the plan languished despite heroic efforts by the president and House Speaker Tip O'Neill and was decimated by interest groups opposed to one or another of its parts. The budget deficit of the 1980s and 1990s is another such dilemma.

A leading Democratic economist joked with me shortly after Reagan proposed his huge 1981 across-the-board tax cut and enormous defense spending increases that if the program worked, "it would set back the economic profession by 50 years," because of the large deficits, rising interest rates, and higher inflation it should cause. In fact, to the average American, the Reagan program worked, despite the incredible deficits it spawned.

It is a myth that Reagan's popularity is mostly due to his charisma, charm, and communication ability. He had all of this in his first two years in office, yet his popularity, because of the 1982 recession, was lower at the halfway point of his presidency than Carter's at a comparable time. Reagan's popularity was powered by the economic recovery that began at the end of 1982 and lasted throughout his term. Indeed, the remarkable expansion that continued through President Bush's first year and a half in office is the foundation of his popularity.

As Haas discusses, those economic experts who month after month, like Chicken Little, predicted the economic sky would fall were wrong. The one short-term crisis, the 1987 stock market crash, was not directly occasioned by the deficit, although it did produce the only significant bipartisan effort of the 1980s to partially close the yawning budget gap.

In fact, the huge deficits, so long decried by Republicans, spurred the recovery. Reagan's budget in 1983, the first year of the recovery, noted that the structural or high-employment deficit—which would exist even with full employment and without a recession—would be a very high 4.7 percent of the estimated 1983 GNP. The budget deficit was a principal ingredient in the 6 percent rise in real GNP between the fourth quarter of 1982 and the first quarter of 1983, the beginning of the recovery. The old Keynesian prescription long endorsed by Democrats—to stimulate the private economy by a public deficit—worked again. So much for supply-side economics. Unemployment dropped to under 6 percent.

Nor did the Reagan deficits of $150 billion to over $200 billion cause higher inflation and interest rates as predicted; both of those measures fell dramatically from the double-digit levels with which we in the Carter administration left in 1981. The dollar strengthened rather than weakened in the face of record deficits, so much so that the Plaza Accords of 1985, negotiated by then–Secretary of the Treasury James Baker, were a concerted effort by the major industrial democracies to reduce the value of the dollar.

Economic "mavens" did not count on the willingness of foreign investors to purchase the Reagan debt and to save us from financing our budget deficit out of our puny domestic savings pool or by printing more money, a sure prescription for inflation.

The budget deficits have had a real and negative impact, but it is a subtle, corrosive, long-term impact that Americans do not feel today. In the absence of public pressure, neither the administration nor members of Congress have the political will or the incentive to impose short-term pain on voters—via new taxes and cuts in popular programs—to achieve the long-term benefits of deficit reduction. Congress is a remarkably democratic institution, which is highly responsive to public opinion. This is both its great strength and its abiding weakness, for Congress, particularly in the absence of presidential leadership, simply will not tackle long-term problems that have not yet aroused the American populace.

Even today, polls regularly show that the American people would overwhelmingly prefer to use whatever "peace dividend" will result from the reduced national security threat from the Warsaw Pact and the Soviet Union for new social spending than for deficit reduction. There is no more boring issue to Americans than the budget deficit, which appears to have no real impact on their daily lives and which consequently ranks low in their order of major priorities, well below crime, drug control, and education. Our Carter administration was criticized when it ran modest deficits in the $30 to $50 billion range. Now there is barely a public murmur or a financial market reaction to far larger deficits.

In fact, the deficit does matter. We are passing on to our children a terrible burden of debt, which is the greatest single impediment to higher productivity, increased real incomes, and an improved ability to compete abroad.

- During the Reagan decade of the 1980s, the national debt, which had taken 200 years under 40 American presidents to accumulate, more than doubled.
- The budget deficit has transformed us in only one decade from the world's largest creditor to the globe's biggest debtor nation, owing more to foreigners than Argentina, Brazil, and Mexico combined.
- The U.S. dependence on foreign investment and the "buying up of America" by foreigners, which has so many Americans and members of Congress upset, is a direct consequence of our budget deficit. Since we have such a low private American savings pool to finance our deficit, we have had to borrow from abroad. We now depend on foreign financing for roughly one of every three dollars we use to finance our debt.
- Household incomes adjusted for inflation have been stagnant since 1973. A recent study showed that from the end of World War II through 1973 average family income more than doubled, from $16,000 to $33,000 in today's dollars. But since 1973 the average family's household income has remained stagnant—only $500 more than 15 years ago, even though we have far more two-earner families today. In effect, many families need two earners to make in real terms what one could earn a decade and a half ago. A study released this year by the Bureau of Labor Statistics showed that real earnings for most Americans fell during the 1980s, the second consecutive decade of loss.
- The budget deficit has led to high *real* interest rates and a strong dollar, which has helped create a massive trade deficit. But it has also helped produce the remarkable situation that U.S. workers, who had higher wages in dollar terms than their Japanese, German, French, and Italian counterparts in 1985, now have lower wages.

But none of these facts has affected the standard of living of the American people dramatically enough to produce the public pressure needed to move the political system. Haas has catalogued with a fine reporter's eye and pen the aborted efforts in the first year of the Bush administration to achieve a political consensus on the deficit absent a perceived crisis.

After reading *Running on Empty*, no one can doubt that the essential difficulty with the deficit is political. With President Ford's domestic advisor, Jim Cannon, I codirected the American Agenda, a bipartisan project chaired by former Presidents Ford and Carter. Our report was presented in person to Bush shortly after his election. The two former presidents, with the assistance of Republican and Democratic experts, like Paul O'Neill (now CEO of Alcoa) and Alice Rivlin (former head of the Congressional Budget Office and now with the Brookings Institution), devised a five-year plan to balance the budget—and provide additional resources for high-priority domestic investments. By holding defense even with inflation, moderating the cost-of-living adjustments for Social Security and federal retirement programs, better controlling Medicare costs—and raising excise taxes on cigarettes, liquor, and oil by $13 billion annually—the goal can be achieved. This is certainly not a draconian program. Indeed, a French official recently commented that it was hard to take seriously a problem that could be solved by a 50-cent-per-gallon gas tax. A recent, commendable package put forward by Rostenkowski follows a similar blueprint. But there is no real indication that it will not be politics as usual from the administration on the Rostenkowski deficit reduction plan.

The third and perhaps most important message of this dramatic book is that the budget deficit has perverted government decision making and prevented us from addressing in a forthright way the problems facing the country.

The deficit has led the country to shorten its vision and to deceive itself on budget numbers to stay within the budget constraints of the Gramm-Rudman-Hollings Act.

The discussion in Chapter 5 of *Running on Empty* of the savings-and-loan bailout underscores these points as well as they have been made anywhere. As Haas recounts, rather than address the issue directly and put the cost on the budget, a device was employed to create a semipublic corporation to borrow the money "off the budget," even though that will end up costing the American people more in the long run.

Although Darman has tried to correct the practice, the early part of the Reagan administration employed shameless duplicity in budget making. For example, absurdly high economic growth assumptions were included with the Reagan budgets to mask the real size of the deficit. Budget director David Stockman's mea culpa memoirs catalogue the outrageous deceits perpetrated on the American people— something no one has done before or since on budget matters in the name of an American president.

Because Gramm-Rudman-Hollings requires only a forecast of the deficit for the forthcoming fiscal year, the actual deficit by year end has regularly exceeded the projection that the deficit will be within the targets required.

But even more damaging to the long-term health of the country is the degree to which the deficit has made all of us in Washington myopic, afraid to directly address the mounting social and economic problems of the nation.

As Carter's chief domestic policy advisor, of course, I always had to be mindful of the budgetary impact of our domestic initiatives. The problem became more severe in our last two years as the economy deteriorated and the deficit grew. But during the Reagan years and into Bush's first year the sheer size of the deficit has made it virtually the only domestic issue, dominating all other issues and limiting the capacity of our great nation to be a leader abroad and at home.

It is not coincidental that in the Reagan era and now in 1990 the dominant domestic advisors around the presidents have been the budget directors and not the domestic policy advisors.

Democracy is breaking out all over the world. The fledgling democracies of the Philippines, Central America, and Eastern Europe desperately need support to make the transformation from authoritarian or totalitarian regimes to democratic ones and to successfully navigate the equally traumatic evolution from state-run to open, free-market economies. Yet Bush, as Haas points out, is left to propose tiny amounts of aid and to look to Japan and Western Europe for more substantial assistance. Japan recently extended more money for export financing to two Eastern European nations on the road to democracy than the United States Export-Import Bank has in its budget for the entire world.

We have enormous future obligations if we are to be everything we should be as a nation. Tens of billions of dollars will be needed to clean up the nuclear waste around the U.S. government's own nuclear facilities and to accelerate the clean-up of our toxic wastes. America's infrastructure of bridges, roads, and highways is in a sad state of disrepair. More children grow up in poverty today than 10 years ago—or 20 years ago. We stand near the bottom of industrial democracies in literacy, math, science, and foreign language capacity; and near the top in low-birth-weight children and infant mortality. Each year a half-million teenagers fail to finish high school and enter the work force without adequate skills to be fully self-sufficient. Some 31 million working Americans and their families have no public or private health insurance. Drugs have infiltrated every crevice of America and have turned some urban neighborhoods into battle zones.

The budget deficit exemplifies our inability to tackle these problems head-on, which is necessary if all of us are to enjoy a prosperous, healthy, safe nation. It punctuates our willingness to present a legacy of debt and inevitably stunted living standards to our children.

This is the ultimate statement of *Running on Empty*, a statement of lost opportunities. The budget deficit has forced us to speak loudly and carry a small stick, to loudly proclaim our intention to address festering problems we are not willing to adequately address. As Haas points out, it is not, as Bush said in his inaugural, that "we have more will than wallet." Rather it is that we lack the will needed to pay for what needs to be done to make this a better country.

Haas has given us a compelling story of the American political system's inability to deal with the overriding issue of the day, the budget deficit, and at the same time told us much about our government and its leaders. In this he has performed a signal service.

PREFACE

In December 1989, the *Miami Herald* took a rather unusual step in promoting a long cover story in its Sunday magazine about the budget deficit. Apparently worried that hardly anyone would read it, the newspaper illustrated the article not with dry charts and graphs, but with tantalizing photographs of a sexy brunette in lingerie. In one, she hugs a picture of President Reagan and smiles widely, as if satisfied moments earlier by the man on a bed behind her. In another, she lies on her stomach and stares out pensively as her mate lies beside her, resting his head on her right shoulder. "How is the national debt like a cheap affair?" the article asks below a headline that blares **Scandal.** "One: It feels good—for the moment. Two: Once you start, it's hard to stop. Three: Your children will hate you for it."[1]

The newspaper could be forgiven for its appeal to the prurient interest. The deficit can, indeed, be a boring subject for discussion, one involving numbers too large to comprehend and concepts not easy to grasp. Nor have the nation's leaders and journalists made the issue any more titillating. Since the deficit exploded in size in the 1980s, they have debated its effects almost solely in economic terms. Would the

---

[1] Joel Achenbach, "Scandal," *Miami Herald*, Dec. 3, 1989, p. 9.

deficit, they ask, stunt economic growth or bring on a recession? Would it bring a new round of soaring inflation? Or higher interest rates?

But to view the deficit in economic terms alone is to miss half of the story—surely the more interesting half, probably the more important half. This book concerns that other half, the *political* half. My thesis is this: Washington—the federal government—does not work very well these days, largely because of the deficit. It hangs like a cloud over nearly all federal activity, sharply limiting the options of America's leaders as they confront national needs. It has turned Washington into a city where penny-pinching, frivolous, even irrational decision making is the norm, not the exception. Unwilling to balance the nation's books—for that would prompt tough choices about what taxes to raise and what spending to cut—officials have decided to address huge needs with piddling sums of money.

Although many of the nation's leaders would like to solve the deficit problem, they have little political incentive to do so. Voters in recent years have voiced support for a balanced budget, but rejected the very steps required to achieve one. In the absence of an economic crisis for which the deficit can be blamed, they are not likely to change their minds. America's leaders, unwilling to jeopardize their own reelections, act in concert with public opinion; they promise to eliminate the deficit, but they shun the tax hikes and spending cuts needed to do so.

To illustrate all this, I chose to write about the Washington of 1989, an appropriate subject for several reasons. It was President Bush's first year in the White House and, if history is any guide, likely to be among his most active. It was also a year to which many people in Washington were looking forward, because they hoped a new president and Congress would reach a deficit-cutting deal to solve the problem for good. That they did not was unfortunate, but no less fascinating. By the end of 1989, the nation's leaders had made little headway on the deficit, which continued to impose perverse incentives on all policy making. The political harm that the deficit caused grew only more obvious.

Running on Empty is really two books with one general theme: the politics of bankrupt government in today's Washington. It is, first of all, a story of how the White House and Congress sought unsuccessfully to craft a "Big Deal" that would solve the deficit problem; of how Bush's promise not to raise taxes, prompting his demand to delay the Big Deal until late 1989, presented obstacles that the parties could not overcome; of how, in essence, a handful of bright, well-meaning individuals could not bring a Republican president and a Democrat-controlled Congress together in the face of overriding political disputes and nasty confrontations on particular issues.

It is also a story of how Washington addresses national needs in an era of huge deficits; of how America's leaders ignore the problems about which there is no public outcry and respond to those for which there is with inadequate or token gestures; of how they choose one policy over another not because they want to, but because they cannot afford the more worthwhile one; of how they focus on the near term (the next election, the next budget, and so on) to the detriment of the future; and, most of all, of how they express interest in cutting the deficit but will subordinate that desire to the more politically palatable one of cutting taxes or raising spending for the constituents back home who decide whether or not they hold onto their jobs.

In 1989, as in most recent years, the deficit attracted the attention, tested the nerves, and ignited the tempers of more key leaders than did any other issue. They struggled to cut it and to comply with Gramm-Rudman, that mischievous contraption of a law that was supposed to force Washington to gradually balance its books but that really has not. In the end, Bush and Congress could not overcome their political differences to make much progress. As Bush addressed a joint session of Congress in early 1989 to present his fiscal 1990 budget proposals, the Congressional Budget Office (CBO) projected that the deficit would stay above $120 billion for at least several more years unless Washington did something about it. When Congress adjourned just before Thanksgiving, that projection had hardly changed.

This is not to say that Bush and Congress left town with no achievements in hand. They accomplished a few things and began a few more. But each time, the deficit limited the options and shaped the outcomes:

- When Washington faced a huge financial problem with failing savings and loan institutions, it borrowed $50 billion rather than raise taxes or cut spending from its cash-starved budget. In doing so, it imposed at least $150 billion in interest costs on taxpayers over the next three decades. To feign compliance with Gramm-Rudman, it circumvented the deficit targets in the most shameless way, choosing to not even record $30 billion of the $50 billion in borrowed funds anywhere in the budget.
- When Washington needed to raise $5.3 billion in taxes for fiscal 1990, it seemed ready to *cut* the tax rate on capital gains until Senate Majority Leader George J. Mitchell rallied enough Democrats in opposition. A tax cut like that, of course, probably would have cost Washington billions in lost revenue down the road, making the deficit even bigger. But it also would have brought a quick infusion of money as investors rushed to take advantage of a lower rate by cashing in assets. In that way, it would have helped officials meet Gramm-Rudman's deficit target for 1990.
- When Washington considered the needs of working-class Americans, it opted to raise the minimum wage rather than to expand the highly regarded Earned Income Tax Credit (EITC). Although the minimum wage was far less popular than the EITC, an increase in the former would not cost the government anything. Not only could Washington not afford to expand the EITC, but its deficit troubles also helped block child care legislation even though child care was a major issue in the 1988 presidential campaign.

It is no surprise that the deficit has become America's biggest political problem. Budgeting, after all, is a quintessentially political exercise. If politics is, as Harold D. Lasswell said in his classic book of 1936, "who gets what, when, how," then the budget provides the answer.[2] Washington allocates resources to various groups: age groups, income groups, geographic groups, interest groups, and so on. As they tried to cut the deficit, the nation's leaders decided who should pay: rich and not-so-rich taxpayers, defense contractors, Social Security recipients, Medicare providers, middle-income families with college students, the poor who get Food Stamps and Medicaid, and others. Who wins? Who loses? These are the most basic of political questions.

What *is* surprising, though, is how one problem has brought such sweeping change to Washington. Cultures are shaped at least partly by the problems they face. The deficit, Washington's biggest problem, has shaped its own culture—a culture that influences how America's leaders think, talk, and act. It is a culture of political cowardliness, constraint, and irrationality, one in which the White House and Congress pretend to address the nation's problems but take steps that are minimal, irrelevant, or counterproductive. Unwilling to do what's needed to solve the deficit problem, they are like mice on a treadmill, expending lots of energy but unable to usefully deploy the machinery of government.

■　　　■　　　■　　　■

Others who have expended a fair share of energy, and in the most unselfish way, are the public officials, lawmakers, staffers, policy experts, journalists, and others who have helped me understand the complicated issues, politics, and mores of Washington. Some did so strictly for this book. Others have offered continuous help since I began to write about budget and tax issues in early 1987 for *National Journal*. This book would not have been possible without their help. I thank them.

---

[2] Harold D. Lasswell, *Politics: Who Gets What, When, How* (New York: McGraw-Hill, 1936).

In particular, several of the major figures in this book gave generously of their time to explain their thinking at various stages of 1989. Among them are Richard G. Darman, Pete V. Domenici, Bill Frenzel, Leon E. Panetta, Dan Rostenkowski, and Jim Sasser. Members of Congress whose conversations with me over the last year or earlier were of great help include Michael Andrews, Beryl Anthony, Jr., Bill Archer, Les AuCoin, Lloyd M. Bentsen, Rudy Boschwitz, Kent Conrad, Silvio O. Conte, Thomas A. Daschle, Tom DeLay, Mickey Edwards, Victor H. Fazio, Thomas S. Foley, Willis D. Gradison, Jr., Phil Gramm, William H. Gray III, Mark O. Hatfield, John Heinz, Ed Jenkins, Nancy L. Johnson, John R. Kasich, Barbara B. Kennelly, John J. LaFalce, Norman F. Lent, Sander Levin, Jerry Lewis, Lynn Martin, Robert T. Matsui, Robert H. Michel, George J. Mitchell, Bruce A. Morrison, Mary Rose Oakar, Bob Packwood, Donald J. Pease, Timothy J. Penny, Ralph Regula, Charles S. Robb, Martin O. Sabo, Charles Schumer, Jim Slattery, Charles W. Stenholm, Thomas J. Tauke, William M. Thomas, Jamie L. Whitten, and Pat Williams.

Among the budget and tax experts upon whom I have relied heavily are Henry J. Aaron, Wendell Belew, Stephen E. Bell, Mark A. Bloomfield, Barry P. Bosworth, John F. Cogan, Stanley E. Collender, Carol G. Cox, Peter J. Davis, Jr., John C. Dill, Gail Fosler, Edward M. Gramlich, Robert Greenstein, Steven I. Hofman, Darwin G. Johnson, John H. Makin, David G. Mathiasen, Victor J. Miller, Joseph J. Minarik, William A. Niskanen, Ellen Nissenbaum, Nell Payne, Rudolph G. Penner, Patricia A. Quealy, Robert D. Reischauer, Alice M. Rivlin, Susan C. Simon, Charls E. Walker, and John C. Weicher. Apologies to those whom I have forgotten.

The unsung-hero awards go to those whose names you will not find here. They are the dedicated staff members in the White House, Office of Management and Budget, executive departments, Congress, and such agencies as the Congressional Budget Office and General Accounting Office. Some are friends, others just business contacts. Each has given me hours of their time to discuss issues of pending importance. They toil, often day and night, in anonymity, keeping the government running while their bosses—the nation's elected and appointed officials—accept credit for what goes right and often shift blame to the staff for what does not. Because these staff members have always spoken with me on the condition that I not use their names, I continue to respect their wishes. But I thank them for everything they have done for me.

Also unsung, except for the few quoted in this book, are my colleagues at *National Journal,* the finest collection of journalists I have ever worked with. They have taught me a great deal about their areas of expertise and about writing. And in the weeks before this manuscript was completed, they have had to endure my constant requests for their help as I checked facts. Past and present colleagues include James A. Barnes, Ronald Brownstein, Richard E. Cohen, Dick Kirschten, Julie Kosterlitz, Margaret E. Kriz, Christopher Madison, Carol Matlack, W. John Moore, David C. Morrison, Jonathan Rauch, Burt Solomon, Rochelle L. Stanfield, Paul Starobin, Bruce Stokes, Kirk Victor, and David L. Wilson. Publisher John Fox Sullivan and editor Richard S. Frank gave me the confidence to write this book, first by hiring me and then by encouraging me to pursue it. Also at *National Journal,* a special thank you to librarian Rose Pool and her assistant, Judith Proctor, not only for putting up with my endless requests for material but for granting them cheerfully. My editor at Business One Irwin, Jim Childs, has been a delight to work with.

The above-and-beyond-the-call-of-duty awards go to Ronald S. Boster, Stanley E. Collender, Richard E. Cohen, John C. Dill, Jeffrey R. Levey, Victor J. Miller, and Joseph J. Minarik, each of whom read parts of one, and in some cases two, drafts of this book and provided very helpful suggestions. They were honest enough to note that some material I liked was more appropriate for the cutting room floor than for these pages. Whatever value this book has is largely due to their input. As much as I would like to share the blame for its faults, I will reserve that to myself.

Finally, a personal word: Not until I began this project did I truly understand the thanks that authors always reserve for their spouses. My wife, Marjorie Segel Haas, deserves the biggest one of all. Although this book occupied the time of a second full-time job, she provided me with warm, loving support throughout the nearly two years of its gestation. It could not have been completed without her. I can never repay the debt of gratitude that I owe Marjie. But I shall forever try.

LAWRENCE J. HAAS

CHAPTER ONE

GOVERNMENT AT ITS WORST

"To all Americans, as the leader of a proud and free people, I address this question," Corazon Aquino, the Philippines' new president, told a joint session of Congress on September 18, 1986, as she asked the United States to help her fledgling democracy. "Has there been a greater test of national commitment to the ideals you hold dear than that my people have gone through? You have spent many lives and much treasure to bring freedom to many lands that were reluctant to receive it. And here you have a people who won it by themselves and need only the help to preserve it.... Today, I say, join us, America, as we build a new home for democracy, another haven for the oppressed, so it may stand as a shining testament of our two nations' commitment to freedom."

It was a moment of high political drama. The petite, bespectacled Aquino, who rode to power seven months earlier on a wave of public indignation against the brutal Marcos dictatorship, had flown around the world to plead her case in Washington, where leaders of the world's richest country allocate resources to a multitude of domestic and foreign interests. Jim Wright, a Texas Democrat who was then the House majority leader, marked the occasion by distributing hundreds of yellow roses so that his colleagues could be-

1

deck themselves in Aquino's trademark color. Some lawmakers wore yellow ties, sweaters, and shirts as well. Secretary of State George P. Shultz, one of several White House officials on hand, sported a yellow shirt and hankerchief. If any foreign aid request seemed meritorious, surely Aquino's did. Not only was she trying to move her nation from dictatorship to sustained democracy, but she was also fighting a growing Communist insurgency. America's national interest demanded that she succeed.

But the United States, with its huge budget deficit, was paralyzed to do much more than wish her well. "She needs help and she deserves help and it's in our interest to help," Shultz had told a group of business leaders a day earlier, "and we've got ourselves in a position where we can't do it. We don't have the money."[1] Aquino got $200 million for her efforts, a piddling sum at a time when Washington was spending $1 trillion a year on domestic, defense, and foreign programs. Even that came only after a struggle. Although the House voted for the money on the day she spoke, the Senate twice turned it down before approving it two weeks later. Philippine officials, reacting bitterly to the Senate's initial position, threatened to retaliate when a pact between the nations involving two American bases came up for renewal in 1991.

Shultz was not alone in his frustration. In the late 1980s, more of Washington's top officials came to share his dismay as the nation seemed less able to grasp new opportunities or to pursue its interests here and abroad. When Solidarity leader Lech Walesa asked the United States in early 1989 for $10 billion to rebuild Poland's economy as his country moved toward democracy, Bush offered a measly $115 million. When Bush proclaimed a "war" on drugs in September 1989, he asked Congress to spend just $716 million more—less than 0.1 percent of the budget—than he had requested to that point. When he and Congress debated America's child-care needs, they haggled over legislation that called for less spending than the $2.1 billion bill President Nixon had vetoed in 1971—before people worried about a child-care crisis. (In inflation-adjusted dollars, the legislation was worth *much* less.) Time after time, Washington could not find adequate funds to address the problems at hand.

"Uncle Sam is running on empty," Sen. Ernest F. Hollings, a South Carolina Democrat, wrote in the *Washington Post* in April 1989:

> To serve in Washington today is to witness the federal government at its worst. We on Capitol Hill preen as we introduce empty 'sense of the Senate' resolutions, sham budgets, and hollow bills and then expect to get a good government award for our efforts.... Meanwhile, under George Bush as under Ronald Reagan, the hollowing out of the federal government continues apace. Profound social problems—the pathologies of the underclass, a failing education system, declining competitiveness—are not addressed in any meaningful way whatsoever. Our government has charted a course of drift, disinvestment and decline.[2]

It was a sweeping indictment, but not an overstated one. Since the deficit soared to mind-boggling heights in the early 1980s, it has warped the art of governing in Washington, constrained America's leaders, and, in a sense, reduced the hopes and aspirations of those they serve. The government is locked in place, its leaders engulfed by this all-encompassing problem, unable to do much else because of it. Pressured by their constituents and by powerful interest groups to protect existing programs and not raise taxes, the nation's leaders lack the means to confront America's emerging challenges in a significant way.

■　　　■　　　■　　　■

"In my opinion, talk, thought, and action about the budget in the government today is a scandal," Herbert Stein, the chairman of Nixon's Council of Economic Advisors, told the House Budget Committee in late 1989. A few days earlier, drug czar William J. Bennett had reportedly explained why he would temper his request for antidrug funds by saying, "I live in the real world." Referring to Bennett, Stein added, "But the opposite is true. He and the rest of us are living in an unreal world, a world in which policy is determined by artificial, self-imposed constraints."

Unreal? Indeed. The nation had not suddenly grown poor. It remained the world's richest, with its people enjoying the highest standard of living. But with its leaders unwilling to eliminate the deficit, Washington pleaded poverty. "We have more will than wallet," Bush said in his inaugural address. But the president had it backwards, as columnist George F. Will pointed out. We had more wallet than will—that is, more money in our economy than we were using wisely, more financial resources than we were willing to tap. What we did *not* have were elected officials who were politically brave enough to balance the budget so that they could, in turn, make suitable federal investments in child care, education, housing, antidrug efforts, and a slew of other areas.

It is here that the economic and political sides of the deficit story come together. Obviously, if the nation's leaders did not view the deficit as economically harmful, they would not feel compelled to control it. Today's deficit of $150 billion or so would grow to $250 billion or more. Indeed, the deficit would have no conceivable limit. Only because they worry that, at some point, the nation will pay the price for its fiscal profligacy do they pay attention. So, unwilling to cut the deficit much, they are equally unwilling to let it grow. They are, in a sense, trapped in a cage of their own making. Rather than admit to it, they hide behind a false veil of federal bankruptcy, a notion that America has run out of money, that its government cannot address today's problems.

As Stein told the budget committee:

> We find ourselves saying all kinds of absurd things. For example, when President Bush announced his space exploration programs, the pundits immediately got busy to say that although we could afford a big space program in the time of John Kennedy, we cannot afford it in the time of George Bush. But, in fact, real per capita consumption in the U.S. today is almost twice as high as when Kennedy was president, and we can afford much more than we could then. The president evidently

wants to extend some economic aid to Eastern Europe, but there is a general consensus that we can only afford to provide aid in the low hundreds of millions of dollars while the Japanese can afford to spend tens of billions of dollars. But the U.S. GNP [gross national product] is at least twice the Japanese.

In late 1989, former Federal Reserve Board chairman Paul A. Volcker complained in the *Washington Post* about the nation's apparent willingness to use its fiscal problems as an excuse to abandon world leadership:

> It has somehow become fashionable to say that we can't "afford" to do important things abroad, like providing substantial help to Eastern Europe, and that we can't afford to do even more obvious things at home, like rebuilding our cities and better educating our people.... Let's not confuse our political problems with lack of the resources required to support continued leadership. The margin of our economic advantage over other advanced countries has indeed narrowed, partly as a desired result of our own policies. But we are still the largest and richest economy the world has ever seen; by any measure, we are far better off materially than when we gave so generously to postwar Europe. So there are no inexorable economic or external forces—no new burdens—that demand we withdraw from leadership; if it happens, it will be of our own choosing.[3]

Similarly, when asked by columnists Rowland Evans and Robert Novak how America could afford his vision of a "war on drugs," New York Governor Mario Cuomo attacked the assumptions behind their question. "A radical government in Quebec invades New York," he hypothesized. "The president declares this an outrage and demands it end. But will you send troops, Mr. President? Oh, no, we can't afford that. Let New York handle that. Let them use the militia. That's how we fight the drug war, and it is a war."[4] War or no war, Cuomo's point was well taken. Washington addressed the drug problem, which Americans said was the nation's most important, with just slightly less lethargy than it faced others. *Time* captured the mood with an article entitled, "Is

Government Dead?" "Abroad and at home," the magazine warned, with a sketch of a teary-eyed George Washington on its cover, "challenges are going unmet. Under the shadow of a massive federal deficit that neither political party is willing to confront, a kind of neurosis of accepted limits has taken hold from one end of Pennsylvania Avenue to the other. Whatever the situation...the typical response from Washington consists of encouraging words and token funds."[5]

Nothing better symbolized this "neurosis of accepted limits," this tendency to plead poverty when confronted by mounting social problems, than did the Gramm-Rudman law, which Washington thrust on itself. Enacted in 1985 and revised in 1987, it was supposed to guarantee a balanced budget by setting lower and lower annual deficit targets, which officials were required to meet. If the White House and Congress could not decide how to meet them, the law would take over by imposing across-the-board cuts on many domestic and defense programs. What Washington has perhaps learned since, however, is that no law can force the nation's elected and appointed leaders to do what they do not want to do. Gramm-Rudman may have brought the budget a bit closer to balance—though nowhere near what it was supposed to. But the deficit remains far too high by almost any economic standard. And any deficit cutting accomplished by Gramm-Rudman has come at great cost to the integrity of government.

As almost any officeholder in Washington would agree, Gramm-Rudman has nourished a silly, if not juvenile, passion for chicanery, for what the politicians call "blue smoke and mirrors," all in the interest of pretending that the deficit is falling fast when almost everyone knows otherwise. The nation's leaders, it is fair to say, were engaged in a conspiracy of sorts. The White House and Congress, Republicans and Democrats, all promised to cut the deficit. And even when failing to do so in a meaningful way, they boasted about their achievements, acting as if they had turned the corner on the problem. With the nation's most important elected leaders saying the same thing, journalists were hard-pressed to report the story accurately. A journalist's common method of expressing skepticism, which is to quote someone else expressing it, was not as readily available. But even the journalists loosened up a bit in 1989 and weaved in their own doubts about how much real deficit cutting the nation's leaders were accomplishing.

To understand how politicians get away with it, remember this: For the most part, budgeting in Washington is prospective; the president and Congress enact tax and spending laws for the year ahead, not in the year in which the money is used. So, for instance, when Bush took office in January 1989, Washington was in the middle of fiscal 1989. But all attention was focused on fiscal 1990, the year that would begin on the following October 1. When Bush addressed Congress a month after his inauguration, he offered up a list of tax and spending ideas for 1990. He did not, however, suggest any changes at all for 1989. For all intents and purposes, that year was over in the minds of officials.

If Washington were truly determined to cut the deficit, of course, it would do so in its *current* year. If, let us imagine, halfway through 1989, the deficit had been on a path toward excessive levels, the president and Congress might have imposed small cuts in some programs or a temporary tax increase. But Gramm-Rudman does not force them to actually cut the deficit. It only forces them to show that, if everything goes according to their hopes, they will have done so in the year ahead. So, because they are unwilling to enact the needed tax hikes and spending cuts, they pretend: They pretend that the economy will grow faster than is likely, generating more in revenues and costing less in unemployment and other benefits. They pretend that Washington will spend less on some programs, like Food Stamps or farm price supports, than is likely or that it will raise more money through tax changes than is likely.

And while they are pretending, they move Washington's funds around like pieces on a board game. They enact policies that would help meet their next Gramm-Rudman target, but might lead to higher deficits in later years. You might think they would eschew such policies for fear that Gramm-

Rudman's target three years later would be that much harder to reach. But politicians do not think that way. They want to "get by" the next year because they focus on the next election, particularly in the House, where it comes every two years. The politicians' first task is to get reelected. So they sell federal loans, which generate short-term revenue bonanzas but can cost even more in loan repayments in later years. They pass spending bills but prohibit the money from being used until a year or so later. And they shift the year's last pay date for government employees by a day or so, enough to push it into the next fiscal year. (In a variation on that theme, the Pentagon in Bush's first year moved *up* a pay date from fiscal 1990 to 1989, helping it to meet Gramm-Rudman's 1990 target but raising the 1989 deficit.)

If this is all a game, the object is *not* to cut the deficit (though many would be pleased if that happened). Rather, it is to let the White House and Congress boast that they have reached Gramm-Rudman's next target. But this is not just a game, for the stakes are high. As Henry J. Aaron, a senior fellow at the Brookings Institution, told the House Budget Committee, "I have the sense that as Congress and the administration are forced to go through these exercises and resort to such devices, that we are all performing childish rituals rather than engaging in adult debate about constructive national policy." So destructive are these rituals that Aaron and others among Washington's most respected experts insist we would be better off scrapping Gramm-Rudman. They have a point. The White House and Congress enacted much more sizable deficit-cutting legislation in the early 1980s than since Gramm-Rudman. What the nation's leaders relied on was not a mechanical device, but common sense. The deficit was too high. They thought it would eventually hurt America's economy. So they cut it. The deficit remains too high. But fewer politicians fear it will cause economic harm. So they merely pretend to cut it by exploiting loopholes in a law that has failed to meet its designers' lofty expectations.

But do not expect the nation's leaders to take Aaron's advice about scrapping Gramm-Rudman. They would like to.

Nobody really cares for the law. Even Republican Sen. Warren Rudman of New Hampshire, who sponsored it with Republican Sen. Phil Gramm of Texas and Hollings, called it "a bad idea whose time has come." Later, Hollings said he wanted a "divorce" from it because of the problems it had wrought. But Democrats and Republicans do not want to be viewed as "fiscally irresponsible" by repealing a law that was supposed to help balance the budget. So they will surely hang on to Gramm-Rudman or a variant of it. And they will probably continue to play their games, moving small sums of money around the budget, while not doing much about the nation's big problems.

■   ■   ■   ■

In a sense, you could hardly blame them. The circumstances in which the nation's leaders labored were at odds with their normal predispositions. Over the years, men and women have come to Washington to *do* things—kick around ideas, debate policy, make laws. Upon seeing a problem, most viewed government as their most potent weapon. The more that the White House and Congress focused on the same problems, the more likely they were to deploy government. Nor was this *modus operandi* confined to the "tax and spend" liberals. Sure, liberals and conservatives tended to view Washington differently, the former as a means to enhance social justice, the latter to provide for the "common defense." But in the great expansion of domestic programs, Democrats did not act alone. In his memoirs, David A. Stockman, Reagan's first budget director, called it "the modern dirty little secret of the Republican Party: The conservative opposition helped build the American welfare state brick by brick during the three decades prior to 1980."[6]

This liberal-conservative consensus took root with the New Deal. Before it, the two sides had debated whether government should grow. As Theodore J. Lowi has written, "Liberal and conservative regimes derived their specific uses of government and policy from their general positions, and differences between the two national parties were for the most part clear within these terms. The perennial issue underlying the dialogue was the question of the nature of government itself and whether expansion or contraction of government best produced public good." But after the New Deal, "the old public philosophy, drawn from the liberal-conservative dialogue, became outmoded in our time because elites simply no longer disagree whether government should be involved."[7]

What began in the 1930s was fortified in the 1960s and 1970s. Party differentiation counted for little. Lyndon B. Johnson's Great Society, a victim of the guns-versus-butter debate of the Vietnam years, gave way to the "Nixon revolution," viewed as the reaction of a silent, resentful majority. Rather than reverse it, however, Nixon helped to expand the Great Society. Sure, he brought nuances of change, appointing conservative Supreme Court justices, restricting the Health, Education, and Welfare Department from using federal aid to advance desegregation, and pushing for block grants to give states the freedom to spend federal aid as they wished. But he left the basic tenets of the New Deal and Great Society unchallenged. Even Reagan, known as an antigovernment crusader, reaffirmed Washington's central role in American life by choosing not to attack key programs on which the citizenry depended.

The growth of federal power was underscored by philosophical change. At issue was the concept of equality. No longer were Americans satisfied with equality of opportunity. Now they wanted results. Pushing for the Voting Rights Act of 1965, Johnson declared, "We seek...not just equality as a right and a theory but equality *as a fact and equality as a result*." Reflecting on the change, Theodore H. White wrote, "It was the explosive renascence of the idea of equality that transformed American politics between 1960 and 1980.... What began as a quest to expand the definition of freedom was to end in the centralization of federal controls on a scale never envisioned by those who dreamed the dreams of the early sixties and still remembered John F. Kennedy calling, 'I say this country must move again.' New words like 'quotas,' 'entitlements,' and the officialese 'protected classes' replaced older words, changing the nature of the American government."[8] Everyone was "entitled" to one thing or another: senior citizens, blacks, women, youth, the handicapped, homosexuals, and others.

As recently as the mid-1970s, the White House and Congress had little trouble finding money to spend. As the economy grew, which it did most of the time, it generated more tax revenues for the Treasury. And as inflation pushed taxpayers into higher brackets, Washington got an even bigger boost in revenues—in essence, a tax hike without voting for one. These boosts were so great, in fact, that budget experts projected that the relatively small deficits of those years would be replaced by surpluses a few years later. So everybody tried to get their hands on the growing pot of money. For instance, the House and Senate Budget Committees, created in 1974, were charged with drafting annual tax and spending plans, known as budget resolutions, for the government. Most committee members would prepare amendments to increase spending in this area or that. Once the resolutions moved to the House or Senate floors, noncommittee members proposed their own spending increases. More for defense, more for housing, more for this, more for that.

Big spending increases often made their way into law. In 1972, a 20 percent increase in Social Security benefits sailed through Congress, having been proposed by House Ways and Means Committee chairman Wilbur D. Mills of Arkansas, then harboring presidential ambitions. Facing overwhelming majorities in both chambers, Nixon reluctantly signed it. Less dramatically, Nixon teamed with Congress to create not only the Comprehensive Employment and Training Act (CETA) and General Revenue Sharing for state and local governments but also the "alphabet agencies": Environmental Protection Agency (EPA), Occupational Safety and Health Administration (OSHA), Consumer Product Safety Commission (CPSC), and others.

Even Washington's budget conventions were prejudiced toward more spending. America's leaders did not really draft a new budget each year. Rather, the president and Congress assumed, as a starting point, that programs in place would stay and, for the most part, receive enough money to offset inflation. Debate centered not on the programs but on proposed changes. Not even Reagan, the most conservative president in a half-century, would change that approach. To be sure, Reagan's rhetorical flourishes against domestic spending, mixed with the soaring deficit, shifted the burden of debate. Rather than easily doing so, those who wanted to create new programs had to explain why, had to convince skeptical colleagues, and had to find ways to pay for them. But at the same time, those who wanted to cut programs faced an equally tough task.

Consider the language of budgeting, particularly the word *entitlement*—the nearly half of all spending that included Social Security, Medicare, and other programs in which individuals were eligible for benefits under certain qualifications, such as age or income. The government, it suggested, "owed" something to someone. Washington's failure to pay would logically represent a breach of trust, of moral obligation. Calls for fiscal restraint would appear cruel, heartless. "On several occasions," William A. Niskanen, a member of Reagan's Council of Economic Advisors, later wrote, "I tried to persuade Stockman and other administration officials, without success, not to use the word 'entitlement,' because it conveys the impression of a right to continued government transfer payments and services."[9]

And consider the rules of budgeting. In the 1960s and 1970s, Congress tied spending on many entitlements to inflation; when it rose by, say, 4 percent, recipients automatically got a 4 percent boost in benefits. "Indexing," as the practice was known, was especially popular in the 1970s. Not only was Social Security indexed, but so were railroad retirement benefits, veterans' pensions, Medicaid, Food Stamps, some federal pay programs, and part of Medicare. Even in the deficit-riddled 1980s, Washington indexed benefits for federal employee retirement, veterans' health care, the Earned Income Tax Credit (EITC), parts of Medicare and Medicaid, and some state and local grants. In 1986, it dropped a requirement that

inflation must rise by at least 3 percent in order for Social Security recipients to receive a cost-of-living increase. By 1988,
one study found, benefits were indexed in 57 programs in
such areas as federal employee retirement and disability, social insurance, cash assistance, housing, nutrition, education
and training, energy, health, and mental health. Another 42
programs of goods and services were indexed, including farm
price supports, medical vendor payments, nutrition, federal
pay and scholarships, and training stipends. Indexing was
also used in intergovernmental grants, user fees and revenue programs, loans and loan guarantees, and regulatory
programs.

The nonentitlement, or day-to-day, programs were indexed in a subtler manner. In the mid-1970s, Washington
adopted the "current services" baseline approach to show
what it would cost in later years to provide current levels
of goods and services. Let's say, for instance, that Washington
spent $100 million for an education program in 1980. If in-
flation were expected to hit 5 percent in 1981, the program
presumably would need $105 million to provide the same ser-
vices. Washington, in its budget rules, assumed as a starting
point in 1981 that the program would get $105 million. Con-
ceptually, this approach makes sense. If inflation is 5 percent,
a worker knows he will need a 5 percent pay raise to keep
pace. If he gets 3 percent, he knows quite well that, although
he has more dollars in his pocket, they are worth less to him.
He has fallen behind. Similarly, a federal program funded at
a level that does not keep pace with inflation would face the
same problems.

But the "current services" baseline biased Washington
toward more spending. You might wonder, after hearing so
much about spending cuts, why the budget kept growing.
Here's why: Washington starts from its baseline. If a program's actual funding turns out to be less than its baseline
amount, the difference is tabulated as a "cut." So, for the
$100 million education program cited above, with inflation
projected at 5 percent, the baseline assumes $105 million to
start. Now, let's say the program receives only $103 million.

Rather than tabulate that as a $3 million increase, Washington records it as a $2 million cut. Conceivably, then, each of Washington's programs could receive more money from year to year and still be "cut" by Washington's standards.

■   ■   ■   ■

But while these budget conventions stayed in effect, a new mood began to sweep through the capital in the late 1970s. Deficits, though only at levels later dwarfed by Reagan's, evoked growing concern. President Ford vetoed 66 bills in his two-and-a-half-year tenure, often citing the deficit as his reason. In his 1975 State of the Union address, Ford said he would not support new programs, except to address America's energy problems. Deficits, he cautioned, caused inflation. President Carter, though a Democrat, nevertheless seemed quite comfortable with constraints on Washington. He had railed against Ford's deficits during the 1976 campaign, and he promised a balanced budget by the end of his first term. "Government," he said in his 1978 State of the Union message, "cannot solve our problems. It can't set our goals. It cannot define our vision. Government cannot eliminate poverty, or provide a bountiful economy, or reduce inflation or save our cities."

Big programs had become passé. Inflation was rising and policy makers blamed deficits. In the budget committees, lawmakers started looking for ways to save money. Witnesses asking for "more, more, more," as they had always done, were no longer taken as seriously. When he wanted to spend, Carter was hemmed in as well, such as on the issue of national health insurance. On one side were organized labor and its chief Senate advocate, Edward M. Kennedy of Massachusetts, who went on to challenge Carter for the Democratic presidential nomination in 1980. On the other side were growing concerns over the deficit. Although Carter was sure to anger labor and Kennedy, he felt constrained by the deficit to limit his plan's first-year cost to $17 billion.

Nevertheless, the Ford-Carter years offered just a taste of what was to come. Spend $17 billion for health insurance?

In one year? Figures like that would seem like pipe dreams a decade later, even after inflation had reduced the value of those dollars. Barring an emergency of cataclysmic proportions, nobody was going to find $17 billion in the budget for anything new. How about $700 million? Well, there you had a fighting chance. With a few exceptions, Washington was now penurious. A House Democratic aide described the atmosphere as "throwing nickels at problems." In the context of huge needs and a budget exceeding $1 trillion by the late 1980s, his characterization was not inappropriate.

As the money got tight, policy making became "fiscalized," in the word of experts. Whether an idea was viewed favorably was more dependent on its cost than its merit. As Lance R. Simmens, a former Senate aide who was lobbying for the United States Conference of Mayors, told me in 1988, "Public policy is driven now more than ever by the bottom line, rather than whether it is a needed program, a useful program, a national priority. We don't decide on national priorities. We decide on whether we can fit it in the box." After working on *American Agenda*, a study that Ford and Carter supervised in 1988 to prepare Reagan's successor for the challenges ahead, former CBO (Congressional Budget Office) director Alice M. Rivlin told the National Economic Commission, "The budget deficit problem loomed over *all* discussions.... The budget deficit has become a defense issue, a foreign policy issue, a health care issue, an education issue."

When it came to spending money, the burden had shifted. Where once those who wanted to cut programs had to make their case, now those pushing to expand them needed to do so. Occasionally, they succeeded. A handful of small but highly regarded programs for the disadvantaged got more money in the 1980s. Certain science and space programs also did well as the nation made efforts to compete with Japan and other advancing nations. A rash of airline crashes prompted the White House and Congress to send more money to the Federal Aviation Administration. The State Department got more money, as did some law enforcement programs. But these were exceptions that proved the new budget rules.

When Washington tried to cut programs, nobody wanted his or her favorite to bear too great of a burden—not defense, not Medicare, not education, not anything. Agencies dug in. So did congressional committees that supervised programs in their domain. One solution seemed obvious: All programs would share equally. As a result, "formula budgeting" took hold. Spending would be cut, across the board, to a certain level. It was no coincidence that Gramm-Rudman required across-the-board cuts in many defense and domestic programs (although Social Security was exempt and other big domestic programs were at least partly protected). The House and Senate dabbled with proposals for spending freezes. A White House-Congress budget summit in late 1987 agreed first on an across-the-board limit to defense and day-to-day domestic programs.

When Congress did choose between programs, its decisions were colored by the deficit. Ideas once viewed unfavorably seemed appealing if they would save money. For example, Defense secretaries had long wanted to close domestic military bases that were no longer needed. But bases brought the promise of jobs, and lawmakers whose districts housed the bases did not want to dispense with them. In 1977, Congress passed a law that, by requiring the economic and environmental effects of a proposed closing to be studied, almost ensured that no more would occur. Fort Douglas in Utah, built to guard stagecoach routes to the Wild West, would remain open. So would Fort Monroe in Virginia, built for the War of 1812.

Not any more. When Rep. Richard K. Armey, a conservative Texas Republican, mounted an effort in 1988 to close the superfluous bases, Congress took a closer look at the idea. Base closings would save at least $1 billion a year. Some experts estimated greater savings. Lawmakers still did not like the idea. But money was so tight that they decided to act. To avoid blame from constituents, they set up an outside commission to recommend which bases to close. Congress would vote on the list as a whole. This way, each lawmaker could blame the commission for particular decisions while voting for the concept of "cutting waste." In early 1989, they let the panel's recommendations take effect.

"Privatization," which called for transferring some federal functions to the private sector, was once just an idea for "Big Government's" biggest critics. By the late 1980s, it had become a mainstream idea for the same reason that base closings had: It offered the promise of cash. Washington debated which of America's physical assets to sell; in 1987, after a long debate, it sold its 85 percent stake in Conrail to the public. Congress also considered selling loans that were issued by agencies; in 1987, it sold education and farm loans to private sources.

Budget constraints also prompted Washington to dump the costs of its policies on nonfederal entities. The federal government required (or "mandated," as the practice is known) that businesses or state and local governments do certain things, whether or not Washington kicked in any money. This way, Washington could answer some voter requests for new programs and not bear the costs. It forced business to notify workers before a plant closing and to extend health insurance for workers up to 18 months after they leave a job. In the late 1980s, business was fighting proposals to force them to pay a higher minimum wage, expand health coverage and offer parental leave for workers, and contribute more to environmental cleanup, such as on acid rain. States and localities were forced to help clean up the air, rid schools of asbestos, clean the lead from school drinking water, absorb more refugees, and give job training to welfare recipients.

Nothing better reflects the overriding role of budget issues in today's Washington than the new powers enjoyed by the Office of Management and Budget. OMB has a proud history. When I asked him why he had joined OMB three decades earlier, David G. Mathiasen, a longtime staffer who left in 1989 for another top-level federal post, responded only half-jokingly, "Why does someone become a priest?" Admittedly, not everyone at OMB views his or her job as a religious calling. But the 500 or so civil servants who worked in or near the Old Executive Office Building, an architecturally magnificent structure that sits just west of the White House, took their roles as the president's budget staff quite seriously.

Before the Reagan years, OMB was a far less conspicuous agency. Originally called the Bureau of the Budget, it was created in 1921 to craft a presidential budget so that departments would stop sending their own requests separately to Congress. First situated in the Treasury Department, the bureau was transferred in 1939 to the Executive Office of the President, where it took the lead role on fiscal, organizational, and managerial issues. In 1970, the agency was renamed OMB, with its management function given equal status with its budget tasks. Still, in those decades, policy making was centered in the departments. Proposals would move "bottom up" from departments to the White House, where the president would decide (with OMB's help) how much he could cram into his budget. With the White House and Congress in basic agreement over fiscal priorities, final decisions were left to the amicable relations between the departments and congressional committees.

Throughout this period, a president's budget was just a plan, something to which Congress could compare its decisions. OMB dropped the budget on Capitol Hill and left the choices to lawmakers. But Reagan, assuming he had won a mandate to cut domestic spending and boost defense, hoped to change the very direction of government. For him to be successful, Congress had to implement at least part of his budget. So, under Reagan, OMB's power soared, turning policy making into a "top-down" operation. OMB directed the strategy on domestic cuts, imposing its own ideas on reluctant departments and trying to do the same with Congress. Stockman spent far more time on Capitol Hill than any previous director, pushing proposals, making deals with lawmakers, and, when needed, offering to substitute one set of cuts for another. His aides, who had hardly ever dealt with Congress, attended the committees' bill-drafting sessions, monitoring progress on the cuts Stockman was promised. OMB installed computers so that specialists could give Stockman more data for his negotiations. An OMB unit whose members tabulated the effects of congressional spending bills was expanded.

As the deficit swelled, OMB's power grew more out of its role in economic forecasting. For all the talk about whether taxes are too low or spending too high, the biggest influence on deficits is the economy. The faster it grows, the more Washington receives in taxes and the less it pays in social benefits. Small changes in GNP, interest rates, and unemployment produce big swings in deficits. Presidents are naturally tempted to forecast optimistically; by projecting stronger growth, lower inflation, and less jóblessness than warranted by available data, they can claim success for their policies. But such optimism gained new notoriety in 1981 when, Stockman said later, Reagan used a blatantly unrealistic projection that minimized the spending cuts needed to balance the budget. Although its forecasting was stronger after that, OMB remained discredited by this "rosy scenario." Meanwhile, congressional reaction to OMB's forecasts was baldly hypocritical. Each year, Democrats lambasted OMB, claiming its forecasts were wildly optimistic. They talked about using CBO's more pessimistic forecasts. But soon, facing the task of enacting bigger spending cuts or tax hikes, they decided that OMB's figures were too tempting to resist.

■   ■   ■   ■

Mathematically, at least, the deficit seemed easily solvable. Washington was spending more than it was collecting. Cut spending, raise taxes, or do a little of each, right? Well, not quite. Interest on the national debt, which comprised 15 percent of spending in 1989, had to be paid; a national default could have produced an unthinkable catastrophe on international financial markets. Leaders on the Left and Right, reading the political tea leaves, left other big chunks of spending alone, principally programs for the elderly, which were ardently supported by voters and powerful interest groups. Social Security, occupying 20 percent of the budget in 1989, was left untouched. Medicare, at 8 percent, would continue providing the same services for senior citizens; limits in that program mostly affected only those who provided the care, such as hospitals and doctors. Nor were officials more willing to cut back on other federal and military retirement programs.

Officials acted with similar discretion on the tax side. Having cut personal and business income tax rates dramatically in 1981 and in 1986, few wanted to raise them. When the 1986 Tax Reform Act was drafted, scores of deductions were eliminated to pay for the lower personal and corporate rates. Whatever deductions survived that process had proved their popularity. Scaling them back—just to reduce the deficit, and not to give taxpayers even lower rates in return—would not be easy. As with spending, then, much of the tax ledger was "off the table." In particular, the personal tax rates set in 1986 acquired a political status not unlike that accorded to Social Security. Only the most courageous would admit to wanting them raised.

Washington, having created a deficit by *commission*, now would ensure its life by *omission*. Almost half of federal spending would be left alone, to grow like what Bush's budget director, Richard G. Darman, called a "hidden PACMAN," consuming an ever greater share of the budget pie.[10] Facing cuts year after year, the remaining programs—defense and day-to-day domestic programs for housing, education, and so on—would shrink as a portion of the budget. Nobody liked the situation, neither the liberals who wanted more for social programs nor the conservatives who wanted more for defense. But too few of either side would question the overriding decisions that left so much of the budget untouched. Budgeting was stuck in place. As a colleague of mine wrote in early 1987, Washington had entered a "fiscal ice age."[11]

Such realities reduced the differences between Democrats and Republicans, once obvious in policy proposals, to mere rhetoric. In the 1988 campaign, Bush effectively tarred Democrat Michael Dukakis as a "liberal," raising the specter of another round of Democratic "Big Government" financed by big tax increases. Dukakis's refusal, until the campaign was nearly over, to do much more than run from the liberal label crystallized the schism between himself and Bush on the role of government. But for all of their supposed differences, Bush and Dukakis both accepted the major assumptions of the fiscal ice age: leave Social Security alone and avoid raising taxes, particularly by boosting tax rates. Thus, on the question of Washington's role in making policy, differences between a future Bush or a future Dukakis White House melted away. During the campaign, Dukakis's aides said that, if elected, their candidate would launch a series of new programs with small down payments, hoping to find more money in later years. And what did Bush propose for fiscal 1990, his first full budget year? A series of new programs with small down payments. He expressed sympathy with those wanting to spend more for some and hinted at helping them to do so in later years.

Politicians were little more anxious to cut programs that were "on the table"—for discussion, anyway. Voters would not allow it. As much as they favor a balanced budget, Americans do not expect their representatives to dismantle the programs on which they depend. Those who try can find themselves out of work. Rep. Leon E. Panetta, a California Democrat who became chairman of the House Budget Committee in 1989, was asked at a conference late that year about possibly giving presidents more power to cut spending. He explained why Congress would object: "The thing that drives the institution is obviously survival, political survival, among the various members who are part of that institution, and they survive by basically trying to, you know, meet the needs of their constituents. And I think they would find it very difficult if suddenly you had a representative that said, 'Gee, I can't improve your benefits, I can't deliver on education, I can't provide better housing, I can't deliver disaster assistance, I can't provide any of this, because somehow, you know, the president has the authority to control it.' Then they'll say, 'Well, what the hell are you good for in terms of your ability to respond to our needs?' "

As Panetta explained, lawmakers of both parties must "bring home the bacon," however much they rail against wasteful spending. Stockman learned all about that, to his considerable disillusionment. His memoirs read like a litany of complaints about this or that lawmaker, each of whom pushed to extend existing programs for parochial reasons, all the while pledging allegiance to Reagan's goal of cutting domestic spending. In one telling anecdote, Stockman related how Sen. Strom Thurmond, a South Carolina Republican and "a man not known for liberal leanings," urged him to save the Rural Electric Administration, which Stockman thought should be disbanded because its original purpose of bringing electricity to rural areas had been achieved. According to Stockman, Thurmond "took me aside and with a gentle smile said, 'Now, we're all behind the President's program, yuh heah? But you take good care of those REAs. Them's some real FINE people.' "[12]

Even GOP congressional leaders, who were most responsible for pushing Reagan's legislative program through the House and Senate, practiced the politics of hypocrisy when the need arose. Having barely survived his 1982 reelection race, House Republican Leader Robert H. Michel of Illinois took no chances when he faced the same opponent in 1988. Under attack for not bringing enough "bacon" to his Peoria-area district, Michel took advantage of a televised debate to boast about "federal goodies he has brought to the 18th District of Illinois: funds for highway improvements, bridges, airports, hospitals, and a $7 million Urban Development Action Grant that is expected to spur the revitalization of downtown Peoria," according to the *Washington Post*.[13] But to give Michel his due, he at least acknowledged the hypocrisy. In mid-1989, he criticized efforts to add a balanced budget amendment to the U.S. Constitution. Why? Well, Republicans supposedly belong to the party that does not raise taxes. If the amendment were enacted, they would have to cut enough spending to balance the budget. But, as Michel told the House, Republicans were little more interested in cutting that much spending than were Democrats.

With the public expressing support for lower defense spending by the late 1980s, the Pentagon seemed likely to bear heavy burdens for future deficit cutting. In fact, defense has not been given enough money to keep pace with inflation in any year since 1985. But defense cuts had their practical limits—not only because some conservatives would oppose them. Future defense spending was substantially beyond control, an outgrowth of yesterday's decisions to build weapons for today and tomorrow.

When Reagan's buildup raised yearly Pentagon expenditures from 23 to 28 percent of spending between 1981 and 1986, Defense Secretary Caspar Weinberger pushed for as many long-range weapons as he could. More than 20 new systems were "locked in"; contracts to build proceeded. Two dozen more went into research and development. The only way to reverse those decisions was to cancel the contracts. If that occurred, Washington would get nothing for the money it had spent. Sen. Sam Nunn, a Georgia Democrat and chairman of the Senate's Armed Services Committee, understood. After arguing in late 1988 that the nation should not build two bombers and that the B-2 was better than the B-1, he nevertheless would not say that the B-1 should be canceled. Pressed on CBS's "Face the Nation," Nunn explained, "It's too late. It's too late. I don't know how you deal with it now, it's very difficult to deal with. We've already spent the money on the B-1."

Weinberger and other top officials acted as if they wanted to block the future "builddown" that normally follows a buildup. For decades, defense spending has alternated between feast and famine, mirroring changes in public opinion or the needs of war. Public support for enhanced military strength gives way to discomfort with the share of resources allotted to the Pentagon, which then gives way to another buildup when the nation feels threatened. For instance, the costly Korean conflict was followed by a defense downturn under Eisenhower. Kennedy, having railed in his campaign against an alleged "missile gap," began a second post–World War II buildup in 1961. As Vietnam wound down, Nixon began a builddown. Although known as the Reagan buildup, the next swing began under Carter as public opinion shifted again. Reagan, though, made Carter's commitment to more money seem weak by comparison.

But, as Pentagon officials said later, Weinberger often brushed aside suggestions that he plan for the lean years, saying that to do so would result in a self-fulfilling prophecy. Navy Secretary John F. Lehman, Jr., predicted that with contracts locked in, Reagan's goal of a 600-ship navy would come to fruition. When news stories of overpriced toilet seats, wrenches, and ashtrays and other examples of fiscal profligacy helped turn the public toward another builddown, Weinberger & Co. refused to adjust their books. Not until Congress got hold of the Pentagon's five-year plan in 1986 did it recognize the game. The Pentagon had assumed it would get almost $400 billion to spend in 1990, not the $300 billion or so it received. The Pentagon would have to cut almost $300 billion from its internal plans for 1990 to 1994 to meet Secretary Frank Carlucci's order in early 1988 that it plan on 2 percent in annual inflation-adjusted spending hikes.

But even before the dramatic changes behind the Iron Curtain in 1989 eased U.S.–Soviet tensions, almost no one thought the Pentagon would get 2 percent increases. "My guess is that zero real growth—only enough to offset inflation—is the very best that the Pentagon can hope for," House Armed Services Committee chairman Les Aspin, a Wisconsin Democrat, said in a late 1988 speech. "What's more likely is more of the negative real growth that there's been in the last four Defense budgets." In his "Face the Nation" appearance, Nunn brought more bad news. To adjust the Pentagon's plans from Carlucci's 2 percent growth rate to a zero-growth level, the Pentagon would have to cut $200 billion more from its plans.

The decisions would not come easily. Some weapons had to be canceled. But these cancellations tended to raise political and substantive problems. On the political side, contracts brought jobs to congressional districts. "When you start a program," Nunn explained, "even people who may have opposed the program to begin with—if you put a plant in that district, it's very hard to vote to kill it." Substantively, cancellations helped little with short-term budget problems. Because weapons were financed with long-term contracts, cancellations provided lots of savings over time but little in the short term. To save more quickly, the place to look was the Pentagon's accounts for maintenance and training, spare parts, and ammunition. But if those accounts were cut too much, the Pentagon would be left with a "hollow force"—the weapons it wanted, but neither the parts nor the people to run them.

■   ■   ■   ■

Rather than search for places to save money, however, the nation's leaders spent more time protecting their favorite programs. After Reagan's military buildup, everything— domestic *and* defense spending—faced the knife. Nobody's pet programs were immune. And nobody sat back to watch them get cut. Each year, CBO and such private groups as the conservative Heritage Foundation issued reports that suggested which programs could be cut or eliminated to reduce the deficit. Such "hit lists" attracted a lot of attention, not only from those searching for things to cut but also from those fighting to save the listed items. Advocates mounted public or behind-the-scenes campaigns to save them.

More lawmakers had a stake in existing programs than ever before.[14] One reason involved institutional changes. After World War II, the number of congressional committees and, more importantly, subcommittees swelled. While the number of regular House committees increased from 19 to 22 since the 1940s, the number of subcommittees rose from 102 to 138. In the Senate, the number of committees inched up from 15 to 16 while the number of subcommittees soared from 61 to 140 before dropping to 86. Each lawmaker now served on more panels. A House member, who might have served on one committee and two subcommittees in the 1940s, later served on two committees, four subcommittees, and maybe a joint, select, or other special panel. A senator, who served on two committees, three subcommittees, and maybe another panel decades ago, later had a seat on three committees, seven subcommittees, and one other panel.

The more panels on which a lawmaker served, the higher his or her stake in existing programs. A member of the House Education and Labor Committee invariably grew to like programs that offered student loans, job training, and other services. He studied them. He knew their purpose. The more the lawmaker knew, the more attached he grew to the programs, viewing them as less expendable than others. He therefore fought any proposals to cut them. This phenomenon was particularly true with subcommittee chairmen, of which there were now more. Subcommittees allotted power to their chairmen. The larger the programs were within their jurisdiction, the more powerful were the chairmen. Whereas the average member of a committee or subcommittee worked hard to protect its programs, the chairman worked harder.

Lawmakers were spurred on by committee staffs, which had grown as well. In the House, the number of staff members serving committees grew from 167 in 1947 to 2,024 in 1987. The Appropriations Committee staff, for instance, grew from 29 to 188, the Energy and Commerce staff from 10 to 153, and the Banking staff from 4 to 99. In the Senate, the number of staffers assigned to committees grew from 232 in 1947 to 1,074 in 1987. The Agriculture Committee staff grew from 3 to 35, the Commerce staff from 8 to 93, the Judiciary staff from 19 to 138, and the Labor staff from 9 to 127. These staffers, who became increasingly powerful as lawmakers' workloads increased and the issues they faced grew more complicated, had the same stake in programs as did elected officials.

External pressures, too, exerted an enormous influence on lawmakers. More interest groups set up shop in Washington. The number of national trade and professional associations (banking, real estate, labor, agriculture, and so on) headquartered in and around Washington numbered about 2,200 by the late 1980s—or one third of all such groups, according to the Greater Washington Society of Association Executives. More groups poured more money into campaigns through political action committees. The number of PACs rose from 608 in 1974 to 4,268 in 1988. Corporate PACs accounted for nearly half the total, with the others tied to labor, trade, health, membership, and other groups. PAC contributions to congressional candidates soared from $12.5 million in 1974 to $147.9 million in 1988. These contributions comprised growing shares of campaign funds—more than a third of House candidates' and nearly a quarter of Senate candidates' funds by 1988.

The larger the groups, the more obvious their presence in Washington; the more money they poured into a lawmaker's reelection coffers, the more pressure they could exert to save their favored programs. When proposals for spending cuts arose, groups pulled out all stops. They sent their Washington lobbyists to Capitol Hill for conversations with lawmakers or staffs or to the relevant executive branch department. Or the groups ordered their hundreds, thousands, or millions of members across the land to write to their congressmen. Or they sent a few unsolicited dollars to this or that incumbent's reelection account.

Pushed, then, by their own sentiments and the power of others, lawmakers went to work. To see how, remember this: Congress makes policy in three steps. First, it passes a budget resolution that sets tax and spending totals and also recommends how to apportion the spending among defense, health, education, transportation, and other categories. Second, it considers bills drafted by its policy-making, or "authorization," committees (Agriculture, Banking, Energy, Labor, Small Business, and so on) that order Washington to do things—boost welfare payments, provide medical assistance, protect wildlife, assist the schools, buy tanks. Third, it passes "appropriations," which are spending bills that have all, part, or none of the funds to carry out the authorizations.

In recent years, lawmakers and staffs of the authorization committees have been spending less time thinking about better policies and more time fighting recommendations in the budget resolution to cut programs they oversee. Staffs attend Budget Committee hearings and monitor budget resolutions on the House and Senate floors. Because no one wants to sacrifice a program he or she helped create or supported, agreements do not come easily. Disputes stretch over weeks and months. Deadlines for adopting budget resolutions, authorizations, and appropriations bills are hardly taken seriously and pass with little notice. Arguments along party, ideological, and regional lines drag on. Hovering above are even more basic disputes between the White House and Congress.

Forced to make decisions for the next fiscal year, which begins October 1, the nation's leaders have resorted to extraordinary steps. For two straight years, before Reagan chastised lawmakers in his 1988 State of the Union message, Congress wrapped all 13 annual appropriations bills into a single measure, sending it to the House and Senate, and then to the White House, for single yes-or-no decisions. Even those bills were not finished until weeks after October 1; Congress kept the government running with stopgap measures. Because his veto would have temporarily shut down the government, Reagan had little leverage to reject these monster bills. Other than party leaders and the Appropriations Committees that drafted the bills, most lawmakers were no happier than Reagan. Unsure even of what was in the bills, they felt disenfranchised from the big decisions of fiscal policy. "If I wasn't on Appropriations," Silvio Conte of Massachusetts, the House panel's senior Republican, told me in 1987, "I'd be leading a revolution.... It's wrong."

■   ■   ■   ■

In this kind of environment, Washington was, well, simply less fun. Lawmakers openly admitted it. After surveying 114 lawmakers and 115 staff members in early 1987, Washington's Center for Responsive Politics concluded: "The message conveyed by the respondents is clear. Members are frustrated and deeply concerned about the way Congress operates."[15] Asked to elaborate on changes needed, 32 percent of the lawmakers mentioned budget process reform, the second most common response. Nearly half of all lawmakers who responded—and two thirds of the senators who did—said the budget process had weakened policy-making.

Washington's ongoing fascination with reforming the process was a surefire sign of discontent. The 1974 Congressional Budget and Impoundment Control Act, which set the framework for Washington's budget procedures, was prompted largely by congressional anger at Nixon's refusal to spend money that it allotted for urban, housing, farm, and other programs. Gramm-Rudman was propelled by congressional dismay with Reagan's refusal to accept big enough defense cuts or tax hikes to significantly reduce the deficit. Unfortunately, rule changes will not make the deficit disappear; if America's leaders are not committed to a balanced budget, they will find ways to circumvent the rules they have enacted. As Rudolph G. Penner, CBO's former director, was often quoted as remarking, "The process isn't the problem. The problem is the problem." Nevertheless, as the political deadlock over the deficit continued, the White House and Congress focused on procedural changes, as if they had simply not yet found the best set of airtight rules.

Meanwhile, some lawmakers were so bothered by the realities of bankrupt government that they chose to throw in the towel altogether. Six senators retired in 1988, including Lawton Chiles, a Florida Democrat who served in 1987–1988 as chairman of the Senate Budget Committee. Unless Washington solves its deficit problem, more are expected to leave in the coming years. Governors, who once viewed their jobs as stepping-stones to the Senate, are changing their minds. "There's less interest in going," Raymond C. Sheppach, executive director of the National Governors Association, told me in 1988. "I think there is a real frustration about their ability to get things done. They talk. They see it."

And yet, in the unhappy Washington of the 1980s, those who quit were in a distinct minority. Most of the nation's leaders stuck around, as if presuming that they would soon fix the deficit problem. After all, the formula for doing so was no mystery. Everyone knew that a deficit-cutting agreement had to include cuts in the major spending categories—defense, entitlements, and day-to-day domestic programs—and a sizable tax increase. Only a balanced approach like that had any chance of attracting the needed votes. The problem was that the president and Congress did not have a politically salient excuse for taking action. With the economy humming along, the deficit did not seem to be hurting anyone. Americans expressed concern about the deficit, but they displayed little inclination to accept the tax hikes and spending cuts required to eliminate it. Only a crisis of some magnitude was likely to stir the nation from its complacency. In the 1980s, the deficit cutters tried to find an existing crisis or invent a new one. They could do neither.

CHAPTER TWO

DON'T WORRY, BE HAPPY

It was 1987. Up in New York, Cuomo was ruminating about Washington when he came to an unsettling conclusion: the nation's leaders were not grappling with America's economic problems in a coherent fashion. The budget deficit was handled as one problem, the trade deficit as another, the debt of Third World nations as still another. Each problem was treated separately, as if distinct, although they were quite interrelated. Cuomo and his staff soon developed legislation that called for a bipartisan panel to study the problems together. Sen. Daniel Patrick Moynihan and Rep. Thomas J. Downey, both New York Democrats, introduced Cuomo's bill in the Senate and House, respectively.

When the stock market plunged a frightening 508 points on October 19, focusing attention on the nation's economic imbalances, Cuomo came to Washington to push his idea. Accompanied by James D. Robinson III, president of the American Express Company, and Peter G. Peterson, chairman of the Blackstone Group, a New York investment firm, the governor met with Senate Minority Leader Robert Dole, a Kansas Republican, and Sen. Pete V. Domenici of New Mexico, the Budget Committee's top Republican. Afterward, Dole told reporters that he favored a commission. Cuomo and the investment bankers next met with Senate Majority Leader Robert C. Byrd, a West Virginia Democrat. He, too, thought a commission could be helpful. With Cuomo's idea streamlined—the focus was placed more squarely on the budget deficit—the commission was established in late 1987 under a provision tucked into a huge spending bill.

The failure of the National Economic Commission, which expired in early 1989, is often blamed on the 1988 presidential campaign, particularly Bush's promises not to raise taxes and to ignore the commission if it recommended that he do so. Any panel of big-name Republicans and Democrats would have been hard put to reach a consensus under those circumstances. But in a larger sense, the panel suffered from the same obstacle that the White House and Congress have faced for years: a healthy economy. Voters are moved by pocketbook issues, such as inflation, interest rates, and unemployment. These determine how well they eat and dress, where they vacation, and where their kids go to camp and college. Only if Americans thought the deficit was hurting them economically would they and, in turn, their elected representatives in Washington accept the steps needed to eliminate it.

The deficit was not that kind of a problem. Its ill effects were less short-term than long-term and less obvious than those of, say, crime or drugs. As Charles L. Schultze, former chairman of Carter's Council of Economic Advisers, put it, the deficit was not quite a "wolf at the door," ready to blow down the economic house of cards. Rather, it was like "termites in the basement," eating away at the nation's economic foundation and likely to impair future living standards.[1] While the nation might enjoy some short-term pleasure, like an alcoholic on a binge, future generations would live less well than otherwise. In a strange way, the public seemed to acknowledge the situation. For although Americans supported the notion of deficit cutting, as if recognizing that excessive borrowing was no better for a nation than for a family, they rejected the short-term sacrifices needed to make it happen.

"Cut the deficit," they said in poll after poll, "but don't raise my taxes, and don't cut the expensive spending programs on which I depend."

The nation's leaders were, in a sense, trapped. They *wanted* to cut the deficit; it had made their lives as politicians exceedingly unhappy. As much as they talked publicly about the need to keep the economy growing, many longed for an economic excuse to take action, such as a sharp rise in interest rates. Typically, when I discussed deficit cutting with a White House aide in early 1989, he noted that "we don't have that luxury" of an economic crisis. He was not *wishing* for such a crisis, he quickly added, only pointing out how it might help Washington take the steps that so many desired. On Capitol Hill, lots of Democrats and Republicans expressed similar sentiments. On the stump, they talked about ensuring that the economy stayed strong, about containing inflation and interest rates. Privately, they acknowledged that when it came to deficit cutting, only a short-term crisis would create a constituency for tax hikes and spending cuts.

Indeed, the deficit "hawks," as those most committed to deficit cutting were known, had spent the 1980s searching for such a crisis. They warned that one was coming soon — in a month, or two weeks, or a week — if they did not act. Or they suggested that one had arrived, such as when banks boosted the prime interest rate a half-point, or when inflation jumped sharply for a month. But the crisis never appeared. The economy kept growing, interest rates never rose that high, and inflation remained in check. So, the nation's leaders tried instead to create a short-term political crisis by enacting Gramm-Rudman, which threatened deep, across-the-board cuts in many spending programs if the White House and Congress could not agree on a more rational deficit-cutting plan. And when that did not work, they set up a private commission that, they hoped, would recommend how to get the job done. The commission's failure was a fitting end to a decade of dismal budget politics. In 1989, a new president and Congress came center stage, hoping to find the elu-

sive formula that would prod the two branches toward a big
deficit-cutting deal. That they could not was hardly surprising, considering the history that preceded them.

■   ■   ■   ■

To begin, think of a nation as you would a farmer. A
farmer must plant now to enjoy a future harvest. He must
decide how much to plant, that is, how much to spend today
on the future. "Should I spend my money on tonight's dinner,"
he might ask himself, "or on seed for tomorrow's crop?" So it is
with a nation, balancing the demands of today's constituents
against the claims of generations in infancy or not yet born.
How much do today's Americans owe tomorrow's? How much
of the nation's resources should they use for their own enjoy-
ment and how much should they invest for their children's
and grandchildren's pleasure?

The questions have no right or wrong answers. Nations,
like farmers, make judgments. Politicians and economists
have grappled with the questions for decades. In 1961, Edmund Phelps, then an assistant economics professor at Yale
University, wrote of "The Golden Rule of Accumulation: A
Fable for Growthmen," suggesting how much of a nation's resources each generation is entitled to for its own pleasure and
how much it owes its successors.[2] President Eisenhower, more
than once in his last year in office, lamented the public debt
that his generation was leaving to the future. In the 1980s, as
the outstanding debt passed $1 trillion, then $2 trillion, and
approached $3 trillion, the nation's leaders complained about
their generation's attitude toward future Americans.

Whether today's Americans explicitly chose to treat their
successors so shabbily is problematic at best. As a candidate,
Ronald Reagan had disparaged the (much smaller) deficits
of earlier years and promised that his supply-side tax cuts
would generate a rush of revenues that would help balance the budget. In sending him to Washington, voters could
hardly be blamed for the fiscal calamity that followed. Nevertheless, through their elected representatives, Americans
had implicitly made a striking decision: Enjoy today. Eat,

drink and be merry, if you will. Or, as suggested by the 1989 Grammy award-winning song that Bush adopted (most appropriately) for his 1988 campaign, "Don't Worry, Be Happy." Tomorrow's Americans would bear the costs.

The nation, in essence, had chosen to *save* less.[3] With fewer savings, it had fewer dollars of its own that it could invest in plants and equipment; in roads, bridges, and dams; in education and child care; and in other ventures to help build a more productive work force and, in turn, ensure the continued growth of living standards. The domestic savings pool has two components: private savings (by individuals and businesses) and public savings (by federal, state, and local governments). Unfortunately, savings took a double whack in the 1980s. Here's how:

The deficit ballooned just as private savings, somewhat mysteriously, sank. The deficit, which averaged just over 1 percent of GNP between the end of World War II and the Carter years, shot up to an average of 4.5 percent under Reagan. At the same time, Reagan's program of supply-side tax cuts was supposed to increase private savings, which by 1980 were considered too low. In fact, the opposite took place. Private savings, which averaged 7.5 percent of GNP in the 1950s and 8.1 percent in the 1960s and 1970s, dropped to an average of 5.8 percent between 1980 and 1987. As budget deficits soared and private savings sank, total domestic savings dipped from well over 7 percent of GNP between 1950 and 1980 to below 2 percent at the end of the Reagan years.

Quite naturally, investment also fell—from the 7 percent or so of GNP that it averaged from 1950 to 1980 to around 5 percent for much of the 1980s. It would have fallen much further had foreigners not met part of our investment appetite by sending money here. Foreign investment, which transformed America from the world's largest creditor to its largest debtor in the mid-1980s, is much better than no investment at all. The nation benefits from the jobs created and from the corporate and personal taxes paid. But, unlike investment of our own funds, at least some benefits flow to sources abroad in the form of profits, interest, and dividends.

To the extent they affect productivity and, in turn, living standards, the saving and investment shortfalls came at a bad time. Productivity, which grew an average of 1.9 percent from 1950 to 1973, was essentially flat for the rest of the 1970s. (Sharp slowdowns also occurred in Western Europe and Japan.) While productivity began to grow again in the 1980s, its growth rate remained far below earlier levels. This phenomenon remains largely unexplained, although experts attribute parts of it to demographic change, the cost and quality of labor, managerial incompetence, federal regulatory policies, inadequate spending on research and development, and economic vicissitudes. Living standards, in turn, have suffered. Real (inflation-adjusted) compensation per worker grew an average of 2.6 percent between 1950 and 1973, but rose only 0.6 percent for the next six years and 0.5 percent between 1979 and 1987. Per-person income grew more rapidly, but only because of other factors. More married women worked, providing families with a second paycheck. Couples had fewer children, reserving their money for fewer people. But because not all Americans could compensate in this way, some suffered absolute declines in living standards.

By 1989, the figures were troubling enough to evoke concerns from the new president. "The Federal deficit absorbs too much of America's savings," Bush wrote in the fiscal 1990 budget proposals that he sent Congress in early February. "No other single measure open to the Federal Government is more likely to raise the national saving rate, and promote productivity growth, than a substantial reduction in the budget deficit."[4] Whether this administration and Congress could agree on how to make such a reduction, though, was another matter.

■   ■   ■   ■

That the public probably wished them well was understandable. Historically, Americans have never been comfortable with deficits.[5] The debt that the Thirteen Colonies ran up to help finance the War of Independence incited a sweeping debate over the role and power of the new government. In the early 19th century, Thomas Jefferson, Andrew Jackson, and other figures who opposed excessive federal power viewed deficits as a symbol of dangerous excess—indeed, as a sign of moral corruption. After the Civil War, the Republican party exploited the nation's budget-balancing fervor by purposely overspending, providing a justification for revenue-raising tariffs that its business constituents wanted. During the Progressive Era of the early 20th century, officials viewed balanced budgets as a symbol of the "efficiency" they favored in government. Gramm-Rudman reflected the same spirit; it set out a five-year schedule of steadily declining deficits. A balanced budget, once a shared social goal, was now mandated by law.

Balanced budgets have had a symbolic value for Americans, showing that their government was just. Budget balance was the norm. Deficits, however often they occurred, were deemed a deviation. As former House Republican leader John J. Rhodes of Arizona, cochairman of the Committee for a Responsible Federal Budget, said at a seminar a while back, "For nearly two hundred years, the norm of budget balance served our nation very well. Our budgets have not always been in balance, but almost everyone agreed they should be—if not every year, then over some reasonable period of time." Nor was the spirit hollow. For the first 150 years or so, policy-makers hued closely to the line. Sure, annual deficits were not uncommon; Washington produced 46 of them between 1789 and 1930. But they were generally caused by unusual circumstances, such as recessions or the extraordinary costs of financing wars. Once the economy picked up or the combat ceased, Washington balanced its books and even produced surpluses to help pay off the debt.

Even in the last half-century, the budget-balancing spirit was not so much abandoned as it was transformed. President Franklin D. Roosevelt, who promised in his 1932 campaign to balance the budget and quickly tried to do so by cutting federal salaries and veterans' benefits, wrestled long and hard with the idea of deficit spending before accepting it. John Maynard Keynes, the English economist, later provided a philosophical rationale, arguing not only that budgets are a legitimate tool of economic policy, but that deficits would pump up a deflated economy. Not to worry, Keynes told the budget balancers. Deficits generated by a slow economy would be replaced by surpluses at times of prosperity.

For much of the postwar period, Keynesianism was king. Its philosophy dominated the economics profession and provided the intellectual rationale for American fiscal policy. One high-water mark came on December 31, 1965 when *Time*, describing a seemingly boundless economy and Keynes' influence over the Kennedy-Johnson White House, produced a cover story about him. Another came in January 1971, when Nixon, a long-time conservative, declared after submitting his budget, "Now I am a Keynesian."[6] To reconcile the deficits of the time with the philosophical aversion to them, presidents and their advisors relied heavily on the "full employment" budget concept; the budget should be balanced, it proclaimed, if the economy were operating at full employment.

With an economic rationale to support them, deficits grew more common in the 35 years after World War II. Only eight times were the federal books in balance or surplus, all but one of those coming before 1961. The last was in 1969, after Washington enacted an income tax surcharge to help finance the Vietnam War. But Reagan's deficits were much different than any that came before—much larger, more intractable, and more economically troublesome. In actual dollars and, more importantly to economists, as a share of GNP, those deficits dwarfed almost all others. Between 1946 and 1981, the last year shaped by Carter, deficits averaged $16.4 billion, or 1.2 percent of GNP. Under Reagan, they averaged $176 billion, or 4.5 percent. As a result, the debt nearly tripled in the Reagan years, climbing from just under $1 trillion at the end of 1981 to $2.9 trillion at the end of 1989. No longer was the nation's debt shrinking as a share of GNP, as it had over the years. Instead, it climbed in the 1980s from 33.3 percent to 55.6.

To understand how out of balance the books have been recently, consider this: In 1986, when the deficit reached its record $221 billion, the government raised $769 billion and spent $990 billion, a whopping 29 percent difference! Even in fiscal 1989, after nearly a decade of gruesome deficit-cutting battles, the government raised $991 billion and spent $1.143 trillion—a 15 percent difference. Nor could the deficits be blamed on a poor economy. Economists distinguish between "cyclical" and "structural" deficits. The former are caused by recessions or slow growth, as Washington receives less in tax revenues and allocates more in unemployment and other social benefits. By their very nature, cyclical deficits are not worrisome; they melt away when the economy rebounds. Structural deficits are, by contrast, built into the budget. They occur as Washington spends more than it can reasonably expect to raise. While the 1982 recession helped nourish them, Reagan's deficits remained structural: Even with a healthy economy in his last six years, the nation spent at least $150 billion more each year than it received. As Bush took office, CBO projected that the deficit would hover between $120 billion and $140 billion for at least several years longer.

Besides, the deficit-cutting progress that Washington claimed in the late 1980s was based on questionable assumptions. Sure, the deficit fell from $221 billion and was projected to drop more. But those projections did not account for huge spending needs, as outlined by the General Accounting Office in late 1988. Immediately, Washington needed $50 to $100 billion to rescue the troubled savings and loan industry; delays would increase the costs. Over the next decade or so, Washington would need hundreds of billions to maintain programs or fulfill plans for others. The Energy Department faced costs of $100 to $130 billion to clean up and modernize its 50 nuclear weapons plants across the nation. The Pentagon faced costs of $11 to $14 billion to clean up hazardous waste pollution at more than 5,000 military facilities; its plans to build the first phase of the Strategic Defense Initiative ("Star Wars") would add $69 billion more. Other agencies' efforts to upgrade computer operations could add scores of billions.

With the public clamoring for more government, not less, Bush and Congress pledged more spending on education, child care, the environment, and other needs. Because Washington enacted a catastrophic health insurance program in 1988, influential lawmakers wanted to expand federal coverage to long-term care, such as for nursing home stays. (The successful 1989 revolt against the catastrophic program put those plans on hold.) If the White House and Congress chose to, upgrading America's crumbling bridges and highways would cost hundreds of billions, although states share these costs; repairing its deteriorating public housing would add $20 billion; maintaining its national parks would cost $2 billion; and adding needed prison space would cost a few billion more.

Bookkeeping practices, too, hid Washington's long-term fiscal problems, while making its job of meeting Gramm-Rudman's short-term targets much easier. Washington calculated the deficit by including Social Security's surpluses, which grew by $52 billion in fiscal 1989 alone and were expected to approach *$12 trillion* over the next quarter-century. With the surpluses invested in U.S. government securities, they helped to finance deficit spending in the rest of the budget. But, needing money in the early 21st century to pay benefits to the retired "baby boomers," Social Security would have to cash in the securities. To replace those IOUs with real money, Washington would have three unpleasant choices: raise taxes, cut other spending, or borrow more from the markets.

How did the deficit grow to such incredible levels? The answer is not complicated. For all of the blather about whether low taxes or high spending brought on the huge deficit, the simple point is this: no one factor produces a deficit. A deficit is, by definition, a mismatch between taxes and spending. Those who blame just low taxes or just high spending are making political, not substantive, arguments.

As Carol G. Cox, president of the Committee for a Responsible Federal Budget, told the National Economic Commission, "If you are a conservative, you go back to the mid-60s, and you point to the really rather rapid and dramatic expansion of not just the domestic programs in the budget but very large new entitlements in the budget, Medicare probably being the most dramatic because it is far and away the largest of the programs. If you are a liberal, you have to go back to 1981. You say it's that darn Reagan defense buildup and tax cut that caused all of this."

On the other hand, certain tax and spending trends surely contributed to the deficit. In the 1960s and 1970s, Washington enacted new social programs and expanded existing ones. Until the 1980s, financing them was not a big problem. Defense spending was cut after Vietnam, freeing up funds for the domestic sector. Even after raising defense spending again in the late 1970s, Washington fulfilled its domestic commitments by capitalizing on the high inflation of those years. As taxpayers were thrust into higher tax brackets, Washington received a big enough boost in revenues to keep the budget close to balance. In the late 1970s, Washington even cut taxes four times to ease personal tax burdens. While doing all this, government experts projected in those years that the revenue boost would soon replace deficits with surpluses.

Such happy relationships ended in the Reagan years. In the early 1980s, not only did the president push for increased defense spending, reduced taxes, and an inadequate amount of domestic cuts to cover the difference, but the Federal Reserve Board (Fed) sent inflation down dramatically with its tight monetary policies. No longer could Washington count on such a large inflation-adjusted boost in revenues. In addition, by 1985, the tax code had been "indexed," so taxpayers no longer would move into higher brackets simply because of inflation. Now, if inflation returned, an inflation-adjusted boost in revenues would not.

The Reagan program—supply-side theory, conservative ideology and post-Carter optimism—actually had deep roots in the late 1970s. The defense buildup, for instance, began under Carter who, in talks with European leaders, committed the United States to a 3 percent annual inflation-adjusted growth in defense spending. Day-to-day domestic spending, which grew significantly in the prior two decades, came under closer scrutiny from a public tired of "Big Government." On the revenue side, House Republicans, fighting the Democrats' fiscal 1977 proposal for $50-per-taxpayer rebates and increased federal spending, proposed an across-the-board reduction in tax rates. Congress cut the tax rate on capital gains in 1978. The congressional Joint Economic Committee issued reports in 1979 and 1980 calling for tax cuts and spending restraint. The Senate Finance Committee, in Democratic hands, passed tax-cutting legislation similar to the plan that Reagan endorsed in his campaign. And Rep. Jack F. Kemp, a Republican from near Buffalo, New York, was holding discussions in his office with a small group of academics, ex-journalists, lawmakers, congressional staffers, and others who would later head up the supply-side movement.

A vacuum had opened in fiscal policy. The Keynesian movement, attacked from several directions, was in retreat. One challenge was mounted in the 1960s by the "monetarists," who believed that monetary, rather than fiscal, policy was key to steering the economy. Another came from the "rational expectations" school, which held that individuals would anticipate future economic conditions and act accordingly. But the most serious challenge was the "stagflation" of the 1970s because, contrary to the facts at hand, Keynesianism had postulated that higher inflation and slower economic growth would not occur simultaneously.

When the going got tough, Democrats largely abandoned Keynes. No longer would they defend deficit spending as a useful tool of economic policy. By 1984, they had run so far from Keynes that their presidential candidate, Walter F. Mondale, disappointed liberals by campaigning. as one put it, as a "Democratic Hoover" who promised only to cut the deficit.[7] Democrats and Republicans practically switched sides on the issue. With deficits soaring under a GOP administration, top Republicans suddenly adopted a new "don't worry, be happy" attitude toward them. Surely the most symbolic moment came in 1981 when Kemp told the House Budget Committee on which he served, "The Republican party no longer worships at the altar of a balanced budget." Democrats were so startled to hear the news, they asked him to repeat it.

Developments at the state level were important as well. With inflation robbing people of their earnings and pushing them into higher tax brackets, antigovernment fever swept across the nation. As inflation rose, so did the public's resentment of it. New York City's fiscal crisis of 1975 came to symbolize government profligacy. Highlighted by California's Proposition 13 in June of 1978, which limited property taxes and made it harder to raise them, voters in at least 10 states considered ballot questions to limit or cut their taxes. Most were approved. The next year, many governors and legislatures cut taxes.

Supply-side economics offered an appealing antidote. The traditional, or "old school," Republican ideology talked about pain and sacrifice to balance the budget. Supply-siders, who dismissed this politically unpopular "root canal" brand of economics, had a sunnier outlook. "The world could indeed be started anew," Stockman recalled thinking at the time. "Its current accumulating economic and social breakdowns could be repaired and its older, inherited ills of racism and poverty vanquished by sweeping changes in the policies which caused or prolonged them."[8] How many supply-siders truly believed that lower tax rates would boost revenues, as economic activity surged, is debatable. Murray Weidenbaum, first chairman of Reagan's Council of Economic Advisors, remembers a high-ranking Treasury Department official predicting that so much revenue would come in that the government would have to increase spending to rid itself of a budget surplus. Stockman believes the school's leading theorists, such as Arthur Laffer and Jude Wanniski, perverted supply-side tenets into happy notions of more revenue for political reasons. Either way, although retaining its adherents, supply-side philosophy has largely fallen into disrepute, blamed for the fiscal profligacy that threatens living standards.

On the spending side, the Reagan program and congressional adjustments to it brought vast change. Of the $1.1 trillion spent in fiscal 1989, defense consumed 27 percent, up from 23 percent in 1981. Entitlements consumed 48 percent, about the same as eight years earlier. Because big deficits added so much to the debt, interest payments represented 15 percent of spending in 1989, nearly double its share of a decade earlier. As the nation's leaders would not raise taxes or limit defense or entitlements enough to cut the deficit much, attention focused on the only place left: the day-to-day domestic programs, such as education, housing, transportation, environmental protection, the FBI, CIA, and IRS—indeed, everything that Americans think of as their "government." Under close scrutiny each year, that portion of the budget shrunk from 25 to 17 percent during the Reagan years.

■   ■   ■   ■

In the abstract, not all deficits are bad. In extraordinary situations, governments would be foolish not to borrow if they had to. Annual deficits averaged a huge 23 percent of GNP from 1942 to 1945, when the nation was financing its participation in World War II, and nobody views that policy as reckless. Similarly, deficit spending is justified, if not praiseworthy, if the nation allocates its borrowed funds to long-term investments. In that situation, future generations who bear the burdens of that debt also reap its rewards. Today's deficits, however, are much different. Almost nobody views them as benign, but how economically damaging they are is debatable. The Reagan era has shaken some deeply held beliefs, shifting the debate over the economics of deficits.

Consider this: In 1980, Carter proposed a fiscal 1981 budget with a projected deficit of $15.8 billion. When private forecasters soon estimated that the deficit would be three or four times as high, Wall Street reacted violently. The bond market sank. Panicked White House officials and Democratic congressional leaders rushed to the bargaining table. Three weeks later, they unveiled an ill-fated plan to replace the deficit with a $16.5 billion surplus. By the late 1980s, even a deficit of $40 billion to $80 billion—that is, in the range that had shaken Wall Street—would seem unfathomably low. Elected officials grew accustomed to deficits of at least $150 billion. More than one lawmaker said that cutting the deficit to below $100 billion would be considered a moral victory. Economists have not grown so accustomed. But the 1980s jolted their outlook, because it broke each of their rules. Big deficits, they thought, would provoke serious short-term problems. But as Washington piled up annual deficits, the economy chugged along.

Before the 1980s, for instance, economists had long warned that deficits would bring higher inflation. Under one theory, deficits would force the Fed to increase the supply of dollars in the economy; as a result, more dollars would be chasing the same amount of goods. Under another, the Fed, seeing no other way to repay the debt, would inflate the currency so the debt would be cheaper. Republican leaders had long warned about the inflationary effects of deficits. Eisenhower and Nixon did, as did Sen. Barry Goldwater of Arizona, the Republican presidential nominee in 1964. In the 1968 elections, other Republicans blamed the 5 percent inflation of that day on deficit spending that financed Johnson's "Great Society." By the late 1970s, many Democrats bought the deficit-inflation link, including some of Carter's advisors. Reagan also accepted the prevailing notions. He warned about the deficit-inflation link in his 1980 campaign and in his 1981 "Program for Economic Recovery." In pushing for more domestic spending cuts in late 1981, Stockman warned that higher deficits would force inflation up. Economists Alan Greenspan, Herbert Stein, and Walter Heller, chairman of President Kennedy's Council of Economic Advisors, sounded similar alarms.

Deficits soared, from $79 billion for the budget that Reagan inherited from Carter, to $128 billion for fiscal 1982, Reagan's first budget, to $208 billion the next year, to $212 and $221 billion in 1985 and 1986. What happened to inflation? It sank faster than even the optimistic Reagan team thought possible. In firm control of the Fed's policy-making apparatus, Volcker was determined to wring inflation out of the economy. In clamping down on the money supply, sending the economy into a deep recession, he helped cut inflation from 13.3 percent in 1979 to below 4 percent by 1982. Deficits moved one way, inflation moved the other.

Interest rates also defied conventional wisdom. Deficits were supposed to send them skyward. In this view, the government, whose borrowing needs had to be satisfied before any other borrowers', would soak up a greater portion of available credit. It would "crowd out" credit for others. The tight competition among private borrowers for whatever credit remained would push interest rates higher. All through the 1980s, the deficit-interest rate connection had been taken for granted. Reagan paid it lip service by approving of tax increases in the early 1980s. Martin Feldstein, the most controversial chairman of Reagan's Council of Economic Advisors, warned about higher interest rates. In the late 1980s, lawmakers of both parties still talked about the connection.

But in the early 1980s, deficits went one way, interest rates went another. From more than 14 percent in 1981, interest rates on three-month Treasury bills had dropped to below 9 percent by 1983. By the mid-1980s, various studies were questioning the existence of any strong deficit-interest rate link. The Treasury Department issued one report in 1984. CBO followed a year later. Some economists began to offer other explanations for the level of interest rates. Some pointed to monetary policy, others to overall economic activity, still others to the international economy. All of this does not prove, of course, that deficits do not cause higher inflation or interest rates. Who knows? Maybe both of those measures of economic performance would be lower if deficits were not so high. And while interest rates were lower than in the Carter years, *real* interest rates (that is, interest rates minus the inflation rate—perhaps a better measure of borrowing costs) were at their highest levels in at least several decades. Some economists said the deficits had indeed forced borrowers to compete more vigorously for credit, sending real interest rates upward.

But by the late 1980s, economists had begun to sound like the "boys who cried wolf." Economic apocalypse? No one had seen much evidence. Liberals began to wonder why they should not spend more on social programs. Conservatives dug in their heels even harder against a tax increase. The hawks, who tended toward the center of the political spectrum, were beginning to feel like a lonely lot. As Bill Frenzel of Minnesota, now senior Republican on the House Budget Committee, told me around that time, "The fact that the sky has not fallen has made Chicken Little an unreliable prophet. And it makes it difficult for us. The folks who do not want to stop spending have a pretty good argument."

Are the deficits that important after all? Experts began to wonder. "I confess to being weary of writing about budget deficits," economics columnist Robert J. Samuelson wrote in October 1988. "It's not only that people don't know what to believe anymore...but I'm not sure what to tell them."[9] Other journalists raised doubts. "Is the deficit really so bad?" the *Atlantic* asked in its February 1989 cover story, which reached the newstands in mid-January.[10] A few days later, the *New York Times* followed with a front-page piece entitled "Is the deficit still dangerous? Maybe not, some start to say."[11] Stories and columns followed, in the *Wall Street Journal, Washington Post*, and elsewhere.

"Well, yes," economists now insisted. "Deficits *do* matter." But the economists' outlook had changed. Years earlier, deficits were the "train wreck" just around the bend. Cut the deficit or else there would be soaring inflation! Higher interest rates! Economic collapse! Now economists focused on the long term. Deficits, they said, were part of a larger problem: national saving. Lower saving led to less investment, lower productivity, and lower living standards. Deficits, they said, were like a slow-moving "cancer," eating away at the nation's economic foundations, or like Schultze's "termites in the basement."

The long-term focus, though, caused big problems for the hawks. Deficit cutting was not pleasant. Taxes would have to rise, spending would have to fall. Voters would not like either option. In a widely cited article in 1984, University of Michigan economist Edward M. Gramlich, who later served as the CBO's acting director, suggested that the effects of deficits on living standards might not be apparent for two decades or more.[12] House members faced reelection every two years, presidents every four, senators every six. Presuming Gramlich was right, why would today's elected officials, whose incentives revolved around electoral needs, want to anger today's voters? Helping future generations would be nice. But short-term needs would not permit it.

Lawmakers admitted to the dilemma in words and actions. Only if a crisis provided the excuse, they thought, could they justify to voters the tax hikes and spending cuts that a big deficit-cutting plan required. In late 1985, they tried to invent a short-term crisis with Gramm-Rudman. If they did not reduce the deficit to a set level each year, the law would do it with a "meat axe" plan of indiscriminate cuts. Wouldn't the nation's leaders, spurred by such a threat, surely find a more rational way? Not necessarily. To prevent the onset of deep across-the-board cuts in 1987, Washington did not replace them with a big deficit-reduction plan. Rather, in September, Reagan and Congress revised Gramm-Rudman by raising the deficit targets, thus making it easier to comply with the law. Deficit cutting was OK, it seemed, if it did not unduly burden anyone.

Around that time, Democrats were pushing for a high-level summit with Reagan to devise a deficit-cutting plan. Reagan was not interested. The Democrats wanted to raise taxes. He did not. Both sides dug in. Tension between Republicans and Democrats, and between Reagan and Congress, was as high as anyone could remember. Of Reagan, a former House Democratic aide snarled, "He'll meet with Gorbachev, but he won't meet with Congress." Some lawmakers continued to hope for a summit, but Reagan privately told GOP leaders that he would take the $23 billion in across-the-board cuts, mandated by the revision of Gramm-Rudman, rather than agree to raise taxes.

A month later, however, Wall Street offered the short-term crisis that Washington had sought. As the stock market fell 508 points on October's "Black Monday," the closely watched Dow Jones Industrial Average lost nearly a quarter of its value in the biggest loss ever recorded. Explanations ran the gamut, from the budget deficit, to provisions of a tax bill being drafted at the House Ways and Means Committee, to the Reagan administration's policy on the international value of the dollar, to the trade deficit, to American strikes against Iranian oil drilling platforms, to Reagan's weakness in governing the nation, to a market-induced correction to 1987's run-up in stock prices. Plenty of analysts disputed each explanation as it was offered.

Markets are strange entities, studied by many but understood by few. Nobody really knows why the stock market, or any other market, moves one way or another on a particular day. Nor does anyone know where the market is headed tomorrow. Such fluctuations result from the thousands of decisions of money managers, traders, investors, and others. Although analysts use the catch all phrase "Wall Street" to denote the financial world, participants operate all over the nation and world. But some of the nation's leading officials hooked onto the deficit-crash connection. Whether they believed it was another question. But a crisis was nothing if not an opportunity. "The theory that the budget deficit caused the market crash thus did not have to be correct in order to be widely accepted and immediately acted upon," Joseph Grundfest, a Securities and Exchange Commission member, wrote in 1988. "Instead, the theory was accepted because it provided a convenient rationalization for actions policy makers wanted to take anyway."[13]

The crash, however, *did* seem to shake some well-entrenched beliefs. The market needed the reassurance that Washington was working on the deficit problem. After meeting with Greenspan (who had replaced Volcker at the Fed), Treasury Secretary James A. Baker III, and White House chief of staff Howard Baker, Jr., Reagan changed course. The president sent the two Bakers and James C. Miller III, OMB's director, to negotiate with congressional leaders. Yes, Reagan said, he would accept a tax hike to help cut the deficit. After a month of closed-door meetings, negotiators brought out a two-year agreement, but it was hardly sizable enough to tackle the structural mismatch between taxes and spending.

Washington remained concerned about Wall Street as Bush took office. A second crash was not inconceivable. But such fears no longer seemed so imposing. After all, the nation had survived "Black Monday," and better than many economists expected—no recession, no noticeable effect on economic growth. Stock prices settled after the crash at about the level at which they began in 1987. As *Business Week* explained it in a story commemorating the crash's one-year anniversary, "A funny thing happened when the market crashed last year. Nothing else did. . . . That puts Oct. 19 in the history books alongside such curiosities as the tulip-bulb mania in 17th Century Holland and the crash of the silver market in 1980."[14] The deficit hawks now had a new concern. If the crash did not hurt the nation much in 1987, then perhaps nobody would care if a second one occurred.

By 1989, the hawks had turned to another short-term incentive. Foreign investors had been buying large chunks of federal government debt, and owned almost 20 percent of the outstanding, privately held debt by the end of 1988. Their purchases helped keep interest rates lower than otherwise. Without them, the Treasury would need to offer higher rates to entice enough American investors into buying the debt. Rates on federal debt influence all other interest rates, from those which banks offer their most reliable corporate clients to those which car and mortgage companies charge to middle-class families. Americans, thus, had reason to welcome foreign participation. But the participation had costs. The nation was now dependent on foreigners. No longer could its leaders worry only about their domestic audience. In late 1989, Japanese economics professor Mototada Kikkawa suggested in an article for the *Journal of Commerce* that Japan consider retaliating against any future American trade sanctions by cutting Japanese purchase of U.S. Treasury securities. Referring to this article, Sen. J. James Exon, a Nebraska Democrat, told his colleagues in a floor speech: "Professor Kikkawa has finally spoken to what I and many of my fiscally conservative colleagues have warned of for many years. There is a danger to U.S. debt and dependence on foreign capital. That danger is a real loss of American economic and political independence."

At issue was foreign confidence in the American economy. The value of the dollar on international markets was one sign of it. Foreigners owned billions of dollars. A fall in the value of that currency would cost them dearly. If some investors began to sell dollars, others might follow, sending the value plummeting. A free fall like that could send inflation rocketing. Why the dollar moves up or down in value—and, particularly, whether the deficit plays a big role—is not much clearer than why stock prices move. But Washington was clearly worried. A sharp drop in the dollar's value just after Bush's election was widely seen as a "warning shot" from foreigners. "Get your deficit down," they seemed to be saying. "We're not going to buy your federal debt forever." The nation's leaders were hemmed in. While the Fed may have wanted to cut interest rates to keep the economy growing, it could not afford to do so. It had to maintain interest rates at levels that were high enough to keep foreigners interested in our debt.

As fears of a dollar sell-off grew, lawmakers and senior aides sought to dampen foreign expectations of a big deficit-cutting deal by early 1989. Relax, they told the investors, bankers and others who visited from Tokyo and elsewhere. The American system of government is slow, clumsy, even messy. Deficit reduction might not come until late 1989, and only after Bush and Congress had fought bitterly. "'My No. 1 message this fall," a top House aide told me in late 1988, "is to talk to as many of these people as possible and to say, 'For God's sake, don't think that we're going to come to a solution in January, February, or March.' This thing is clearly going to take until autumn, maybe even until there is snow on the ground. We're going to spend the whole spring trying to figure out where we are, and then the whole summer probably bashing each other." For foreigners accustomed to the smooth workings of parliamentary government in which, by definition, the same party controls the executive and legislative branches, it was a rude lesson.

■   ■   ■   ■

Had the foreigners visited Washington months earlier, they might have received a more heartening message. In early 1988, lawmakers, lobbyists, and private experts had big hopes for the National Economic Commission. Why not? "Government by commission," as some called it, was a growing phenomenon in Washington, reflecting a weakening of the political process. The rationale for it was simple: The nation's leaders could not solve the more ticklish political problems as well as they once could. Private interests were powerful enough to block steps they opposed. Deadlocks would ensue between the White House and Congress, Democrats and Republicans, northerners and southerners, and urban and rural interests. Solutions were delayed; problems grew.

Let's say, for instance, that a federal program was going broke. A lawmaker might suggest that, to rebuild its finances, the program's beneficiaries should pay a fee for its services. Groups that represent the beneficiaries would react swiftly. Lobbyists would travel to Capitol Hill or to executive branch departments, asking their friends to denounce the idea. The group might begin a national letter-writing campaign, stirring up its members through stories in the group's newsletter and reaching other sympathetic Americans through newspaper advertisements. Before long, the proposal would die unceremoniously, opposed by more than enough executive branch officials or lawmakers. So, getting nowhere, the White House and Congress would set up an independent commission to study the problem. The commission might, in fact, recommend the same proposal as had the lawmaker. But in this case, the commission would provide "political cover" to others. To the angry beneficiaries, lawmakers who voted for the fee could say: "It was not my idea. This commission of experts suggested we do it. To solve the problem, we all decided to go along."

Since the early 1980s, Washington had created commissions to perform a number of functions: devise a plan for the financially troubled Social Security system; study United States policy toward Central America; draft a plan for land-based nuclear weapons; decide which domestic military bases to close; suggest how to provide long-term and other health care; recommend new pay levels for lawmakers, judges, and top federal officials; and, finally, craft a plan to eliminate the deficit. Only a last-minute snag in late 1988 prevented Congress from setting up a commission to look at the nation's savings and loan mess. Some panels worked, some did not.

Most interesting, the Social Security commission, chaired by Greenspan, is considered the standard by which to judge others. But despite broad perceptions to the contrary, that commission was not really the success many think. Set up in early 1982, it collapsed in partisan squabbling at year's end. Republicans opposed tax increases, while Democrats opposed cuts in benefits. At that point, a rump group of some commission members and White House officials negotiated a Social Security rescue plan in private and then took it to the commission. The commission, in turn, adopted the plan as its own and sent it to Congress, where the House and Senate adopted it without much change. Payroll taxes were raised and benefits limited in some ways. Social Security, America's most cherished program, was again financially secure.

So in the late 1980s, Congress would try again. But if Social Security was a tough challenge, the deficit promised to be even more difficult. Commissions work best when the nation faces an immediate, observable crisis. Social Security fit the bill. After all, it was running out of money and would be bankrupt by July of 1983. Checks would be delayed. What would happen then? Demonstrations, mass panic, or worse. And what would happen to the already tenuous bond between government and its people? No longer would today's and tomorrow's elderly be sure that Uncle Sam would meet his obligations. The system simply had to be saved. The deficit, as we have noted, was a wholly different problem. Only if it precipitated another stock market crash, a run on the dollar, or another economic malady would it be viewed as an immediate crisis.

Nevertheless, in early 1988, hopes were high in Washington. Nearly everyone drew analogies to Greenspan's commission while ignoring the differences between Social Security and the deficit. Hopeful, too, was the commission itself, a panel of 12 (later expanded to 14), whose well-regarded staff worked in a townhouse on Lafayette Park, across from the White House. Early on, the panel set a December 21, 1988, deadline for submitting its report, although the law did not demand one until March 1, 1989. By reporting early, members hoped to have some input into the next president's first budget plan, which presumably would come in early 1989. The law enabled the new president to make two appointments to the commission, boosting its membership from 12 to 14. But because he could not officially do so until after December 19, 1988, when the Electoral College confirmed his victory, the commission would wait until then before issuing its report; before then, the president's two choices could work informally with the commission to shape the report.

Commission membership was impressive enough. With two members appointed by Reagan, the others by congressional leaders of both parties, the panel included past and present lawmakers, former officials, and business, labor, and civic leaders. All were "movers and shakers"—powerful, respected, politically well connected. In particular, hopes centered on the two cochairmen. Robert S. Strauss, known in Washington as "Mr. Democrat," had served as the Democratic National Committee chairman and was Carter's U.S. special trade representative. Drew Lewis, a major force in Pennsylvania Republican politics, had served as the number 2 man at the Republican National Committee and was Reagan's first Transportation Secretary. They were accustomed to getting what they wanted in politics through smarts, savvy, and connections. What they clearly wanted this time was for the commission to work, to issue a significant report, to play a role in early 1989 when, presumably, a new president and Congress would face the deficit head on.

To do all this, though, the commission had to proceed quietly through most of 1988. Candidates were running for president. If the commission began to openly consider specific tax hikes or spending cuts, reporters invariably would ask candidates how they liked the ideas. The candidates, in turn, would be tempted to curry favor with particular groups. An increase in the gas tax? No way, the candidates might say, particularly if campaigning in southern or western states where voters rely so heavily on cars. Once the candidates were locked into such positions, the commission would have two choices: recommend those proposals anyway and risk irrelevance, or choose from a narrower list of options. As the *New York Times* editorialized, "The whole undertaking will be doomed if the commission itself becomes a campaign issue."[15]

So the panel moved slowly, its members displaying surprising candor only about their own ignorance. The first of three public hearings in early 1988 was especially revealing, as budget experts walked the members through the complicated world of numbers, rules, and the "current services" baseline. The commission's four lawmakers did not need much tutoring. Domenici and Rep. William H. Gray III, a Pennsylvania Democrat, had chaired the Senate and House Budget Committees, respectively. Moynihan served on the Senate committee. Frenzel, a former House Budget Committee member, would soon be tapped as its top Republican. Nor did former Defense Secretaries Weinberger and Donald Rumsfeld need a refresher course, having helped draft Pentagon budgets.

But to the others, budgeting was an eye-opening experience. After a short talk from Timothy J. Muris, a former top

OMB official, about the "current services" baseline, Strauss said, "Thank you. I've never understood that before. Thank you. You've taught me something." "Well," Muris replied, "I think quite frankly if someone with your knowledge and expertise in Washington doesn't understand it, that shows you we've got a problem." To which Strauss countered, "Shows you I've got one, anyway." Chrysler Corporation chairman Lee A. Iacocca, a commission member, had a harsher judgment about the budget rules. Commenting after the meeting, he said, "If we did this in business, they'd lock us up."[16]

At the same time, the commission was receiving some of its 1,200 written submissions from lawmakers, economists, business and labor leaders, and average citizens, all suggesting how, or how not, to cut the deficit. Up to three quarters were generated by a letter-writing campaign on the part of Fuel Users for Equitable Levies (FUEL), a coalition of groups opposed to raising the nine-cent-a-gallon federal tax on gasoline to cut the deficit. The American Petroleum Institute, Automobile Association of America, and other groups, whose members would be hurt financially by measures that discouraged gas use, hoped to head off such a recommendation at a time when Greenspan, Volcker, Ford, Carter, powerful lawmakers, newspapers, and columnists had urged that the tax go up to cut the deficit and boost conservation.

More privately, the members learned about the budget by playing a computerized game. Created by a commission staffer, it let them choose among tax and spending options and learn how much, alone or together, these options would cut the deficit. For those who could not play at commission headquarters, staffers brought computers and disks to their business offices: Moynihan at the Capitol, Weinberger at his Washington law office, Rumsfeld in Chicago, and Iacocca in Detroit; the car magnate played without interruption for more than three hours. Had the commission followed its plans, the members each would have used a revised version of the computer game to draft a one-page budget outline—so much in cuts from defense, entitlements, and day-to-day domestic programs and so much in tax increases. With those drafts as a framework, the members then would have chosen from among hundreds of pages of specific tax and spending options from a staff-written resource book. To get a consensus report, the members would have negotiated not only the broad numbers of cuts and tax hikes but also the specific proposals.

■   ■   ■   ■

As it turned out, they never got that far. In several ways, the commission was doomed from the start. An early blow was struck by its legal framework, which required that negotiations among members take place in public. By their very nature, such negotiations were unlikely to bear fruit unless done privately. In a closed room, members could let their hair down. "Sure, Cap," AFL-CIO president Lane Kirkland, a Democratic appointee, might say to Weinberger, "I will agree to cut Social Security benefits—if you will agree to cut defense." "All right, Bill," Dean R. Kleckner, president of the American Farm Bureau Federation and a Republican selection, might tell Gray, "I'll agree to cut farm subsidies, if you'll cut programs that help cities like your home town of Philadelphia." Lewis might deal with Felix Rohatyn, an investment banker and Democratic appointee. Strauss might do the same with Rumsfeld. As such deals developed, the group could come together and draft a report. When the report was made public, each member could deny that he was the source of particular tax hikes or spending cuts.

Private, informal conversations of that sort had taken place among individual members. Lewis and other Republicans, for instance, figured they could craft a report, signed by perhaps 10 or 11 members, that called for cutting the deficit by $100 billion or so over three years. If the report included recommendations for a tax increase, they knew that Kleckner would not sign on. Kleckner's federation had mounted a "*no* to more taxes" campaign, complete with buttons and bumper stickers. With the effort coordinated through the various state farm bureaus, farmers were encouraged to express their views in letters to their senators and House members.

To support a tax hike, Kleckner would have to buck his own constituency. He showed no inclination to do so.

Others, however, seemed more open. In their testimony to the commission, such figures as Volcker and William E. Brock, a prominent Republican who had served in the White House and Congress, suggested raising the gas tax or other excise taxes. Republicans, thus, had the "political cover" to propose such steps. Presuming they could raise $50 billion or so in taxes, they planned to add another $50 billion in spending cuts to fashion their three-year, $100 billion package. Republicans figured that the Democrats would go along, although they might have to entice some by offering to recommend new social spending. But if negotiations were held in public, candor would not last long. Kirkland would be pressured to protect the interests of labor, Weinberger and Rumsfeld of defense, Gray and Moynihan of social programs, and Domenici and Frenzel of Republicans opposed to higher taxes. If they hinted at compromise, interest groups would react strongly, forcing them to back off. Consensus would prove elusive. Indeed, Greenspan's commission and the rump group that sprang from it and the 1988 commission that recommended domestic base closings had worked privately.

The National Economic Commission would have no such luck. As legislation to create it was completed in December 1987, the Senate Governmental Affairs Committee urged that the panel be covered by the Federal Advisory Committee Act. Nobody objected, so it was. Along with providing guidance on such routine matters as where to get furniture, the act generally forced commissions of this sort to hold their meetings in public. The Senate committee, which took its jurisdiction over the act quite seriously, had learned not long before that some panels had not complied. Staffers were even thinking about amendments to strengthen the act.

At least some members of the economic commission quickly grasped the ramifications of an open-meeting policy. When the two Bakers (White House chief of staff, Treasury secretary) hosted an informal get-together for the commission in March 1988, Strauss asked his law firm colleague

Alexander D. Platt to brief members on legal matters. Platt, who became the commission's counsel, mentioned the open-meeting requirement. "What!" Rohatyn exclaimed. Others raised their eyebrows. You could hardly blame them. Kirkland and Moynihan had served on Greenspan's commission, and Kirkland and Strauss had served on the 1984 panel that studied United States policy toward Central America. When the economic commission tried to close its meetings in late 1988, some news organizations sued. In December and January, a federal judge blocked the panel's plans.

The judge's actions, however, came after the commission had probably been mortally wounded anyway. Despite its hopes, the panel was gradually drawn into the 1988 presidential fray. An early salvo came from Bush, who had never liked the commission in the first place. It probably didn't help matters that Strauss was a close friend of Dole, who challenged Bush for the presidential nomination, and that Lewis ran Dole's presidential campaign in Pennsylvania. At a news conference in May 1988 in Kennebunkport, Maine, where he was meeting with economic advisors, Bush said, "As far as that commission goes, it should shape its recommendations based on what the American people say in the election.... Because it seems to me that commission might well come up with a tax increase and I'll be saying, 'Wait a minute. I've taken my case to the American people to hold the line on taxes. Workingmen and workingwomen in this country don't need to pay any more in taxes.' That's what I would be vociferously insisting on as a newly elected president. There might be other parts of the thing that would be useful."

Nor did Bush's aides take kindly to the panel. When officials from Dukakis's campaign asked the commission's staff for an update on its activities, top staffers decided they should give such information to both campaigns. In July, Platt and Mathiasen, the former OMB aide who served as the commission's executive director, visited Bush's campaign headquarters in Washington. Among those on hand were John H. Sununu, later appointed as the White House chief of staff. Some Bush aides seemed disinterested, others hostile. They

asked about the commission's legal standing and about how
and when Bush, if elected President, would make his two appointments. Nobody asked about the budget. One Bush aide
said Dukakis had a "secret plan" to raise taxes as high as
possible.

By the fall, the commission had added to its own problems, with members issuing some rather undiplomatic remarks. That the most harmful ones came from Strauss, considered as savvy a political insider as Washington offered, was
only more startling. In a September 20 speech, he brought the
commission more directly into the presidential campaign by
suggesting what the panel must target to cut the deficit. "We
have to go to Social Security. We have to go to Medicare, entitlements generally, and we have to go to defense," he said at
an international economics conference in Washington. Asked
after his speech about Bush's "read my lips" comment against
a tax increase, he said, "I take heart in one thing. I know
George Bush, and I think he knows better."

Even if he did, Bush would not admit it. Predictably,
he and Dukakis immediately distanced themselves from
Strauss's remarks. A Bush spokesman in Washington repeated the candidate's pledge to cut the deficit without raising
taxes or cutting Social Security. From Boston, the Dukakis
campaign issued a prepared statement vowing to oppose Social Security cuts. Even Strauss's commission colleagues de-
serted him. Moynihan and Kirkland said that they, too, would
oppose Social Security cuts. Within days, two Republican
members denounced the tax-hike talk: Frenzel, a long-time
congressional opponent of raising taxes, and Kleckner.

In a broader sense, Strauss's comments had confirmed
the suspicions of tough, hard-nosed conservatives throughout Washington. The commission, they had warned from the
start, was just a "tax hike Trojan horse," a tool through which
the next president and Congress could raise taxes. Columnists Evans and Novak called it "Mario Cuomo's tax increase
time bomb."[17] The notion was so widely held that the Chamber of Commerce's chief economist, Richard W. Rahn, dis-

cussed it openly when testifying before the commission in late
1988. His comments brought a pointed rebuke from Lewis. "I
think one thing you should be aware of as far as the commission itself is concerned," Lewis lectured Rahn, is that "we are
not a tax commission nor are we proposing taxes."

By then, disappointment with the commission had engulfed Washington's policy-making community, except among
those who viewed a tax increase as more harmful than
the deficit itself. "Right now, I'd have to say we're discouraged," Warren Lasko, executive vice president of the Mortgage Bankers Association of America, told me at the time. "I
was really hopeful that the commission was going to bite the
bullet and raise taxes. You do all the cutting that you can,
and then you bite the bullet." Christopher Zimmerman, an
official with the National Conference of State Legislatures,
said of the commission members, "There is more and more
feeling that they don't seem to be moving towards each other
at all."

As the campaign wound down, the Bush team did not
know what to do about the commission. Bush's no-tax pledge
had risen above the level of mere rhetoric. It was a measuring
rod by which to judge his integrity. If Bush broke it, according
to some of his advisors, his credibility, if not his very presidency, would be ruined. Domenici made that point privately.
Before the November 8 election, well-connected Republicans
in Washington had sent encouraging signals to the commission, suggesting that it not worry about Bush's pledge. Even
if the commission suggested a tax increase, it still could play
a role in 1989. After all, Bush had said "no *new* taxes." He
could, as many insiders expected him to do, raise the old ones.
But such signals stopped coming after November 8.

The commission's Republicans had little room to maneuver, as the Democrats openly, if unhappily, acknowledged.
They could not buck their new president on such a symbol-
ically important issue as taxes. If Bush said that he could
balance the budget without raising taxes, they, too, would
say so. Politically, the Democrats were boxed in as well. Sure,

they viewed Bush's promise as a sham, an artful ploy to help him get elected. But they could not suggest that taxes be raised. To do so would leave them twisting in the wind, under attack from the commission's conservative critics, who had long warned of such things. And it would burden the national Democratic party, which Republicans had effectively tarred in recent years as the party of "tax and spend."

By Election Day, Lewis had talked occasionally with James A. Baker III, Bush's campaign chairman, and with Nicholas F. Brady, the Treasury Secretary and a close friend of Bush's. They discussed the panel's activities and tossed around the names of possible Bush appointees. Whom to appoint was dependent on what role Bush wanted the commission to play. Richard G. Darman, a campaign advisor whom Bush later appointed as his OMB director, was a possibility, particularly if Bush decided that the commission could be useful. Another was Paul Craig Roberts, a supply-side Treasury official under Reagan and a vociferous opponent of tax hikes. His selection, they figured, would kill any tax hike talk.

Bush had a related decision to make. The law offered him the chance to extend the commission for six months beyond its March 1 expiration date. Domenici suggested that he exercise the option. Under Gramm-Rudman, the president and Congress would focus in the fall on whether they had sliced the deficit enough to avoid across-the-board spending cuts in fiscal 1990. If they had not and a deadlock over what to do ensued, Domenici figured that the commission could play a useful role. Lewis and Frenzel disagreed, saying that the commission was beyond hope of success. If it died, Bush could move on and try to work with Democrats in Congress. If the commission stayed alive, debating tax hikes or spending cuts, it could complicate Bush's congressional relations.

Bush sided with Lewis and Frenzel; he wanted the commission out of the way. And before it went, he didn't want it to complicate his life with an embarrassing report. Required to appoint a Democrat and a Republican, Bush settled on former Rep. Thomas L. "Lud" Ashley of Ohio, a close friend and Democrat, and Paul Laxalt, the former Republican senator from Nevada. The conservative Laxalt was chosen not only to block any tax talk, but to do so in a less combative way than the high-profile Roberts might. That way, Bush would not ruffle any Democratic feathers.

The commission split into two: the seven Republicans and Ashley issued a majority report, the other six Democrats drafted a minority version. Even though it was an embarrassingly skimpy seven pages, lacking in much substance, the majority report was no easy matter to compose. A draft of just four paragraphs, submitted by Lewis's aide, Gary Schuster, to start the process, was met with broad criticism. Weinberger sent in six pages, four of them dealing with defense. Rumsfeld rewrote the Weinberger draft. Kleckner proposed major changes. Everyone else offered ideas. Because the judge had prohibited the commission's majority from meeting privately, ideas flowed in by telephone or fax machine to Schuster, who coordinated the editing process.

Schuster wrote a final draft and circulated it for two weeks among the members. Their aides visited Schuster's office in Washington with Union Pacific Corporation, where he and Lewis worked, to suggest changes. Members phoned in their comments. (Rumsfeld called from the Caribbean, working through a Spanish-speaking operator.) Weinberger and Rumsfeld wanted the defense budget protected. Domenici wanted the question of Social Security's growing surpluses addressed; Kleckner and Weinberger, on the other hand, wanted Social Security to be ignored. Frenzel and Ashley wanted to discuss budget process reforms. Rumsfeld and Ashley wanted some mention of the savings and loan crisis. Compromises took shape as negotiations ensued over sentences, words, and punctuation.

By the time it expired, the National Economic Commission had become what its members most wanted to avoid: a politically split body, Republicans on one side, Democrats on the other, divided over basic issues of how much Washington should tax, how much it should spend, and for what. It had become, in essence, a miniaturized version of the Congress itself, unable to free itself from the interparty split over fiscal policy. For all the hoopla surrounding its creation more than a year earlier, its death was barely noticed. The major newspapers tucked their small stories about the commission's demise well inside their editions.

■   ■   ■   ■

It was a portent of things to come. The healthy economy had long been a huge obstacle for the deficit hawks. In 1989, they would face a few more in the aftermath of the presidential campaign and changes in the public mood. While Bush had paid lip service to the idea of deficit cutting, he and the public seemed predisposed toward other things. Bush's no-tax pledge alone might make it impossible for his aides to craft the big deficit-cutting deal with the Democrats that each side said it wanted. As for the public, it seemed more interested in higher spending to address social needs, and less interested in the belt-tightening required to cut the deficit. To see the trouble ahead, one needed only to look at the budget proposals that Bush unveiled three weeks after his inauguration, reflecting his and the public's prejudices. It is to the campaign, to public opinion, to the domestic problems about which Americans fretted, and to the Bush budget that we will now turn.

CHAPTER THREE

"I DO NOT HATE GOVERNMENT"

Even the Democrats admired his chutzpah. Forget all that talk of sacrifice, of tough choices facing the nation, Bush suggested. The ship of state was steady, the nation healthy. "Many presidents have come to this chamber in times of great crisis," he said early in his February 9, 1989, budget speech to a joint session of Congress. "War. Depression. Loss of national spirit. And eight years ago," he said, gesturing behind him to where Vice President Dan Quayle was seated, "I sat in that very chair as President Reagan spoke of punishing inflation and devastatingly high interest rates, and people out of work, American confidence on the wane." By contrast, he said, "Our challenge is different. We're fortunate—a much changed landscape lies before us tonight. So I don't propose to reverse direction. We're headed the right way."

Only with a reference to Winston Churchill as he wrapped up did Bush display much concern at all. Instead of talking about programs to cut and taxes to raise as if Washington were going to reduce the deficit, Bush devoted most of his speech to suggesting ways to spend *more* money in fiscal 1990, which would begin October 1. After all, even if the nation were healthy, Washington had neglected some problems. Bush wanted more for education, for antidrug and crime-fighting efforts, for science and space, for research and development. If the Bush plan were adopted, there would be more money for AIDS research, child care, aid for the homeless, and nuclear waste cleanup. He hoped, in effect, to help bring about the "kinder, gentler" nation of which he had spoken in his 1988 convention address.

Bush's vision may well have been a sincere one, for he is considered a thoroughly "kind, gentle" fellow himself. But for all the grandiose rhetoric, his budget was severely limited. Bush had few options for doing what most presidents before him had done—that is, putting his own stamp on government, molding it in his own image. The deficit acted as a tight brace on such hopes, particularly if, as he vowed, he would not raise taxes, cut defense or Social Security, or do much to rein in other soaring entitlement programs. With little room to maneuver, Bush could just tinker at the margin of government, proposing piddling amounts for new or expanded programs that were aimed at huge social needs. (It was not surprising that he talked so hopefully about America's "thousand points of light"—its network of volunteer organizations—as a means of accomplishing social goals; relying on them would cost Washington virtually nothing.) As the *Wall Street Journal* put it, "President Bush is proposing to change the face of government. But his new budget provides mostly lipstick and rouge."[1]

On paper, the budget that Bush unveiled in February (a revision of Reagan's 1990 budget) would have cut the deficit from $163 billion—then estimated for 1989—to below Gramm-Rudman's $100 billion target for 1990. But there, too, his rhetoric was excessive. For in that 193-page document, entitled "Building a Better America," Bush had not specified all of the spending cuts needed to reach that target. Instead, he suggested that he and the Democrats sort out those unpleasantries together. "I make this pledge tonight," he said. "My team and I are ready to work with the Congress, to form a special leadership group, to negotiate in good faith, to work day and night—if that's what it takes—to meet the budget targets, and to produce a budget on time."

To average Americans, Bush's offer probably seemed eminently reasonable. But the Democrats did not think so. "Frankly, I am disappointed with the particulars of President Bush's budget that I have seen so far," Panetta, the House Budget Committee chairman, commented the next day. "The test of leadership for a president is whether he is willing to confront the American people with the realities and the tough choices we face in reducing the federal budget deficit." Zeroing in on the political crux, he said, "Mr. Bush chose to give us only the good news. He left it to the Congress to give the American people the bad news." In other words, Bush was the guy who wanted to spend more for this or that. The Democrat-controlled Congress, which had to pass bills that specified how to meet Gramm-Rudman's deficit target, would stop him from doing so.

Panetta and his Democratic colleagues were in a tough spot. As he promised in his inaugural address, Bush was "putting out my hand" to the Democrats; was this not what they had always urged Reagan to do? They could insist that Bush specify which programs he wanted to cut, but he did not have to. They could resist his invitation to negotiate, but they risked looking obstinate, if not whiny. Or they could accept the offer, and let him off the political hook. "Let's face it," a House Democratic aide told me back then, the White House "won the PR [public relations] battle on the budget for the short term." Democratic discontent was matched by GOP euphoria. House Republicans were "very pleasantly surprised at how well things are going," said an aide. Republicans, nearly as unwilling to embrace Reagan's proposals for deep domestic cuts as were the Democrats, finally had a budget from their president to be proud of. "For once," the aide said, "the Republican administration has left the House Republicans with something to do. Our slogan the last few years has been, 'What do you mean *we*, kimosabe?' "

So, for Bush, it was an early tactical victory. But however suited for the political exigencies of early 1989, Bush's budget had begun to take shape much earlier—in fact, one can safely say, years earlier. A president's budget does not only represent *his* priorities and hopes for the nation. In an age of sophisticated opinion polling, it also represents his response to the *nation's* changing desires. And the America of 1989 was a different place than that of 1981, when Reagan took office. The nation wanted Washington to respond more to domestic problems, which seemed more serious in such areas as housing and children's issues. It worried less about its military and more about its economic strength, as the specter of Japanese and West European power sowed fears on which some politicians tried to capitalize.

However much he associated himself with his former boss, for whom the public expressed deep affection, Bush was a man for the new times. An experienced public servant, he was comfortable with Washington's political customs and folkways, and he surrounded himself with others who felt similarly. While paying lip service to fiscal constraint, he proposed numerous tax and spending programs, most to address problems about which the public had raised concerns. Moreover, he promised greater efforts down the road. But to follow through, he needed to craft a major deficit-cutting deal with Congress, one that would put the deficit on an assuredly downward path and, thus, enable the nation's leaders to confront other problems. Unfortunately, the tools of effective campaigning are not always those of governing. Indeed, the former can interfere with the latter. What one says to get elected can seriously impair one's options in office. So it was with Bush, who had vowed to cut the deficit but offered an unrealistic plan for doing so—and who had constructed a further obstacle with his seemingly unalterable no-tax pledge.

■   ■   ■   ■

Americans associate periods of their history with presidents—the Roosevelt era, the Eisenhower era, the Nixon era, and so on. But in the United States, the transfer of power is as much a sideshow as it is the main event. Historical currents, though influenced by presidential elections, do not necessarily begin with the departure of one man and the arrival of another. They can cover part of one presidency or the tenure of two or more. They can bring new activism in foreign affairs, environmental regulation, and racial tolerance. Or they can reverse it. In this sense, presidencies are as much products of ongoing historical eras as they are catalysts for new ones. The nation, already moving this way or that, chooses a president for the times. Viewed in this way, Inauguration Day is but a small blip on a screen, one that brings a change of leaders but not of broader trends.

And so perhaps it was in early 1989, when Bush assumed power. As Arthur M. Schlesinger, Jr., the liberal historian and former Kennedy aide, had written three years earlier, "At some point, shortly before or after the year 1990, there should come a sharp change in the national mood and direction—a change comparable to those bursts of innovation and reform that followed the accessions to office of Theodore Roosevelt in 1901, of Franklin Roosevelt in 1933 and of John Kennedy in 1961."[2] In the late 1980s, fiscal limitations almost surely would preclude the kind of open-ended swing toward federal activism that Schlesinger foresaw. But his prediction of a new public mood, of a new focus on Washington as a tool for social change, was not off base at all. Americans, who had welcomed the Reagan crusade as a fitting antidote to bloated, mismanaged government, had had enough of it well before his departure. They wanted to again change course, to use Washington to address the emerging social problems at home and the challenges from abroad.

At home, the nation seemed confused, troubled, even fractured. Rather than preparing for its future, the United States was letting itself decay. The American Dream was becoming a lost hope for many, particularly minorities. The unusually long recovery from the 1982 recession had brought a peculiarly selective prosperity. Whether told in terms of income, after-tax income, or tax burdens, the story of the United States had become, as Cuomo suggested at the 1984 Democratic National Convention, more of a "tale of two cities," with the chasm between rich and poor growing wider. "The incomes of low-income families rose only slightly or fell between 1979 and 1986," CBO wrote in early 1988, "while incomes of wealthier families rose sharply."[3] The gap between rich and poor families was the widest in at least 40 years, according to the private Center on Budget and Policy Priorities.

For everyone, the cost of big-ticket items soared. Take, for instance, college costs. Tuition prices in the 1980s rose not only faster than prices in general but also faster than such high-cost items as medical care and new housing. At the same time, college participation rates, though rising among students above certain incomes, fell for those at the bottom. Experts feared a two-tiered higher education system, based on income. Housing, too, had become less affordable. Homeownership rates, after rising for decades, were falling. Average down payments absorbed a greater share of income, and mortgage payments ate up a greater share of monthly earnings. More young adults lived with parents, other relatives, or friends, some in overcrowded apartments.

The homeless, of course, were the most shameful symbol of housing problems. An estimated 200,000 to 3 million roamed the streets of cities and towns, seeking a place in a public shelter or a safe spot outdoors. Causes included the lack of affordable housing, cutbacks in federal aid to the poor, persistently high unemployment and other economic factors, and the "deinstitutionalization" of the mentally ill from psychiatric institutions, which was not offset by the needed increase in community facilities. The fastest growing group among the homeless was families with children, and the numbers were growing. Of 27 major cities surveyed by the United States Conference of Mayors in 1988, all but two reported increases, averaging 13 percent, in demands for emergency shelter. Almost all of the cities expected the demands to increase in the next year.

Statistics on children were particularly disturbing, and they raised questions about how federal resources were allocated among age groups. While poverty among the elderly had plummeted in recent years, largely because of Social Security, poverty among children rose from 14 percent in 1969 to more than 20 percent in the 1980s. Children—the nation's future—were America's poorest members, and their problems were growing. Children were poorer, less healthy, and less educated in America than in many other countries. Their problems cost the nation billions in lost earnings and taxes. Meanwhile, a handful of highly regarded, cost-effective federal programs for children reached only a fraction of those in need.

While domestic problems jeopardized living standards from within, Japan and other countries seemed to be doing so from abroad, selling their products here and taking away jobs. The public was worried. *Americans Talk Security*, a year-long survey of public attitudes financed in 1988 by Boston businessman Alan Kay, uncovered a remarkable change: most Americans viewed national security no longer as a mostly military matter but rather as an economic one. "America may be on the verge of a landmark debate challenging historic definitions of national security," the survey concluded. "The relative stability of U.S.–Soviet relations and the rapidly changing international environment may allow discussions of national security to shift into new realms, where a nation's power and international influence may be defined as much by its economic power as by its military power."[4]

Part of the change was no doubt attributable to Mikhail Gorbachev, the charismatic Soviet figure who seemed far less threatening than his austere predecessors. During a December 1987 visit, Gorbachev stopped his limousine in downtown Washington, walked briskly to a curb where a crowd of lunchtime onlookers had gathered, and smiled widely as he worked the crowd with all the skills of an adroit American politician. Mikhail and his wife, Raisa, were the Soviet answer to the Kennedys—Camelot at the Kremlin, if you will.

But another part of the public's change in attitudes was rooted in new fears about the Japanese. Our enemy in World War II and an ally ever since, Japan seemed to represent an awesome challenge. Asked in April what posed the greater threat to national security, 59 percent of respondents to the *Americans Talk Security* survey chose "economic competi-

tors," while only 31 percent chose "military adversaries."
Most also believed that economic power was more important than military power in determining a nation's place in
the world, and that America's trade deficit and the strong
economies of Japan and Western Europe threatened national
security. Americans saw more tangible evidence all around
them. The Japanese and others had money. We did not. They
lent money or bought things. We borrowed or sold off our assets to make payments on our earlier borrowing. Washington
issued monthly trade reports, each in recent years showing
American indebtedness growing. The Japanese, West Ger-
mans, and others made what consumers wanted to buy.

The Japanese, in fact, seemed to be everywhere. New
York City offered a host of examples, as Daniel Burstein
noted in *New York* magazine in early 1989.[5] Some of that
city's 60,000 Japanese jokingly referred to it as "the 24th
ward," a reference to Tokyo's 23. About a third of all customers
at Tiffany's were Japanese and some of its salespeople were
learning to speak Japanese. Macy's and Saks had Japanese
shopping guides. The number of Japanese restaurants had
risen from 60 to 600, and the Japanese were becoming more
active in New York's art world. By 1988, Japanese investors
owned the corporate buildings of Exxon, Mobil, ABC and part
of the Citicorp Center, the Tiffany Building and Algonquin
Hotel, and prime office buildings in Manhattan. Japanese-
owned hotels included the Manhattan Inter-Continental and
the 99 others in its worldwide chain, the Essex House, and the
Stanhope.

Western Europe posed a separate challenge. West Germany, France, and other members of the European Community were preparing for "EC 1992," a project through which,
by that year, more than 300 trade barriers between the nations would be lifted. By late 1988, the effort—first called
for in the 1957 Treaty of Rome, which established the European Community—was moving through more than 280 working groups. While "EC 1992" was expected to boost economic
growth, cut prices, and create jobs throughout Europe, it represented a huge challenge for the United States. Europe, with

320 million people, would become the world's single largest market. To compete in the new environment, European companies were acquiring, or making alliances with, their competitors. Some American firms feared a "fortress Europe" that would put up new barriers to outsiders as it lowered them among its homegrown companies.

■   ■   ■   ■

Politicians had spoken years before about the end of American world dominance. In the early 1970s, for instance, Nixon and Henry Kissinger, his top foreign policy aide, said they envisioned a world of five economic powers: the United States, Soviet Union, Japan, Western Europe, and China. If the world were now evolving as Nixon and Kissinger predicted, nobody should have been surprised. World War II had devastated Japan and Europe. Escaping with its mainland intact, the United States occupied an unusual position, able to dominate a world economy without competition. After the war, the nation made a concerted effort to rebuild the world. Other nations would grow stronger. We *wanted* them to. They would provide markets for our products. And they would not be tempted, in a time of economic despair, to follow the Soviet political model. That these nations were now full-fledged economic competitors was a credit to our successes, not to our failures.

Some of the most thoughtful presidential candidates of 1988 tried to make that very point. Democrats Gary Hart of Colorado, Bruce Babbitt of Arizona, and Albert Gore, Jr., of Tennessee all addressed the issue. They described how the bipolar American-Soviet world was ending, replaced by a multipolar world of diffuse economic powers. The American challenge, they said, was to prepare for the economic competition. Public anxiety, however, tempted more demagogic appeals. A multipolar world seemed threatening. Americans did not want to relinquish their nation's role as the world's leader, though they feared it might already be gone. Asked in 1988 about America's place in the world economy, just 22 percent of respondents to the *Americans Talk Security* poll

said the United States was still the world's top economic power
(although, in fact, it was); 41 percent put it on the same
level with Japan and Western Europe; 34 percent put it below
them.[6]

Hart fell victim to social indiscretion, Babbitt to poor TV
skills. Gore stayed in the race until the New York primary
in April. Other Democrats, tapping into public anxiety, offered voters a more emotional economic appeal up through
Election Day. Richard Gephardt, an ambitious, well-regarded
House member from Missouri, was not getting far with his
cerebral approach before the all-important Iowa caucuses in
February. So, donning a windbreaker and cap, he struck up
a populist "us versus them" message. "It's your fight, too,"
he told the working classes. Within weeks, he came from the
back to finish first. Jesse Jackson, the lone black in the race,
gathered more white votes than experts had expected with his
message of economic empowerment. He addressed the struggling working class, which was increasingly worried about its
living standards. He called for higher taxes on the wealthy
and corporations and more aid for those of low and moderate
income. He wanted corporations to provide jobs at home, not
to send them abroad.

The most striking sign of populist appeal, however, came
from Michael Dukakis. Behind Bush in the fall and losing
ground, he took off on a philosophical turnaround not unlike Gephardt's. Having earlier derided Gephardt's "protec-
tionist" proposal to force other nations to cut their trade surpluses with the United States, Dukakis reversed course and
embarked on a message of economic nationalism. He decried
the "middle class squeeze," referring, he said, to Americans'
growing difficulties in affording housing for themselves and
college for their kids. And he decried Bush's proposal to cut
the capital gains tax rate, calling it an unwarranted break
for wealthy investors. Dukakis did not win, but according to
pollsters, the economic appeal may have been his most effective.

As they responded to such political appeals, Americans
read books that attempted to explain the nation's changing
world role. *The Rise and Fall of the Great Powers*, a 540-

page scholarly tome about world empires since the Ming dynasty of 14th century China, jumped aboard national bestseller lists after its release in 1987. America, wrote Yale University's Paul Kennedy, "now runs the risk, so familiar to historians of the rise and fall of previous Great Powers, of what might roughly be called 'imperial overstretch': that is to say, decision makers in Washington must face the awkward and enduring fact that the sum total of the United States' global interests and obligations is nowadays far larger than the country's power to defend them all simultaneously."[7]

Kennedy's impressive work was just the best known of a new "decline school."[8] What several authors argued in the late 1980s was that economic health was the key determinant of military strength. The economically strong nations built military forces and deployed them across the globe, eventually assuming too many commitments. As their commitments grew, their economies sank. The nations, in turn, lost influence. David P. Calleo argued in 1987 that the United States no longer had the economic might to maintain its alliances. What the nation needed, he wrote in *Beyond American Hegemony*, was for it and its European allies to restructure the North Atlantic Treaty Organization (NATO). Europeans, he said, should assume a greater share of the common defense.[9] Similarly, Walter Russell Mead wrote that year in *Mortal Splendor* that "The decline, and ultimately the fall, of the American Empire is the basic political fact of the current period in world history" Rather than fight it, he said, the nation should prepare for a smooth transition.[10]

Decline, one must remember, was a relative, not absolute, term. For the most part, American living standards were not falling. They were rising. Today's children, on average, would live better than their parents. Decline, instead, involved America's place in the world. The United States was still the world's dominant economic power, but its lead was slipping. Where it once was an unchallenged first, now it was a first among equals. No longer could the United States call the shots alone. With its budget and trade deficits, it was dependent on other nations to continue lending and to help straighten out its finances. Some economists, comparing U.S.

worker productivity against that of other nations, predicted that America would be surpassed in economic power in the next century.

■   ■   ■   ■

With so many challenges to address, Americans no longer viewed government as "the problem," as Reagan had put it in his 1981 inaugural address. No, government was once more a solution for social ills. One clear sign came in 1986, when Democrats regained control of the Senate by turning back Reagan's campaign efforts on behalf of several GOP incumbents elected on his coattails in 1980. Another came in opinion polls. In 1987 and 1988, Americans said too little was being spent on health care, education, the environment, cities, public transportation, Social Security, blacks, the poor, antidrug programs, and crime-fighting efforts. Americans said they would pay more in taxes if the money went for long-term health care, student aid, housing, or child care.

The Bush-Dukakis race, popularly cast as a fight between continuity and change, was not about that at all. The public wanted change. Even Reagan acknowledged as much when he declared, in a boost for Bush, "We *are* the change." The race, instead, was one about what *kind* of change it wanted. Bush accepted the terms of debate without hesitation, even if he paid due allegiance to the Reagan legacy of low tax rates and a "peace through strength" defense policy. For Reagan's view that "government is the problem," Bush had a contrasting outlook. Announcing his presidential candidacy in late 1987, he declared, "I want to add here that I do not hate government. I'm proud of my long experience in government. I've met some of the best people in the world doing the people's business in the Congress and the agencies. A government that serves the people effectively and economically, and that remembers that the people are its master, is a good and needed thing."

Bush was a man for such times. The son of Prescott Bush, a businessman and 10-year Republican senator from Connecticut, he held a House seat from Texas from 1967 to 1970, when he ran unsuccessfully for the Senate against Democrat Lloyd Bentsen. Nixon appointed Bush in late 1970 to be the American ambassador to the United Nations, and then selected him to chair the Republican National Committee in early 1973. Ford sent him to China as the American envoy in late 1974 and to the CIA as director in 1976. In 1981, he began eight years as Reagan's understudy.

Government, Bush suggested, was a tool for the well-off to help others. In his 1987 autobiography, *Looking Forward*, he wrote approvingly of his father's first and unsuccessful Senate run in 1950. "It didn't surprise me because I knew what motivated him. He'd made his mark in the business world. Now he felt he had a debt to pay."[11] Bush expressed similar sentiments in his inaugural address:

> My friends, we have work to do. There are the homeless, lost and roaming, there are the children who have nothing—no love and no normalcy—there are those who cannot free themselves of enslavement to whatever addiction—drugs, welfare, the demoralization that rules the slums. There is crime to be conquered, the rough crime of the streets. There are young women to be helped who are about to become mothers of children they can't care for and might not love. They need our care, our guidance, and our education, though we bless them for choosing life.

Bush himself had known the benefits of federal largesse. As a young oil man in Texas, he attracted investors to his drilling ventures at least partly because they could write off losses and, thus, cut their tax bills. A particularly important investor was Eugene Meyer, then owner of the *Washington Post*, who plopped down $50,000 of his own money and some of his son-in-law's in the early 1950s for Bush and a partner. "You say this is a good tax proposition?" Meyer asked as Bush and his partner departed Meyer's limousine in front of Washington's Union Station. As Bush recalled, "We nodded enthusiastically." The three were in business.[12]

What the tax code had done for him, he wanted it to do for others. In what was considered a huge achievement, Reagan and Congress agreed in 1986 on the most sweeping overhaul of federal taxes in decades, if not ever. Personal and corporate rates were slashed, and scores of deductions were eliminated. Strengthened minimum taxes would, it was hoped, ensure that wealthy individuals and businesses no longer escaped taxation. Economists who had long dreamed of making the code fairer embraced the law enthusiastically. Bush, however, was ambivalent at best. In August 1988, he told *Business Week*, "The [Reagan] Administration has been unwilling to open up the tax code for various reasons. Fine, I've been a part of this Administration. We're going to change in 1989. I will open up the tax code."[13]

Specifically, he promised to push for a cut in the capital gains tax rate on long-term investments to 15 percent, a step that surely would reopen the debate over tax reform; in hopes of closing tax shelters, the 1986 act had ended any preferential tax treatment for capital gains. In addition, Bush proposed tax breaks for the oil and gas industries, a tax-free "individual savings account" for funds held at least five years, a tax-free savings bond to help families pay college costs, a child-care tax credit to help the poor with young children, and an expansion of the existing dependent care tax credit. Bush wanted to make permanent the existing tax credit for business research and development, and he proposed to set up urban and rural enterprise zones, giving businesses tax breaks for locating in run-down areas.

Even as he tarred Dukakis as an old-fashioned liberal, Bush ran a strikingly progovernment campaign on the spending side, too. His proposals for new spending, while often modest in size, were broad in scope. Bush wanted more money for Head Start, the preschool program for disadvantaged kids, so that all eligible kids would eventually be helped, and he wanted more for educational remediation. He hoped to set up a system of "merit schools" to reward those that sharply improved student education, particularly for the disadvantaged, and to provide money to encourage educational experiments. He wanted to expand the income-based college loan program. He supported more money for child immunization and nutrition programs, such as the Women, Infants, and Children (WIC) program, and he promised funds to combat infant mortality. To expand health care, he wanted to allow workers to buy Medicaid coverage and to expand coverage for low-income Americans.

Bush wanted more money for antidrug efforts and for AIDS research. He promised to help rural hospitals. He suggested increased financial aid for local law enforcement, and he said he would double the budget for prison construction within four years. For the homeless, he suggested more money for low-income housing and local mental health clinics. He vowed to strengthen the Small Business Administration, and he promised a new worker retraining program that, for the first time, would help farmers. He hoped to beef up the Coast Guard so that it could track down environmental polluters. He promised to commit the United States to developing an operational space station by 1996, and he asked for a national commitment to manned and unmanned space exploration.

■   ■   ■   ■

The 1988 presidential race, in which all of these ideas arose, had been a particularly nasty one. Because Bush began it with unusually high "negative ratings"—as many as half of registered voters thought poorly of him during the summer of 1988—he and his top aides believed that, to win, they had to raise public doubts about Dukakis. Off they went, slamming Dukakis for vetoing a Massachusetts bill that would have forced teachers to start the public school day with the Pledge of Allegiance; the "liberal governor," they suggested, was somehow less of a patriot than was Bush. Bush finished his 1988 convention speech by reciting the Pledge of Allegiance, talked about how the sale of American flags had risen during the Reagan years, and even visited a flag factory. Dukakis's objection to the Pledge of Allegiance bill on constitutional grounds was buried under the superficial attack.

Bush's broadsides also were aimed beyond Dukakis to the Democrats who ran Congress. With Congress held in such low esteem, these were easy shots, but offensive ones nonetheless to Democrats. "The Congress will push me to raise taxes, and I'll say no, and they'll push, and I'll say no, and they'll push again," he declared in his convention speech. "And I'll say to them, 'Read my lips: no new taxes.'" The Democrats, he implied, had an almost insatiable thirst for raising taxes. But Americans need not worry; Bush would protect their wallets. By Election Day, Democrats were angry and disgusted. Soon afterward, some threatened to "make Bush pay" by forcing him to do as he had promised: to show how he would cut the deficit to below Gramm-Rudman's $100 billion target for 1990. To do that, they figured, he would have to cut popular programs or back off his no-tax pledge. Despite Dukakis's loss, Democrats felt rejuvenated, strengthened. In an unusually good performance for a party that lost the presidential race, they picked up a seat in the Senate and increased their huge House edge by three. If Bush could claim a public mandate, the Democrats said, so could they.

But with their anger waning, influential Democrats soon began to talk less about fighting Bush and more about working with him. Yes, he had unfairly, even cruelly, battled their presidential standard-bearer. But Dukakis had never been a favorite of the Democrats in Washington. He had taken them from the buoyancy of their convention in July, when polls put him 17 points up, to a crushing loss—largely, they thought, because of his awful campaigning. In demeanor, he was as aloof to them as to everyone else. To put it simply, Dukakis was not "one of them." He did not live in Washington and so did not belong to the inside-the-Beltway crowd of national leaders. Had Bush leveled his dirty campaign at, say, Gephardt, Democratic anger might have lingered. But if Gephardt was a brother to them, Dukakis was never more than a distant cousin.

Congressional Democrats had had enough of outsiders. First came Carter, a born-again Christian who strolled into town after Watergate as a kind of moral white knight, promising "a government as good as its people." Then came Reagan, an antiestablishment conservative who rode in as a conquering hero, preaching the values of states' rights and denouncing the Washington political structure. From this perspective, a Bush presidency looked mighty appealing. Party affiliation was beside the point. Republican presidencies were nothing new. Only Carter had interrupted the GOP's lengthy grip on the White House. Democrats had worked with Nixon on much legislation. And they had had as many problems with Carter as with any Republican. The issue was whether one was an insider, someone who understood Washington, respected the political establishment, and felt comfortable with its leaders and mores.

"It might sound grandiose to describe the Bush inauguration as 'a new era in politics,' and that description may sound suspect coming from someone known as a partisan Democrat," House Majority Whip Tony Coelho of California said in a speech in January 1989. "But I do believe we are at the dawn of a new era in our national politics.... In fact, most Democrats feel energized by the coming Bush administration. We're eager to work with the president-elect. Democrats believe the outsider era of Carter and Reagan is ending and that Mr. Bush can be an effective activist president. George Bush is a product of the federal system. He's the son of a senator. He's served in government for 20 years.... When he sits with us at the White House, we won't have to explain to him what a budget is or what OSHA and EPA were created to do. He'll know."

Not only had Bush served in Congress, but he seemed comfortable with its traditions, its role in the political process, and the needs of its members. Friendships begun in the late 1960s were nourished through the years. As vice president, Bush continued to play paddle ball and exercise in the House gym, renewing old ties and creating new ones. A stream of letters, thank-you notes, and phone calls from Bush to his friends on Capitol Hill engendered much good will. Among his many friendships with lawmakers were certain potentially important ones. One was with Democrat Dan Rostenkowski of Illinois, who had served with Bush on the Ways and Means Committee in the late 1960s and was now its chairman. In the Senate, although Bush had engaged in a long-running feud with Dole, he had a close friend in the second-ranking Republican, Alan K. Simpson of Wyoming. Bush's and Simpson's fathers had been close. Other important lawmakers of both parties counted Bush as a friend.

Upon taking office, Bush talked about cooperation with friend and foe alike. He traveled to Capitol Hill to massage hurt feelings left over from the campaign, spending hours there on the first day of the 101st Congress to swear in newly elected and reelected senators and to pose for pictures with them and their families. "Just call me George," he told Gray, the House Democrats' new caucus chairman, during one phone conversation.[14] He called in Democratic leaders for chats about the deficit. He invited rank-and-file lawmakers over for a tour of the White House family quarters, snapping pictures of individual lawmakers and their wives as they sat on a Victorian bed upstairs in the Lincoln Bedroom.

"To my friends—and, yes, I do mean friends—in the loyal opposition—and, yes, I mean loyal—I put out my hand," he said in his inaugural address. Then, turning to the distinguished guests seated beside him on the Capitol's West Front, he gestured first to Wright, the House Speaker, and then to Mitchell, the Senate majority leader. "I am putting out my hand to you, Mr. Speaker. I am putting out my hand to you, Mr. Majority Leader. For this is the thing: this is the age of the offered hand." Three weeks later, he told Congress in his budget speech, "It is comforting to return to this historic chamber. Here, 22 years ago, I first raised my hand to be sworn into public life. So tonight, I feel as if I am returning home to friends."

Another hopeful sign for the Democrats was Bush's top aides, as comfortable with government as was he. "There are no Jim Watts among them," Coelho noted in his speech, in reference to Reagan's controversial Interior Secretary. Whereas ideologues were heavily represented within the Reagan team, Bush surrounded himself with pragmatists who were more interested in solving problems than in crusading on behalf of ideas. Many were veterans of government, insiders who had served Reagan, Ford, or Nixon or even Carter or Johnson. Most still lived in the Washington area. They believed in government, although a moderate alternative to the Democratic kind they considered excessive. Also telling was the outlook with which right-wing Republicans approached the Bush team. As if adrift in unfriendly seas, conservatives decided early on that their best hope of influencing the White House might be through Quayle, the former conservative senator from Indiana. They wanted to repair his image, which was so marred in the 1988 race, and then to exploit their ties to him.

Darman, who would play the leading role for Bush on budget issues in 1989, represented perhaps the single most striking change from the Reagan years. Reagan's OMB, after all, was home to his most fiercely antigovernment conservatives. Stockman spoke disparagingly about dozens of programs, suggesting not only that they did not work, but that Washington had no business running them. Only when the deficit soared and he realized that Congress would not end those programs did he adopt a more flexible approach, calling for some spending limits along with tax hikes. Stockman was followed by Miller, a far less accommodating ideologue. Whereas Stockman's star fell in the White House for pushing tax hikes, Miller's main problems were on Capitol Hill, where he earned neither affection nor respect. Unwilling to compromise much, Miller pushed for the same proposals to terminate programs that Reagan sent up each year, even though Congress clearly would not accept them. By the time he departed in late 1988, he was not only unwelcome in some congressional offices but also disliked throughout OMB, where the career professionals were embarrassed by his largely ineffectual tenure.

Darman, by contrast, believed deeply that American government could work, if only because it had worked so often before in addressing big challenges: Southern secession, the Great Depression, or war. A veteran of six sub-Cabinet posts and the White House, Darman was an earlier favorite of Elliot Richardson, a progovernment Republican whom he served at the Departments of Health, Education and Welfare, Defense, and Justice. Hooking up later with James A. Baker III, Darman worked his way up in Reagan's White House. First a deputy assistant to the president, he soon became the fourth most powerful official under Reagan and the ruling troika of Baker, deputy chief of staff Michael Deaver, and presidential counselor Edwin Meese. Active on everything from the budget to issues involving the Third World, Darman served as a key behind-the-scenes player in White House-congressional negotiations in the early 1980s to beef up the Social Security system. When a tired Baker departed the White House for Treasury, so, too, did Darman, hooking on as deputy secretary. Before long, the department became known as the "Baker-Darman Treasury," with Darman playing a key role in molding the 1986 Tax Reform Act.

No one doubted his brainpower. At OMB, senior staffers praised his ability to quickly absorb information and to dissect policy issues. A teacher for awhile at Harvard, from which he had received B.A. and M.B.A. degrees, students marveled at his knowledge. He wanted to learn more himself. Paying a postelection call on Mitchell, who had just been picked as majority leader by his Senate Democratic colleagues, Darman eagerly asked about his race against two other contenders, as if searching for clues to the "power game" on Capitol Hill. His strength was in grand strategizing, in mapping plans to achieve long-term goals. "The trick," he told the *New York Times* in 1986, "is to arrange a context in which several competing politicians can step forward together to simultaneously share what credit and blame there is for something that's going to at least be ambiguous."[15] Such maneuvering bothered some colleagues. Howard Baker, Jr., a Tennessee Republican and the former Senate Majority leader, coined the adjective "Darmanesque" for schemes that were a bit too clever.

In fact, if Darman's experience and his service as a Bush campaign advisor made him the logical choice for OMB, his selection was nevertheless controversial. Darman had ruffled more than a few feathers over the years. He was a man of no small ego and no large tolerance for the less intelligent, as related in numerous accounts; Rostenkowski eventually would not deal with him during the tax reform deliberations. Mediocre performances grated on Darman, as did criticism by others; when Reagan spokesman Larry Speakes publicly tabbed him "the ultimate second guesser," Darman sent him a letter warning of retribution. He was avowedly ambitious. In winning his new post, it did not hurt that he artfully played the part of Dukakis to prepare Bush for the debates.

Acknowledging the hurt feelings that remained from his earlier battles on Capitol Hill, the new OMB director worked hard to massage them. Upon his selection, he paid courtesy calls on dozens of congressional leaders and rank-and-file members. A frank talk with Rostenkowski cleared the air between them. Others noticed a marked change. Darman seemed less brash, more patient, more eager to listen. Denny Smith, a House Republican from Oregon, joked about a "kinder, gentler" Darman.[16] Nevertheless, Democrats were wary, as they had to be. Personality improvements aside, Darman assumed his post with numerous constraints that Bush, through his campaigning, had imposed on himself and his aides. Campaigns profoundly affect how leaders govern the nation. Rhetoric matters. Slogans matter. Bush's actions in the White House, at least on budget matters, were shaped by the words he uttered on the stump.

■   ■   ■   ■

Bush uttered his most significant remarks in early 1988, as he trudged through the snow of New Hampshire to battle Dole for the GOP nomination. It was here that Bush, a loser a week earlier in Iowa and fighting to save his campaign, insisted he was unalterably opposed to raising taxes—certainly more so than was his rival. According to one of Bush's tough TV ads, Dole was the senator who "straddled," who opposed tax hikes on some occasions but favored them on others. Bush, by contrast, would not straddle. He would not waiver. In a state known for its staunch GOP conservatism, Bush's attack was deadly. When Bush took New Hampshire, he essentially won the race, although Dole hung on for several weeks.

Actually, *both* men had worked to prove they would not raise taxes. Dole, who made deficit cutting his key pledge, proposed to achieve it by freezing all spending from year to year. Mathematically, his plan made sense. As long as the economy grows, Washington collects more revenues from year to year—more personal and corporate taxes, user fees, and so on. If spending were restrained, Washington could cut the deficit simply by keeping the economy growing. The difference between what it collected and what it spent would gradually balance the books. To counter Dole's mechanical freeze, Bush offered up a "flexible freeze." He, too, would freeze spending, but not for each and every program. Instead, he would limit the *total* increase in spending from year to year to the rate of inflation; Social Security, for which spending rises faster than inflation, would be exempt. Within his freeze, Bush would raise spending for some programs and lower it for others. He might spend more on education or environmental protection. He already had pledged to raise defense spending enough to cover inflation. In contrast to Dole's plan, Bush said he wanted the leeway to set priorities.

Bush's flexible freeze might cut the deficit, but it would not balance the budget any time soon. To finish the job, Bush planned to rely on economic fortune. Budgeting, as we have said, depends greatly on economics. The more that the economy grows, the more taxes it generates and the less Washington has to pay in unemployment and other benefits. But with the onset of huge deficits, budgeting grew more dependent on the economy than ever. As the debt tripled to nearly $3 trillion, the federal costs of financing it swelled. Interest payments nearly doubled, to 15 percent, as a share of all spending. Because much of the debt was financed in short-term securities, more than half of it came due for refinancing every two years. As a result, even small changes in prevailing interest rates had a major impact on financing costs.

Bush hoped to turn Washington's economic dependence into an opportunity. Financial markets had long called for a broad deficit-cutting plan to ease inflation and interest rate pressures. If, according to Bush's economic advisors, Congress enacted the flexible freeze in early 1989, the markets would respond by cutting interest rates a few points. This, in turn, would slash federal financing costs. Coupled with savings that accrued from the freeze itself, interest rate savings would help balance the budget in about four years. Whether or not the plan made sense, however, was an open question. Would interest rates drop the necessary few points? Well, the advisors said, a similar drop took place when Gramm-Rudman was enacted and the markets thought Washington was addressing the deficit problem. If the markets viewed the flexible freeze as credible, they said, another drop would follow.

But the drop was no sure thing, since Congress was unlikely to enact anything like a flexible freeze. Lawmakers of both parties would want to make changes. While Bush did not say so, his freeze assumed some dramatic cuts in programs. Most notably, Medicare, which occupied 8 percent of spending, was growing two or three times faster than inflation. So, to hold total spending to inflation, Washington would have to make one of two tough decisions: drastically cut Medicare, the health program on which the elderly relied, or cut deeply into other programs. Writing in the *New Republic* magazine in mid-1988, in a piece cleverly entitled "Bushlit," Harvard lecturer Susan Irving said: "Holding Medicare's total growth rate to inflation means *cutting* each person's benefits, perhaps radically. To hold Medicare to the growth of general inflation, it must be cut by *30 percent in 1993*." Because other spending was also rising at rates exceeding inflation, she said, programs providing for such needs as economic development, sewage treatment, and transportation would have to be slashed or ended altogether to make up the difference. Other experts came to similar conclusions.[17]

Besides, by the time Irving wrote her piece, candidate Bush had already vowed to *increase* spending in various ways and would soon promise more. Although pressed by reporters, he mentioned few if any places where he would cut. The numbers did not seem to add up, as even Bush's economic advisors admitted. One advisor told me at the time, "Now, where the pain comes in is with new programs. To the extent that Congress or the new president want a lot of new programs, they won't be able to do that with this framework. And given the pent-up demand in Congress, that's what the issue is.... That's where the rub comes in." The issue was not mathematics. It was politics. Washington *could*, if it chose, hold spending to the inflation rate. But the decisions would be too difficult, and the pain on some groups too harsh. "I could find that many cuts—if you made me a dictator," Penner, the former CBO director and a Bush advisor, told *Business Week* in August 1988.[18] He and others made the same point at a Bush strategy session that month. At the meeting, according to an account months later in the *New York Times*, economist Paul A. MacAvoy said of the freeze, "that's bunk-o."[19]

■　　　■　　　■　　　■

Maybe it was. But before addressing that question, Bush had others to consider. Reagan would send Congress his fiscal 1990 budget on January 9, 1989. Bush, who would assume office 11 days later, had to decide how to present his own ideas. He could incorporate them into Reagan's budget. He could offer general ideas about how to change it. Or he could send a detailed alternative budget a month or two later. Earlier presidents had provided precedents for almost any approach. FDR and Harry Truman did not propose revisions to their predecessors' budgets. Eisenhower proposed a series of separate revisions in early 1953. Kennedy sent Congress two sets of revisions in March 1961, the first modifying domestic spending and the second focusing on defense. Nixon outlined his proposed changes in an April 1969 message to Congress, and followed with four detailed documents. Carter proposed major budget changes in February 1977. Reagan outlined his program in a February 1981 address to Congress and followed it a month later with a detailed book of revisions. But Bush's situation was unusual. Not since Herbert Hoover in 1928 was a president elected to succeed one of his own party.

The Reagan and Bush teams, some of whose members were part of each, advised early on that Bush should not incorporate his ideas into Reagan's budget. For one thing, Reagan's plan could serve as his own ideological legacy. For another, Bush did not need to use Reagan's budget. To get his administration off to a fast start, he could send his own proposals to Congress. A Reagan-Bush budget also would have raised difficult questions. However close their relationship, the two men hardly agreed on all policy. Take capital gains, for example. Reagan had agreed in the 1986 Tax Reform Act to tax capital gains like ordinary income. It was a—if not *the*—key provision around which the act was constructed. To tax reform's strongest supporters, later proposals to cut the capital gains rate were viewed as threatening to tax reform itself. Bush, however, had vowed to push for a lower rate. To incorporate that proposal in his final budget, Reagan would have signaled a certain disloyalty to tax reform—one of his major achievements. And by offering it later himself, Bush would look like he was fulfilling a campaign promise.

But whether Bush would propose any budget revisions at all was an open question. Darman, in his visits on Capitol Hill, floated an idea. Instead of sending revisions, Bush would call for negotiations so that White House aides and congressional leaders could quickly draft a fiscal 1990 budget. At one point, it seemed like that decision had been made. Appearing on NBC's "Meet the Press" in late November, Domenici said Bush was not required to suggest budget revisions. When Gray, the departing House Budget Committee chairman, asked, "You don't think he should submit a budget?" Domenici replied, "He won't." If Bush was leaning that way, however, he changed his mind soon after. Democratic leaders did not like the no-budget idea, as Republicans had warned Darman. They wanted Bush to show his own spending cuts. If he would not resort to tax hikes, Democrats figured, Bush's proposed cuts would be drastic indeed; how else would he reach Gramm-Rudman's $100 billion target? Thus, Bush's budget would provide a tool with which Democrats could attack him. Even when Darman suggested that Bush would send only an outline of a budget, Democrats balked. They wanted specifics. Which programs would Bush cut? Which policies would he change? Would he raise taxes?

At the time, Darman was preparing to help answer those questions. In December, OMB's deputy director, John F. Cogan, began to brief Darman for a couple of hours every day or so on the details in, and the decisions behind, Reagan's 1990 budget. He explained how it was structured, which programs were growing and why, how the budget process worked, which process changes Reagan was recommending, how Darman might try to cut spending, and so on. Often, Darman requested more information on one topic or another. "Can I get a paper on this?" he asked. "Can I get a better explanation of that?" He wanted to know, for example, whether Washington needed all the lawyers serving in its agencies. And he wondered whether Bush needed to spend as much on the Superconducting Super Collider, the proposed energy project, as Reagan requested. Such requests were funneled from Cogan to OMB's career staff.

As Bush assumed office, top aides were already translating his campaign pledges into a budget. Pushed by his staff and conservative Republicans like Sen. Phil Gramm, Darman employed a potentially radical approach. Rather than use the "current services" baseline, which assumed that each program got an inflation-based raise each year, he first asked how much Washington would collect in revenues. With that figure in hand, he allocated funds for Washington's legal obligations—paying interest on the debt and cutting the deficit to $100 billion. Because not enough revenue was left to finance all existing programs at inflation-based levels (much less cover Bush's promises to create new ones), Darman and other White House aides had to decide how to cut spending and raise more revenues and determine which campaign pledges to fulfill. Campaign promises hovered over the deliberations. Where Bush had made a clear pledge, aides worked to fulfill it. Where he had been vague, they used whatever leeway they had, provided they did his words no injustice. Hammering out the proposals were Darman, Brady, Sununu,

Michael Boskin, chairman of Bush's Council of Economic Advisors, Roger B. Porter, Bush's assistant for economic and domestic policy, and Robert M. Teeter, a senior advisor for Bush's 1988 campaign. Bush, of course, made the final decisions.

At OMB, Darman and Cogan searched for ways to save money in entitlements. Reagan had included some proposals in his budget. Darman had to decide which to suggest. Here, too, campaign pledges proved important. If Bush had talked about expanding Medicaid, the federal-state health program for the poor, he would look silly in endorsing Reagan's ideas to cut it. And while Bush was vague in the campaign about how he wanted to treat child nutrition programs, a proposal to cut them would conflict with the notion of a "kinder, gentler" nation. The savings in entitlements would determine how much Bush could spend on his campaign promises. To translate promises into actual proposals, Bush's top aides set up a series of working groups. Groups were created, for instance, to craft programs on education, the environment, housing, and antidrug efforts. Serving on each were staffers from OMB, the vice president's office, the relevant federal agency, and perhaps the White House, the White House counsel's office, or both. Meanwhile, Sununu and other White House officials briefed Republicans on Capitol Hill, outlining tentative ideas and asking what political hurdles might arise. When the time came, another working group wrote the budget, which contained a running commentary to explain its figures. Darman, Cogan, other OMB political appointees, and some career staffers submitted drafts on certain sections. Darman and Cogan, for instance, wrote a blistering criticism of the "current services" approach to budgeting, saying it had "a curious Wonderland quality" to it.

Within the administration, major policy disputes were rare. Few Cabinet secretaries had taken office, so departments had no leaders to complain about proposed cuts. A sizable battle erupted over defense, however. When Darman and other White House aides proposed that the Pentagon get only enough to cover inflation in 1990 and later years, objections came from the Joint Chiefs of Staff, National Security Advisor Brent Scowcroft, Secretary of State James A. Baker III, and William H. Taft IV, then serving as the Pentagon's acting secretary. The defense community wanted a 2 percent increase, in inflation-adjusted dollars, for 1990 and increases in later years. A compromise ensued: Bush would propose just enough to offset inflation in 1990, but then add more in later years.

On the tax side, campaign promises were equally important. Bush said, "No new taxes." What did that mean? Meeting often in Brady's conference room at the Treasury Department, Darman, Brady, and the others agreed that the small tax hikes and other revenue items in Reagan's final budget were not *new* per se. They could be, and were, adopted by Bush to pick up $6.4 billion. Beyond that, aides stuck as close to Bush's campaign speeches and position papers as possible. For capital gains, Bush promised a 15 percent tax rate. For child care, he pledged a $1,000 tax credit for children of poor families. Also specific were his oil and gas incentives. For adoptions involving children with special needs, he had been less precise. But Darman insisted that a tax break of some sort be included because Bush had promised one. Bush also had left wiggling room with his promise to create enterprise zones.

Brady was nominally in charge, sitting at the head of the table, but the strong-willed Darman dominated. As OMB director, only he understood Washington's fiscal constraints in their entirety. Only he, then, could judge what was affordable. All major tax breaks except for that on capital gains were expected to reduce federal revenues in fiscal 1990. All, then, made it harder for Darman to draft a budget that met Gramm-Rudman's $100 billion deficit target. After discussing campaign promises and fiscal constraints, the group turned to O. Donaldson Chapoton, Bush's old lawyer and golfing buddy from Houston who served as Assistant Treasury Secretary for tax policy. Receiving his marching orders, Chapoton would leave the meeting and turn to his own staff, who, in turn, drafted detailed proposals and estimated the costs. Once they were completed, Chapoton returned, presented the proposals, entertained criticism, ordered changes by his staff, and returned again until the group approved.

The more money that Bush had to spend, the more promises he could fulfill. Consequently, when proposals were drafted, budgetary considerations at times clashed with the desire to make good policy. This was most apparent with regard to capital gains, where revenue questions had long been controversial. Conservative economists argued that, over the long run, a lower tax rate on such gains would bring in *more*, not less, in revenue. With the incentive of a lower rate, investors would buy and sell assets much more often than otherwise. Because they would pay capital gains taxes each time they sold an asset, the increase in such activity would bring in more than enough revenue to offset the lower rates. Other economists disagreed, saying that while buying and selling might increase, it would not do so enough to offset the lower rates.

Before Bush took office, the Treasury Department was split on the issue. Its Office of Economic Policy thought a lower capital gains rate would raise money in the long run. Its Office of Tax Analysis disagreed. Pressured by such Republicans as Rep. Bill Archer of Texas to join conservatives on this issue, the department began a study in the summer of 1988. Although due in November, it was not completed until late January, just in time to incorporate its findings into Bush's budget. Relying on the study, Treasury officials structured Bush's capital gains proposal to maximize revenues, although policy considerations were important, too. For instance, the "holding period" that investors had to endure before getting a lower rate represented a compromise between those concerns; longer holding periods would better encourage savings, whereas shorter ones would generate more revenue. The Treasury Department estimated that Bush's proposal would generate $4.8 billion more in 1990 revenues.

■   ■   ■   ■

More central to hitting Gramm-Rudman's deficit target, though, was Bush's assumption that the economy would perform well in the coming months. This was a debatable proposition. While Bush's projection of robust economic growth was chancy enough, his more controversial forecast was that interest rates would drop sharply. Greenspan agreed, as diplomatically as any Fed chairman would, that the assumptions were optimistic. Questioned at a Senate Budget Committee hearing in February, he said, "Would I, if I were making the estimates, be somewhat more cautious in some of the forecasts? Yes, probably I would." Reagan's fiscal 1982 assumptions were dubbed the "rosy scenario," but Bush's were perhaps a bit rosier. For fiscal 1982, 6 of 35 private economists surveyed by *Blue Chip Economic Forecasters* projected economic growth as high *and* interest rates as low as Reagan had assumed. For fiscal 1990, none of the 37 economists surveyed had done the same in comparison to Bush's numbers.

It was not just that Congress would surely balk at Bush's budget—delaying a big deficit-cutting deal and consequently the interest rate drop on which Bush was counting. It was that interest rates at the time were rising. The longer this continued, the greater the gap would be between prevailing rates and those projected. At some point, Bush's assumptions would turn from unlikely to laughable. In early 1989, however, Bush's aides were not ready to concede defeat. In February, for instance, an aide interrupted Darman's meeting with reporters to bring him news that the Fed had just raised the discount rate—that charged on loans from its regional banks—from 6.5 to 7 percent. I asked whether, based on that and other news, Bush's assumptions should now be deemed implausible. "No," Darman replied, evoking laughs.

The Fed's discount rate hike was just the latest step in its yearlong effort to boost interest rates in the hope of curbing inflation. The producer price index, a key inflation gauge, rose an eye-opening 1 percent in January. The increase was announced a day after Bush released his budget proposals. Later in February came an announcement that the consumer price index, another closely watched standard, had risen 0.6 of a point in January. A month later, February's reports looked almost as dismal, evoking fears that inflation was taking off. Analysts offered various explanations. Unemployment, at 5.1 percent, had hit a 15-year low in February. Industry was using a greater share of its plant capacity, nearly 84 percent, than at any time since the late 1970s. Because the economy had little room to expand, a weak dollar on international markets was purportedly generating inflationary pressures.

Worldwide, inflation was rising. Goldman Sachs & Company, the New York investment firm, forecast that it would go up in Great Britain, Italy, France, Japan, West Germany, and the United States. In the latter, the concern was not that inflation had risen so much. It was, rather, that the small increase might be sowing the seeds of a larger one. As Greenspan told the Senate Budget Committee:

> I do not think we can realistically assume that the inflation rate will stay at the current level indefinitely into the future.... The reason why most economists feel uncomfortable at an inflation rate that currently prevails is not that it is doing clear, significant, corrosive harm to the economy at the moment; but it has built into it the seeds of an acceleration which, if not dampened—if we do not endeavor to bring the current inflation rate lower over the longer term as a policy matter—then we risk it accelerating.

So the Fed, which influences the direction of all interest rates, went to work. For a year beginning in March 1988, it pushed up the federal funds rate—that which banks charge on overnight loans to each other—to nearly 10 percent, its highest level in four years. It pushed the discount rate to 7 percent, its highest point in three years. Rates on other lending followed. Those on Treasury's 30-year bonds, which Bush projected to be 7.2 percent in calendar year 1990, rose to more than 9 percent in February. Banks raised the prime rate—that charged to their best corporate customers—from 10 to 10.5 percent in November 1988, and to 11 percent and then 11.5 percent in February. Mortgage rates zoomed toward their highest levels since the 1987 stock market crash. Home sales consequently dropped in early 1989, prompting lenders to offer new bargains.

Bush and lawmakers grew anxious. It was not that they dismissed Greenspan's concerns; nobody wanted a return of the 1970s-era inflation. But they, and not the nonelected Greenspan, risked voter retribution if higher interest rates provoked a recession, throwing millions out of work. Traveling in Asia when the discount rate hit 7 percent, Bush said of Greenspan, "We've got a little difference of interpretation at this point as to how you read the indicators on inflation." At the Senate Budget Committee hearing, Domenici said of the Fed's decision makers, "I am firmly convinced that... some of them clearly do not understand the impact of their decisions and their suggestions on the American people and the American economy."

In March, 70 of the 174 House Republicans wrote to Greenspan, urging him to cut interest rates to avert a recession. They also asked that he commit to even lower rates if Washington agreed on "real and significant deficit reduction." Their request was surely unnecessary. Everybody assumed that if Washington accomplished it, the markets would respond positively enough to "real and significant deficit reduction" to trigger lower rates. But as years of experience showed, deficit cutting was no easy feat. It would depend not only on political calculations in the White House and Congress but also on the personal dynamics between a few key leaders. Bush, surely one of them, made his own pitch early.

■   ■   ■   ■

"Let's not question each other's motives," Bush told Congress in his February 9 speech. By constructing his budget proposals as he did, the president hoped to push both sides to the bargaining table quickly. Bush had taken Darman's advice. As the OMB director argued publicly and privately, Reagan and Congress had clashed so mightily, at least in part, because Reagan had specified every last program that he wanted to cut, thus igniting the emotional opposition of lawmakers and powerful interest groups. If Bush did the same, he, too, could expect a hostile reception. Tempers would fray, relations sour. Another fight would ensue.

Bush chose not to. Yes, he called for $11.8 billion in specific cuts in entitlements and similar programs. But he did not do the same for day-to-day programs. Instead, he took $136 billion worth of programs, most of them domestic, from 1989. For 1990, he suggested only that, *in total*, they get no more than the $136 billion. In a variation on his flexible freeze, Bush suggested that these programs not get anything to offset inflation. Under this scenario, he and Congress would negotiate how to allocate the $136 billion: which programs would get more, which would get less, which would be eliminated. At a briefing before Bush's speech, Darman explained: "It is meaningless for the executive branch—and it has been proven so—to write down exactly what it proposes to cut under those headings; it doesn't happen. What we need to do is first agree on a cap and then we can have serious negotiations about what goes up and what goes down within that small heading."

Or could they? The Democrats cried "Foul!" Bush, they said, had proved their point: A flexible freeze would not work. The needed cuts would be politically untenable. That, the critics said, was why the Bush team did not specify which of the $136 billion in programs to cut. "They said they could produce a budget that met the Gramm-Rudman targets without raising taxes," a Democratic advisor said. "And the people who were skeptical said, 'When you get down to the detail, you will see that is impossible.' So what they did is, they ducked." Bush's budget looked suspicious in other ways. While Bush proposed that the $136 billion in mostly domestic programs not get an inflation increase, he sought one for defense. Yet Bush used the word *freeze* to describe both ideas. "The Bush budget has a 'flexible' notion of what a freeze is," sniffed Sen. Jim Sasser, a Tennessee Democrat who became chairman of the Senate Budget Committee in 1989.

Critics, seizing on Bush's failure to specify spending cuts, had a field day with the $136 billion pot, which they dubbed the "black box." Panetta, in a March 16 speech to the Chamber of Commerce, called it "the first multiple choice budget." "This is a thousand points of light," Sasser said, borrowing

Bush's campaign line, "but unfortunately the batteries aren't included." Hollings called it "the phantom of the budget" and a "covert budget." A House GOP aide labeled it "the Jimmy Hoffa budget. We know there are bodies in there, but we don't know where they are." Everyone wanted to know more about the black box. Which programs were in it? What would happen if, instead of choosing among them, Washington froze them all at 1989 levels. Private experts went to work. The Center on Budget and Policy Priorities discovered that if the WIC program did not get a boost to cover inflation, 150,000 fewer people would be able to participate. Similarly affected would be maternal, child, and other health programs.

Democrats bugged Darman for more information. So did the press. Details dripped out slowly. Pestered by reporters at a February 10 breakfast, Darman revealed that to keep pace with inflation, programs in the black box needed a total increase of $9.6 billion in 1990. That figure was important, since Congress had no plans to scrap its inflation-based "current services" approach. Thus, the Democrats said, Bush had proposed a $9.6 billion cut in programs, some vital for low-income Americans. But Democrats wanted more details. Byrd, the former Senate majority leader and now the Appropriations Committee chairman, asked Darman to supply specific proposals for all programs in the black box before his February 23 appearance at Byrd's committee. Darman never did so. The key budget players meanwhile threatened to boycott Darman's call for high-level talks until they got such data. They warned that they could draft the required tax and spending bills for 1990 on their own.

But their threats were not credible. The Democrats needed Darman. Working alone, they would have to show how *they* would meet the Gramm-Rudman target. They could not forever withhold the details, as Bush did, because eventually they would have to pass spending bills to finance the government. If they broke with the administration, they surely would get little help from congressional Republicans. At the same time, they would be hard put to keep their own troops in line. Particularly in the Senate, Democrats were as divided between liberals and conservatives as was the nation at large. The former opposed domestic cuts, while the latter hoped to block defense cuts. Neither wanted to raise taxes, fearing Bush's inevitable public tongue-lashing.

Darman needed the Democrats as well. A split between them would doom Washington to another year of the inter-party stalemate over fiscal policy. Only if the nation's leaders could enact a long-term plan for sustained deficit cutting would Bush have a chance to mold government as he hoped. If they could not, Bush would be relegated to the "lipstick and rouge" approach, tinkering at the margin rather than re-ordering priorities. Victimized, for instance, would be plans to substantially shift federal resources more toward investment, as Darman had discussed. Spending would stay basically un-changed, as if stuck in place.

Deficit cutting required cooperation. Bush and the Democrats, while taking credit for the achievement, would have to share blame for the specific, unpopular tax and spending changes needed. With Bush offering cooperation, the Democrats could hardly refuse. Panetta and Sasser, the budget chairmen, agreed to preliminary talks with Darman. But insiders did not hold much hope for an early deal. The deficit had not suddenly become an easier problem to solve. If anything, it was now a harder one. Nobody had any new ideas, because each had been considered before. Besides, Bush had taken away an old one—a tax hike. In the White House and Congress, among lobbyists and reporters, observers expected talks to drag into the summer or fall, with no guarantee of success.

CHAPTER FOUR

AND PORT MORESBY

"The budget agreement does not complete the whole deficit reduction job that is to be done by fiscal year 1993, not by a long shot," Bush told the nation on a warm, sunny April 14.

> But I am convinced that we will only be able to complete that job if we tackle it in manageable steps, on an orderly basis, in a constructive, bipartisan spirit. And this is a first manageable step, and this budget agreement is the first such agreement reached ahead of schedule and not framed in the context of crisis. This is not an insignificant point; it shows that we can make the system work, even with the branches of government controlled by different parties, and if we approach our jobs responsibly and are willing to stay with it, to stick with the task.

He and several of America's most powerful elected officials had gathered in the White House's Rose Garden to display their handiwork. At Bush's side were the House Speaker, House and Senate Democratic leaders, and Republican whips. On the steps behind him were Bush's top budget aides and the chairmen and senior Republicans to other important congressional committees. The congressional leaders who spoke each praised the seven White House aides and lawmakers who had struck a deal for fiscal 1990, still a half-year away, after two months behind closed doors. With their pact, negotiators had set the terms for all 1990 budget action. Included in it were spending limits for defense, international aid, and day-to-day domestic programs, and deficit savings to be achieved by boosting revenues and cutting entitlements. From it would flow the budget resolution, 13 appropriations bills, and the reconciliation bill of tax hikes and entitlement cuts.

As Bush suggested, though, it was not the substance of the agreement that mattered to these leaders but the fact that Democrats and Republicans had reached one. Consider, for instance, Wright's comments. After noting that "this is not an heroic agreement," he nevertheless called it "a very good start in the direction of better cooperation and better performance." On that point, Mitchell said, "The most significant aspect of this agreement is its existence, and that is no small accomplishment. For the first time, early in the process, outside the atmosphere of last-minute crisis, a genuine good-faith effort has been made and an agreement has been reached.... In establishing an atmosphere of cooperation and bipartisanship, for which the president deserves great credit, it sets us on the right course." House Majority Leader Thomas S. Foley, a Washington Democrat, called it "a very important movement on the part of the Congress and the executive branch, Republicans and Democrats, to establish an early consensus." From the Senate, Minority Whip Alan Simpson, a Wyoming Republican, termed the agreement "a very significant thing."

But at the same time, these leaders told the nation something that they themselves did not believe—that their deal would cut the deficit to just under $100 billion. The negotiators and other top officials knew the agreement was a sham, a kind of "paper tiger" that was more dependent on Bush's optimistic economic assumptions and accounting gimmicks than on serious deficit cutting. Sen. Lloyd Bentsen, the Texas Democrat and chairman of the Senate Finance Committee, thought so little of the deal that he boycotted the Rose Garden ceremony. Even those happy about its existence were hard put to defend it. "There's smoke, and there are mirrors," Frenzel told me. Others admitted to the gimmickry, but said an agreement like this, in allowing Washington to avoid a year-long gridlock over the budget, was better than no deal.

The basic idea here, after all, was *not* to cut the deficit. Not really, anyway. It was, rather, for the key leaders to quickly resolve their Gramm-Rudman problems for fiscal 1990, to build trust and "a spirit of cooperation" among themselves, and to set the interpersonal groundwork for a big deficit-cutting effort in the fall. This strategy—to tackle the deficit in two stages, not one—was dictated by Bush's no-tax pledge which, as even the Democrats acknowledged, precluded him from signing on to a major tax increase early in his first year. Bush would instead have to "get by" the first year, to put the 1990 decisions in place, to show that he had lived up to his campaign promise. Only then could he partake in the kind of assault on the deficit that everybody knew would include a sizable tax increase.

In the meantime, other key players would use the opportunity afforded by Bush's campaign constraints to get acquainted, to work on the fiscal 1990 problem, to learn one another's likes and dislikes. This was no waste of time, for Washington is a very human place. Politicians make decisions as much on the basis of personal relationships as on the merits of positions. Those who get along with their colleagues tend to prosper, to push bills to enactment, to move up in their party ranks. Those who do not often languish. Good personal relations were even more important in 1989, when members of different parties and of different branches of government planned to confront the deficit. Each would have to share not only the credit for their achievement but also the blame for the ensuing tax hikes and spending cuts. Only if they did so *together* would neither side suffer. But to believe they would stick together and not stick one another with blame later on, the individuals had to trust one another. Trust like that was not easy to build.

Standing in the Rose Garden, the seven negotiators thought they had nourished the personal ties that could prompt a serious deficit-cutting effort in the fall (although Bentsen's boycott signaled that big hurdles lay ahead). The negotiators had spent many hours together, sharing mornings, afternoons, and evenings in various rooms of the Capitol. They had chatted and gossiped, sipped coffee and eaten bagels, told stories and laughed at or with each other. They had not cut the deficit much. But if personal friendships could set the stage for more in the fall, it would have been worth it. That would remain unknown for months.

■   ■   ■   ■

In his February 9 speech, Bush had called for a "special leadership group" to negotiate a White House-congressional 1990 budget. In talks with Bush's top aides a month or two before, Domenici and Frenzel had pushed for this tack, thinking that it would expedite budget decisions. Both lawmakers had been through enough battles to know what the normal budget procedures would bring: Bush would propose a budget, Democrats would reject it, and the two would fight for months, tying up much other action. Domenici liked the idea of a summit because, through his participation in earlier ones, he knew they could work. Frenzel thought that unless Bush got involved early, Congress would make the key tax and spending decisions alone, leaving him only to sign or veto their bills.

At the time, though, Bush had not decided just how to approach his talks with Congress. His main concern had to be the tax issue. How he handled it would have a major impact on the deficit-cutting effort; from this issue, others would flow. The less that revenues increased, the more Washington would have to cut spending to meet Gramm-Rudman's target. Liberals wanted to protect domestic programs, while conservatives hoped to shelter defense. Neither would take sizable cuts in their favored programs if the other would not do so. And, particularly for liberals, tax hikes would have to accompany spending cuts so as to minimize the latter. "No new taxes," said Bush? Well, then, no big spending cuts, said the Democrats. And, they both said, in effect, no significant deficit cutting.

Politically, Bush was in a tight spot, tighter than any faced by Reagan. While Reagan always expressed contempt for the idea of a tax hike, threatening to veto any sent his way, his actions did not match the rhetoric. Reagan signed more than a dozen tax increases into law during his presidency, including sizable ones in 1982 and 1984 to cut the deficit and a big one in 1983 to help rescue Social Security. However many he signed, though, nobody doubted his antipathy toward them. That, and perhaps public ignorance of his record, enabled him to sign them and not suffer politically. It was, as Washington pundits liked to point out, like Nixon's hugely successful trip to China in 1972; because he had been such an anti-Communist warrior throughout his career, few questioned whether Nixon had grown "soft" on the Communist nation.

But on the tax issue, Bush was different. Many Republican lawmakers and aides, particularly the more conservative ones, did not trust his no-tax commitment; they feared that Bush, whom they suspected of being a closet moderate, would break the pledge to get a deficit-cutting deal with the Democrats. By the late 1980s, as we have said, the GOP had tarred Democrats as the "tax and spend" group. Hoping to regain Senate control in 1990 or 1992, and even holding out hopes of taking the House in the latter year, Republican lawmakers did not want their new president to shatter the distinction between the two parties by accepting tax hikes. House members were especially suspicious. They portrayed themselves as a kind of conscience for Bush, always there to monitor his activities.

Consequently, Bush's "no new taxes" line assumed a symbolic profile. Instead of reading his lips, lawmakers, lobbyists, and others tried to read his mind. Some thought Bush was committed to a no-tax policy for his presidency, but most assumed his pledge covered only the first year. Some thought Bush had merely barred any changes in income tax rates;

others believed that even excise taxes were off limits but that Bush would agree to close tax loopholes. Observers searched high and low for signals, not unlike the way Western diplomats study the words emanating from the Kremlin or the way Wall Street monitors the Fed chairman's remarks. Bush obliged by offering a few hints. A day after his election, Bush said he did not deem the fee that senior citizens paid to finance the catastrophic care program a "new tax."

In January, Darman offered quite a few more hints, though not necessarily the kind he had planned. In written responses to questions from the Senate Governmental Affairs Committee, which had to approve his nomination for OMB, Darman seemed to open the door to other kinds of tax measures. He hoped to keep the door open when he testified to the panel later in the month. The White House, he said, had a commonsense notion of "new" taxes—the duck test. "If it looks like a duck, walks like a duck, and quacks like a duck, it is a duck," he told the panel. What Americans would view as a tax hike, so would the White House.

Unfortunately for Darman and, in turn, the deficit-cutters, senators would not take his definition at face value. They wanted to pin him down. In particular, Sen. Carl Levin, a Michigan Democrat, asked question after question about what was and was not a "duck." Would the taxation of employer-provided fringe benefits be a duck? What about the elimination of the home mortgage interest deduction or deductions for other interest? And for what purpose might Darman ever recommend that Bush violate his no-tax pledge? In this setting, with cameras rolling and the administration just under way, Darman thought he had to turn back efforts to puncture Bush's credibility on the no-tax front. So Darman dug in, leaving few hopes for those who wanted to raise taxes. But the more he did, the harder his budget talks on Capitol Hill would be. As Panetta told me later, "It was not too helpful at that point in time, because we had just begun the process of discussions. And even at that point, I felt that Darman was trying to keep the tax [issue] open.... Politically, to some extent, in an effort to pin down the administration, we were also limiting his flexibility."

Darman's duck test was soon immortalized. Sen. Joseph I. Lieberman, a Connecticut Democrat, asked Darman if he was practicing "high-level quackery." Sen. John Glenn, an Ohio Democrat and the committee chairman, presented three rubber ducks to the OMB nominee. A reporter gave him a plastic duck at one briefing. In his testimony, Darman had said ducks were "off the table." An aide to the Senate Budget Committee, hosting a party at his home, wanted to *prove* Darman was wrong, that ducks were "on the table." So he put plastic ducks on his own tables, near the cold cuts, bread, chips, and silverware. Fuel Users for Equitable Levies distributed yellow ducks with cards saying "If it quacks... it's a duck" to the offices of some 325 House members who had not signed a resolution opposing an increase in the gas tax. The Employees Council on Flexible Compensation, incensed by Darman's suggestion in his written responses that taxes on employee fringe benefits might be acceptable, passed out buttons that displayed a duck with lipstick marks on its side and read "kiss my tax." A new language sprang up among tax watchers. If Bush would not accept ducks, which animals would he take? There was talk of ducklings, as opposed to ducks. Tax ideas of questionable acceptance were tabbed "geese," "birds," and so on.

Bush recognized the political importance of his no-tax pledge. Between his election and inauguration, he told Rostenkowski over lunch: "You've got to give me something other than a tax bill the first year. There's no way I'm going to sign a tax bill." The pledge was central to discussions among Bush, Sununu, and Darman in early 1989 about how to approach the deficit problem. At what point could Bush accept a tax increase? How long must he wait? Darman figured on at least six months, and only then if circumstances permitted. What those circumstances might be was anybody's guess. But Darman had served in Washington long enough to know that the future was unpredictable. He thought, for example, that Congress never would have passed Reagan's 1981 tax cuts had the president not been shot, prompting a wave of public sympathy for him. Another wild card was the economy. With a crisis, like a big jump in interest rates, Bush might be free to discard his campaign rhetoric in the interest of deficit cutting.

Darman suggested that Bush pursue a comprehensive, deficit-cutting agreement from the start, one that would cover at least two years. Because a deal like that could take months to complete anyway, Bush might not have to accept a tax hike until the second half of 1989. Sununu asked about another approach, one on which Darman had not focused. Could Washington address the deficit in more than one step? Well, sure, Darman replied. That approach had one clear-cut benefit: Bush could cut a deal for 1990 that did not include a tax hike. He could boast that he had fulfilled his no-tax pledge (as he did in the Rose Garden in April). Then he might have the political leeway to back off of it. After discussions, the president decided to pursue Sununu's idea. The negotiators would aim for a 1990 deal in "Stage I." They would seek the "Big Deal" on the deficit in "Stage II" in the fall.

■   ■   ■   ■

Expectations that Washington would move quickly on Stage I were not high, however. The nation's leaders were accustomed to making deals only when staring at important deadlines. Not until at least summer, when OMB revised its 1990 deficit projection, might Gramm-Rudman's pending across-the-board cuts encourage a negotiated settlement. In fact, Bush and Congress had until October 15, when OMB certified whether or not the cuts must occur, to slice the deficit to $110 billion (the $100 billion target, plus a $10 billion "cushion" before cuts kicked in). Based on earlier years, the parties were likely to eschew compromise in spring and early summer, and to blame one another for intransigence. As *Time* wrote in February, "A budget concordat with Congress would, of course, provide the tonic that Bush craves, but the Oct. 15 Gramm-Rudman deadline all but ensures that serious negotiations will be delayed until late summer."[1]

But the prognosticators, including myself, forgot to factor in a few things. For one, we assumed the parties would fight over the same tax and spending issues that had tied them up for a decade. What the nation's leaders did, instead, was to sidestep them, to replace "real" savings with phony ones, to use economic and accounting chicanery rather than tax hikes and spending cuts. For another, we had grown so accustomed to yearlong fights, we forget how it was in everyone's interest to avoid one. Bush, for example, needed to show that he could govern, that he could make the political process work, that he would not be bogged down with the same interbranch feud over fiscal policy that had haunted Reagan. Mitchell, also in his first term as a leader, had much the same incentive. He strongly supported the idea of high-level budget talks, and he avoided attacking Bush in early 1989 over such issues as his capital gains cut, fearing that would poison the well for negotiation.

The Democratic leader with perhaps the most to gain, though, was Wright. On one hand, he was quite leery of the high-level summit approach. With budget policy fashioned by just a few individuals, the House's normal processes would be short-circuited and the prerogatives of its members, particularly its committee chairmen, would not be fully protected. On the other hand, the negotiations afforded him a great opportunity. Wright had faced an avalanche of bad publicity since the prior year resulting from questionable financial dealings to allegations that he had pressured federal regulators to lay off some troubled savings and loan institutions in Texas. The only praise he had received of late was in making the House's "trains run on time," such as by pushing appropriations bills to enactment before the October 1 start of the fiscal year. If negotiations would produce a quick deal, he might be able to do this again.

The five original negotiators—Darman, Panetta, Sasser, Frenzel, and Domenici—had their own reasons to hope for success. Darman had earned praise in earlier negotiations, such as over Social Security in 1983 and tax reform in 1986. But he was always someone's understudy—Richardson's in the 1970s, Baker's in the 1980s. At OMB, he ran his own shop. Success would free him from the shadow of his former bosses. Failure could stain his image. Whether or not he succeeded also might determine Bush's ability to address many other issues in his first year. A budget stalemate could block work on items that cost money. Bush seemed to view bipartisanship as the key to success, having followed up his "offered hand" with an early deal that Baker negotiated with the Democrats concerning aid to the Nicaraguan Contras. This deal enabled Bush to set aside one of the most politically divisive issues of the 1980s. Bush now wanted Baker's old sidekick to craft a deal on another vexing problem.

As for the lawmakers, Panetta and Sasser were first-year chairmen who were under pressure to prove their leadership skills. As Panetta told me early in 1989, "Everyone is watching to see whether or not you have the capacity to kind of run through all of the hoops that you have to run through in this job." In particular, Panetta wanted to avoid the difficulty that James R. Jones of Oklahoma, House chairman in the early 1980s, had encountered in trying to build an effective, united Democratic response to the popular Reagan. Forced into a leadership role, Sasser now had a chance to improve his own reputation. Frenzel, too, faced the challenge of leading the Budget Committee's GOP troops for the first time. Domenici, though an old budgetary war horse, anticipated new challenges. With Darman and Panetta building an easy relationship, he did not want to be left out. Although his former staff director at the Senate Budget Committee, Stephen E. Bell, had clashed with Darman, Domenici hoped to work with him.

Up against Darman and the experienced Republicans, Sasser and Panetta seemed an odd pair, so different in background, demeanor, and reputation. The former was soft-spoken and boyish, tentative about budgeting, and wary of negotiations with a Republican administration and its minions on Capitol Hill. The latter was aggressive, intense, experienced in budgeting, a participant in various bipartisan budget negotiations in the past and predisposed toward that tack on almost any occasion. The elevation of these two in early 1989—a product of fortuity as much as ambition—went far in shaping the negotiations and events later in the year that helped doom chances for further progress.

Sasser never wanted his job in the first place. When Senate Budget Committee chairman Lawton Chiles announced in late 1987 that he would not seek reelection a year later, attention turned to the two Democrats next in line in committee seniority. But Senate Democratic rules bar members from chairing more than one committee. Hollings chose not to part with his chairmanship of the Commerce Committee. J. Bennett Johnston of Louisiana decided to retain his at the Energy Committee. Sasser, next in line, was openly disappointed. Asked in late 1988 if he would take the budget job, he said, "Well, I haven't been able to convince Senators Hollings or Johnston to take it."[2] His reluctance was understandable. A budget chairman needed a broad perspective on Washington. If government spent more than $1 trillion a year, he had to know how it was allocated. How much went for defense, Social Security, education, housing, and interest? He had to understand how programs worked and the politics behind them. Why, for instance, had Medicare grown at rates far exceeding inflation? And what were the national security implications if Congress gave less for defense than the president wanted?

Sasser had never been a big-picture guy. According to the 1987 edition of a textbook on American politics, he had "spent a decade in the Senate without finding a major focus for a career that has usually gravitated to the minutiae of public policy rather than the larger issues behind it."[3] For much of Sasser's tenure, the other Tennessee senator was Republican Howard Baker, Jr. While Baker spent most of that time as the Senate's minority or majority leader, studying major issues, Sasser worked to protect programs that allocated money to their economically poor state. His leadership in opposing Reagan's request for Contra military aid in the mid-1980s was considered the exception that made the rule.

While he had served on the Budget Committee since 1977, Sasser had never displayed much interest in fiscal issues. He participated less often than others in committee debates and rarely offered amendments to budget resolutions. Only when programs from which Tennessee benefited, like aid for local development, were at risk did he get energized. But Sasser did not come to his job without ideas. He had learned a lot by watching his father. In the 1950s and 1960s, Ralph Sasser ran Tennessee's soil conservation service, a state branch of the federal agency that helped farmers with conservation, flood control, and other efforts. Not only did the elder Sasser's name help his son win a Senate seat in 1976 (over incumbent William E. Brock). His father's experience also taught the young Sasser that government can be a force for good, that it can help those who just want a fair shake. That outlook was well-suited for a state rich in populist tradition, exemplified by Estes Kefauver, the senator and presidential candidate for whom Jim Sasser had worked.

Panetta, too, was a 12-year veteran of Congress. That's about where the similarities between the two new chairmen ended. If Sasser was tentative about his new job, Panetta wanted to jump into his with both feet. Thoughtful, hardworking, and aggressive, he was considered the most knowledgeable House member on budget issues, even though House rules forced him to leave the Budget Committee after 1985 and not return until 1989. His climb to power had been an unusual one. Although his Italian immigrant parents were New Deal Democrats, he was drawn to the Republican party by the progressivism of California's GOP. A Washington aide to House Republican Whip Thomas H. Kuchel of California in the 1960s, Panetta served as director of the civil rights office in Nixon's Health, Education, and Welfare Department before his aggressive enforcement of federal law prompted his firing in 1970. While an aide to New York Mayor John V. Lindsay in the early 1970s, he grew disgusted with Nixon's civil rights record and his administration's targeting of liberal Republicans for defeat. Although a fiscal conservative, Panetta was liberal on social issues. Thus, his switch to the Democrats in 1971 was more natural than it may have seemed.

Once in Congress, Panetta quickly found his niche on budget issues. He and three colleagues formed the "gang of four"—young Democrats who used their Budget Committee posts in the early 1980s to push for more domestic funds. In 1981, when Reagan's spending cuts moved through Congress, Panetta headed up the Budget Committee's task force to monitor whether other committees, ordered to make cuts, were doing so. Though a junior member, he found himself in private meetings with House Speaker Thomas P. "Tip" O'Neill, Jr., budget chairman James R. Jones, and the powerful chairman of one committee or another who was not anxious to slash programs he had helped to create. Panetta's effort to convince House Democrats to change their rules, and let him chair the budget panel in 1985, was opposed by party leaders and, thus, defeated. Nevertheless, the leaders picked him for the House-Senate conferences in 1985 and 1987 that drafted both versions of Gramm-Rudman and for the 1987 summit that followed the stock market crash. Although two other respected House members announced plans to run for Budget Committee chairman for 1989, they dropped out of the race early, as if acknowledging that Panetta had earned the role.

If Sasser concentrated on "minutiae," Panetta was, at least on budgetary matters, a big-picture man *par excellence*. By examining the structure of the budget, he long ago came to a simple realization: that a big deficit-cutting package would have to include cuts in defense and domestic programs and in popular entitlements, particularly Social Security. To convince Democrats that the package was "fair"—that beneficiaries of domestic programs were not the only ones asked to sacrifice—Republicans would be forced to go along with higher taxes on those who could afford them. Americans, he insisted, would accept such bitter medicine. Panetta had voted for a huge but unsuccessful proposal like that in 1985. He had repeatedly preached the same message to his constituents. And they had rewarded him every two years with sizable re-election margins.

When the two chairmen began their talks with Darman, Domenici, and Frenzel, Panetta seemed better situated here as well. For one thing, he could easily match wits with the Republicans. Sasser could not do so until his knowledge of the budget grew. For another, Panetta's personal ties were stronger. Sasser was hesistant about Domenici, whom he had watched battle Chiles relentlessly even though Domenici and Chiles were hunting buddies. Panetta and Domenici, on the other hand, had developed a close friendship, rooted in respect for one another's abilities. So it was no surprise when, as talks among the five began, Panetta and Sasser approached them differently. Panetta became a kind of unofficial chairman, leading the discussions, trading views with Darman, and setting the agenda for future sessions after consulting the others. Sasser was quieter, as if content to hear the talk among the principals and aides.

■   ■   ■   ■

From mid-February to early March, the five proceeded slowly, deliberately, meeting wherever they could scrounge up a room—in the Capitol, in one of the three Senate office buildings to its north or one of the three House buildings to its south. Of the seven sessions, each was generally devoted to a broad topic: defense, entitlements, day-to-day domestic spending, and so on. Discussion centered on where to cut and how much each option would save. Lawmakers pressed for information on how the White House viewed programs in its $136 billion "black box." What the negotiators had at the end of each session, then, was a range of options from which to choose down the road. And from discussions, each learned what might or might not be acceptable to others. Aides, when not attending, met among themselves. Because staffers provided the backup detail for their bosses' decisions, those on Capitol Hill needed as much data on Bush's budget as possible. OMB sent hundreds of pages of computer runs.

Panetta ran the show, with Darman participating heavily. Others, including top staffers, talked with varying frequency. Frenzel, for instance, hardly spoke at all in these sessions, preferring to fixate on his elaborate doodles. How they interacted was as important as what they said. The negotiators watched one another, talked, and listened. The slick Darman worked to build a relationship with the laid-back Sasser. So, too, did the intense Panetta try to get along with the curmudgeonly Frenzel. Everyone needed to know that private comments would remain private, particularly involving the touchy subjects of tax hikes and spending cuts.

"It took some testing between the different personalities to see whether that was going to be the case," Panetta told me later.

Trust did not come easily. A few days after his February 9 speech, Bush saw a news report that suggested the White House was not sending the backup data that Democrats sought. The next day, for the first of Darman's meetings with lawmakers, Bush sent Sununu. The report was wrong, Sununu assured everyone. Bush would send what the lawmakers wanted. Sununu left, and the meeting continued. But not all tension had evaporated. At one point, Sasser accused Darman of not providing much information. Darman shot back, "I take issue with that, sir." Those two clashed again a few weeks later, less heatedly but in a more embarrassing situation. At a breakfast with reporters, Sasser revealed Darman's private comment that, for years after fiscal 1990, he would be willing to suggest a tax increase to Bush. Darman, meeting with reporters later that day, denied saying that. Still later, Sasser backed down, saying that he would defer to Darman. Sasser phoned Darman to fix any personal problems he might have caused. He had not been wrong, of course, only tactless. Darman had indicated, and not just to Sasser, a willingness to push for taxes. But Sasser's remarks evoked temporary discomfort among the negotiators, all of whom wanted to build trusting relationships.

Sasser seemed tentative, although his confidence grew as the talks progressed. He declared early on that he would not work evenings or weekends, as if unaware that most of Washington's deal-making seems to take place at odd hours. While lawmakers had agreed to bring only two staff members into the meetings, Sasser often brought four or more. The other lawmakers were not pleased, since the rooms tended to be cramped even without the extra bodies. Sasser was heavily dependent on the aides, who constantly whispered in his right or left ear while staffers briefed the group or negotiators talked. So, too, was the seating arrangement around the table reflective of Sasser's uncertainty. Panetta and Darman situated themselves across from one another, as would the top negotiators from General Motors and the United Auto Workers.

Darman, meanwhile, seemed hell-bent on erasing his reputation for arrogance and manipulation. He assured the others that there would be "no surprises" down the road—such as in July when OMB had to recalculate its deficit projection for 1990, based on new economic assumptions and other information. Conceivably, the negotiators could have struck a deal, only to have OMB later find it inadequate for avoiding Gramm-Rudman's across-the-board cuts. Don't worry, Darman suggested. If Congress implemented the steps agreed upon, he would see to it that lawmakers would not face more Gramm-Rudman problems over the summer. The OMB director also poked fun at himself and the White House more than once. When an issue would arise, he might say, "It's all there, on page so-and-so of the 193-page Bush budget. What a masterful piece of work that was!" Others would laugh. Darman began to grow on them.

He also grew on reporters, a group that would help shape his reputation. His humor was consistently self-deprecating. At a briefing in February, he asked reporters if he could say something "off the record." When a few refused, he asked again, protesting with a smile that he did not, for the record, "want to be my old arrogant self." Reporters laughed. Asked in early March whether Bush's bitter and unsuccessful fight to have former Sen. John Tower of Texas confirmed as his Defense Secretary had affected Darman's dealing with the negotiators, he said, "In all the conversations I've had, they've been amazingly good-spirited. . . . I'm considered the least mature of the crowd." By spring, some reporters seemed convinced that Darman was a new man. "The Charming New Darman," the *Washington Post* called him in May. "This is the new Dick Darman—congenial, witty, a darling of Congress."[4] *Newsweek* followed with a one-page profile, accompanied by a picture of the smiling OMB director and headlined "Say Hello to Charmin' Darman: the budget director checks his ego at the door."[5]

By early March, the negotiators had fully surveyed the budget. Panetta and Sasser asked their leaders if they could proceed. "We propose that the budget task force discussions enter a new phase: an exploration of areas of possible compromise between Congress and the administration on a fiscal year 1990 budget," they wrote March 8 to Wright and Mitchell. "These negotiations would begin immediately within a tight time frame of two weeks," they said, promising to report back on "progress" and "areas of agreement" by March 23. With permissions granted, negotiators resumed their talks, now joined by Brady and Foley. But the group still had some groundwork to finish. What they needed, in effect, was a common scorecard, a budget outline on which everyone could agree. However commonsensical that sounds, the task of constructing one was not simple. OMB and CBO classified some programs differently. For negotiators to debate how much to cut from entitlements, how much from day-to-day programs, and so on, they needed to agree on precisely which programs were in each category. If they contemplated revenue increases, they had to know what, precisely, was a tax, and what was a user fee.

By March 14, staffers had developed such a scorecard. Along with broad tax and spending categories, it contained totals for key entitlements, such as Medicare, farm price supports, and pensions. Revenues, user fees, other federal collections, asset sales, deposit insurance costs, debt financing costs, and other items were also distinguished. The table showed savings from various broad options: freezing programs across the board, freezing them but exempting those for the low-income, providing 2 percent increases across the board, and so on. The table served as a bible of sorts for the group. Also on March 14, congressional and budget leaders had one of their periodic meetings with Bush, at which more cheerleading than decision making took place. This did not stop the negotiators from describing its importance in grandiose terms. With markets in New York and overseas watching, negotiators wanted to send a message of hope to creditors who wanted the deficit reduced.

"Today's meeting with the president and congressional leaders represents a giant step forward...a historic step," Domenici said in a prepared statement. What had the partic-

ipants done? They had engaged in such "historic" actions as
updating Bush on their talks and, as Panetta put it, "for-
malizing" the negotiating group. Domenici said they had
done more, that Bush and congressional leaders agreed to
focus their talks on four broad categories—defense, international aid, entitlements, and day-to-day domestic programs—
and to consider revenues separately. But they had not. The
Democrats were not ready to approach the talks that way for
another month. Because Bush wanted a separate guaranteed
allotment for international aid, Democrats had a chit to play.

The contrast between words and deeds produced some
funny moments. On the White House driveway, Bentsen was
asked for details about the meeting.

> **Question:** How did it go?
>
> **Answer:** Oh, I think it was a productive meeting. We
> were discussing the schedule and trying to set forth some
> of the priorities. And you—I think you saw a good deal of
> cooperation between the administration and the Congress
> in the comments that were made.
>
> **Question:** What are the priorities?
>
> **Answer:** The priority is trying to balance the budget....
>
> **Question:** Well, Senator, is there any indication yet as to
> where the president would like to cut spending? Or did
> that come up at all in the meeting?
>
> **Answer:** No, we did not get that specific.

■   ■   ■   ■

International aid offered the longest-running humor of
the negotiations. For one early discussion, Darman brought
along Robert M. Kimmitt, the State Department's undersec-
retary for political affairs, to discuss Bush's international aid
proposal and answer questions. Sasser and others, suggesting
that Bush would have to accept cuts in this area, raised questions about his plan to build a new embassy in Port Moresby,
in Papua New Guinea. When the conversation turned to other
matters, a staff member slipped a note to Sasser and ex-

plained that the proposed embassy was, in fact, a good idea. Part of the State Department's "small embassy program," it was to be a prefabricated structure that would cost only $10 to $12 million—about a third of the usual cost. Sasser piped back in, saying that after hearing from the staff, he thought the Port Moresby project was a good one. His father had been a marine, Sasser told the group, one who had fought in the Pacific where so many others had shed blood. From then on, Port Moresby was a source of lighthearted giggles. One negotiator would urge the group to protect this or that program. Another would chime in, "and Port Moresby."

But to the administration, international aid was no joking matter. Because Bush cared so much about it, his aides hoped to craft a deal like that following the 1987 stock market crash. Reagan had won a big victory by convincing Congress to allot nonentitlement monies among three categories: defense, day-to-day domestic programs, and international aid. Had that not occurred, international aid would have been clumped together with day-to-day domestic programs in a single "nondefense" category, forcing it to compete for funds in Congress with housing, science, transportation, and other programs. Categorized separately, Congress was obliged to fund international aid at an agreed-upon level.

Presidents tend to care more about international aid than do Congresses. Because presidents take the lead on foreign affairs, they are more interested in distributing American dollars around the globe to nourish relations and influence events. Lawmakers, especially in the House, do not see as much of that world. They know what makes voters happy— the domestic programs from which Americans benefit. Voters, who tend to dislike foreign aid, are notoriously ignorant about how it works and how much America distributes. When they speak to various groups, budget experts often are asked whether Washington could balance its books simply by cutting foreign aid. I have been asked the same question more than once in my occasional appearances on a C-SPAN call-in show. That such aid totals less than $20 billion a year is not well known.

The White House also cared more about defense than did the Democrats, many of whom would have cut it to save domestic spending. Here, Bush had a key ally. Domenici was not only concerned about the Pentagon's budget, after four years of funding that did not keep pace with inflation. He also wanted to avoid the political problems he had faced in the 1980s. When, as Budget Committee chairman, he agreed to cut Reagan's defense requests to gather votes for a budget resolution, some White House officials chastised him almost as harshly as they did the Democrats. To avoid such compromising situations, Domenici had a simple demand. As he told Sununu and Darman, if he were going to agree to a defense figure below Bush's request, he would have to get an OK from Bush himself.

As good Democrats, Panetta and Sasser wanted to protect programs for low-income Americans. Although not coordinated, the two men followed a kind of "good cop, bad cop" routine. Panetta plowed ahead for an agreement. Sasser, fearing that one was taking shape too quickly and that domestic programs would not be adequately protected, worked to slow things down. "We're wasting our time," he complained more than once, as if threatening to walk out. He did not plan to do so. He was seeking leverage for domestic money. To protect those programs and still cut the deficit, Panetta and Sasser openly discussed the need to raise taxes. Despite Bush's rhetoric, his budget seemed to support their argument.

Bush had proposed some small tax changes that, when added together, would raise $5.3 billion. But he proposed other revenue measures, too, such as fees for federal services and sales of federal assets. Together, the tax and other measures would have raised $14.2 billion in 1990. So, the Democrats said, Bush obviously agreed that Washington needed more money. The only question was, How should it be raised? Well, they said, Bush's ideas were counterproductive. Asset sales, for example, amounted to one-shot savings. Washington sold the asset and took the money. But unlike a tax increase, such sales would not create a permanent stream of revenue to help cut the deficit in later years. Worse, some asset sales cost Washington money in the long run. If, say, a portfolio of student loans were expected to generate revenues in later years from loan repayments, then selling it would rob Washington of revenues. In the end, the lost revenues might more than offset the onetime saving. To cut the deficit more effectively, Democrats wanted to take Bush's $14.2 billion and convert it into a $14.2 billion tax hike.

Addressing the Chamber of Commerce on March 16, Panetta pushed this point in a fiery speech to the antitax group. "So my argument is," he thundered, "if you want $14.2 billion, damn it, make it real!" Four days later, he privately surrendered. To move the talks along, Panetta offered his proposal for an agreement. If, as was true, Washington needed to find about $28 billion in savings to reach Gramm-Rudman's target, he suggested that half come from revenues and half from spending. More specifically, Panetta said in outlining the plan on a blackboard, he would raise $5.3 billion by increasing taxes, $5 billion by imposing fees on federal services, $3.4 billion by selling assets, and $0.3 billion by beefing up the Internal Revenue Service's tax-collecting capabilities. But while basically accepting Bush's revenue framework, Panetta tried to shift the content of the spending cuts. He proposed that negotiators match the $14 billion in revenues with $14 billion in cuts—half from defense, half from nondefense programs. Bush, as we have seen, had proposed that defense grow with inflation.

Meanwhile, the economy was threatening the relaxed nature of the talks. If growth slowed, Washington might be blamed for not doing more deficit cutting. During the sessions, such political risks were never far below the surface of discussion. The Fed's half-point hike in the discount rate, to 7 percent, on February 24 evoked a public statement from Panetta, who urged that it serve as a "wake-up call for both the administration and Congress. It adds to the urgency of the need to cut out the political gamesmanship and adopt a bold and realistic budget plan." In mid-March, Frenzel added, "The credit markets won't wait forever for a deficit reduction compromise." Nor would Brady let anyone forget the mar-

kets, even if some staffers thought his rhetoric was excessive. After an April 2 meeting in Washington with representatives of the other major industrial democracies, Brady
insisted that, yes, the world really was monitoring the discussions. "I spent 13 hours on Sunday with the G-7," Brady
said at one point, referring in shorthand to representatives
from the United States and the six other nations. "And four
hours of it was on the budget process. We've got to meet the
[Gramm-Rudman] targets. The whole world is watching."

Consequently, negotiators tried to calm the markets for
as long as they could. Even when one or more negotiators
could not attend—and, thus, no progress could occur—the others still met; failing to do so, they feared, might prompt the
markets to view the talks as stalemated. If that happened,
investors might grow nervous, prompting a jump in interest
rates. Thus, with no real agenda themselves, the negotiators
spent time listening to technical discussions between staffers;
it was not glorious work. Their public comments were just as
calculated. Although no real progress was made in March, negotiators pretended otherwise. They coordinated their statements to the press before emerging from closed doors.

But Easter beckoned. Congress would officially start its
recess on March 24. As much as others did, congressional negotiators wanted to enjoy the holidays. Whether they dared
to do so was still unclear. February's producer price index,
announced on March 17, had risen a startling one percentage point; that followed a one-point rise in January. All eyes
focused on the consumer price index. January's figure was
a 0.6-point rise. If February's figure, due out in a few days,
matched it, inflation fears would skyrocket—with the deficit
at least partly blamed. Negotiators would have to meet over
the recess, if only to calm the markets. February's figure
showed only a 0.4-point rise, low enough to send negotiators
home. Not everyone was relieved. An aide to one negotiator,
noting the political impact of economic data, lamented, "I
was sort of hoping that February's CPI would be somewhat
higher."

■   ■   ■   ■

Negotiations would not resume until April 4. Time was running out. April 15, the date by which Congress was supposed to adopt its fiscal 1990 budget resolution, was closing in. Surely Congress would not meet the deadline. But lawmakers wanted to come close. To do so, negotiators would have to hatch a quick deal. Panetta tried to move everyone along. Pressured by Wright, and confident that Bush wanted a deal to prove he was an effective leader, Panetta threatened to leave more than once. "I'm going to mark up," he would say, using the technical term for committee sessions in which bills or resolutions are drafted. Panetta was threatening to convene his committee and draft a resolution, even without an agreement among the negotiators on which to base it.

Republicans snickered privately. They pictured Panetta as a guy holding a gun to his head, threatening to pull the trigger. "Wow, what a threat!" they joked. "Leon's going to mark up!" If Panetta quit the talks, Republicans almost certainly would not help draft the resolution. Democrats would have to do it alone. They could call for a tax increase, but that would practically prove GOP charges that tax-raising was in their blood. Or they could cut defense or domestic programs. Democrats might even agree on a budget resolution, but not before igniting a war between their conservative and liberal wings over how to do it.

No, Panetta was not leaving. Nor was anyone else. Back again in early April, the group got down to business. Hoping to avoid their pre-Easter problem of finding convenient, suitable rooms in which to work, the negotiators gladly accepted Foley's offer of two adjoining rooms in his office suite, located on the Capitol's main corridor. It was an ideal setup. When negotiators wanted to talk by themselves, as they occasionally did, they could send aides to the next room. Democrats could meet privately to consider offers by Darman and the Republicans. Darman and the Republicans could do so for Democratic offers. The negotiators worked, on and off, mornings, afternoons, and evenings for two weeks. Panetta, flanked by Frenzel and Domenici, sat on one side of a rectangular table. Across from the House chairman sat Darman, with Brady to his left and Sasser to his right. Foley sat at one of the ends.

One or two staffers for each negotiator usually sat behind, although a few sometimes gravitated to an open place at the table. In the mornings, the group of 16 or 18 drank juice and coffee and ate bagels, rolls, and doughnuts. For afternoon sessions, they enjoyed cheese and crackers, fruit, and soda. One complained later of an expanded girth.

Sitting together, the negotiators' trust in one another seemed to grow. They exchanged quips and stories. The most memorable story came from Darman. One day, when the group was discussing the savings and loan mess, Darman told about the first time he had met the Senate Banking Committee's chairman, Michigan Democrat Donald W. Riegle. As a student at the Harvard Business School, Darman and his classmates were scheduled to begin an important test at a certain time. The class was divided into seven sections, each with its own proctor. But at the appointed hour, Darman's proctor, also a student at the school, did not distribute the exams. Instead, he began to talk to those in his section. He introduced himself; it was Riegle. The students, Riegle told them, would soon be graduating. Because Harvard had a tradition of public service, he said, many would surely seek jobs in government. The students, losing valuable minutes, hissed and stomped, praying he would stop. Riegle wrapped up with his main point: He was running for Congress that year and looking for campaign workers. It would be a good experience, Riegle assured them. Anyone interested should see him after the test. When Darman finished telling the story, the room erupted in laughter.

As for negotiating, discussions in the first week in Foley's office centered on revenues and entitlements. Since Panetta had presented his proposal on March 20, matching Bush's $14.2 billion in revenues with the same total, negotiators had pretty much agreed on that figure. How to raise it was a different matter. Outside events had already made the job harder. Legislation, as Bush requested, to raise $2.1 billion by opening the Arctic National Wildlife Refuge to leasing for oil and gas exploration was approved by the Senate Energy and Natural Resources Committee before Easter and was headed for the floor. But in late March, the Exxon *Valdez* plowed into Bligh Reef in Alaska's Prince William Sound, causing the worst oil spill in U.S. history. With environmental concerns moving to the forefront of public debate, the leasing proposal died; negotiators would have to find $2.1 billion elsewhere.

On some tax matters, the White House showed flexibility. To make the deficit cutting easier, Darman offered to part with some of Bush's proposed tax cuts, each of which would have cost Washington money. At one point, he pulled out a table that listed the cuts, showing what each would cost. One in particular, costing $1.7 billion, that he offered to sacrifice was a break for firms that had foreign operations. Nevertheless, Darman and Brady pushed hard for Bush's tax ideas, particularly his proposal to cut the tax rate on capital gains. Panetta and Sasser were only two of the important lawmakers who had raised objections.

Although not part of the negotiating group, the chairmen and senior Republicans on Congress's tax-writing committees had to be consulted. After all, of the $14.2 billion in revenues, negotiators wanted those committees to raise $5.3 billion in taxes. Panetta could assign the task to Ways and Means, but he could not force Rostenkowski to pursue it. So, too, was Sasser dependent on Bentsen. Acknowledging such realities, Darman and Brady talked privately about taxes with the House chairman on April 5 and the Senate chairman the next day. From the former, the talk was blunt. The White House had to understand a thing or two.

Rostenkowski said he would not go out on a limb to raise taxes. He had done that before, and it was not a pleasant experience. In 1987, the fiscal 1988 budget resolution called on Ways and Means to raise $19.3 billion for that year. Because Reagan insisted he would veto a tax increase, Ways and Means' Republicans refused to help the Democrats. Democrats pushed a bill to the House floor by themselves. The committee, which often exhibits an easy bipartisanship, was torn apart. It stayed that way for more than a year, until Democrats and Republicans pooled their efforts to draft a technical tax measure in late 1988. With his members working together again, Rostenkowski did not want to see the 1987 experience repeated. Only if Bush agreed to support the committee's tax-raising efforts would Republicans feel free to help. So, without that pledge from Bush, Rostenkowski said, he would not even try.

By mid-April, as it turned out, Rostenkowski had secretly offered to help Bush fulfill his campaign pledge on capital gains by pushing for a one-year rate cut, in exchange for some tax-related items. But although he served as chairman, and a powerful one at that, Rostenkowski had just one vote on the 36-member Ways and Means panel. His support for a tax idea was often necessary, but never sufficient. If he pushed for a capital gains cut, he could expect an outcry from liberal Democrats who would view it as an unfair tax break for wealthy investors and as a threat to the heralded 1986 Tax Reform Act. The problem was that if they did not accept Bush's capital gains proposal, the nation's leaders would need another way to raise the $4.8 billion in revenues that this tax cut was projected to bring in. In terms of revenue raising, this was the most significant item that Bush brought forth.

Some of Bush's other revenue-raising proposals faced even bigger hurdles. Reagan had long tried to extend Medicare payroll taxes to all state and local workers, some of whom did not pay but were covered for benefits, such as through a spouse's participation. Congress repeatedly rejected the idea, which would have affected lots of workers in large states, including Bentsen's home state of Texas. Opposition to the proposal, which was worth $1.8 billion, had not subsided. Nor would Bush have an easy time convincing Congress to raise $900 million by stopping a scheduled drop in aviation taxes from taking effect. Congress, angry that money in the airport and airway trust fund was not being spent, voted in 1987 to cut the tax if that practice continued. Many lawmakers had not changed their minds.

But whether he wanted to work with Rostenkowski or not, Bush had political problems of his own. House Republicans grew even more convinced in early 1989 that the no-tax issue was a political winner. Although, in the spring, Democrats won two of three special elections for House seats, the Democratic winner in Illinois was a no-tax candidate who took advantage of her GOP opponents' vulnerability on the issue. Republicans therefore hoped to pin Bush down. Around that time, Rep. Mickey Edwards of Oklahoma, chairman of the House Republican Policy Committee, collected signatures from more than 100 of his GOP colleagues on a letter to Bush, pledging to support his veto of any tax hike. Also, Rep. Richard K. Armey of Texas proposed a resolution through which House Republicans, as a group, could vote to support Bush's no-tax pledge. Whether Bush and Congress would agree on tax hikes would not be known for months. Darman and Brady said Bush was amenable to closing tax loopholes. But the Treasury Department had privately compiled just $500 million worth of loophole-closers to offer. At Darman's request, top staffers of the Ways and Means and Finance Committees, Congress's nonpartisan Joint Tax Committee, and the Treasury Department met in early April to exchange ideas. With nobody willing to offer proposals, the meeting faltered. No more get-togethers were held.

When negotiators turned to entitlements, Rostenkowski and Bentsen would have to play key roles again. Although known as tax-writing committees, the Ways and Means and Finance panels have jurisdiction over the nation's largest entitlements, including Social Security and Medicare. If negotiators wanted to save money by cutting the skyrocketing Medicare program, as they almost certainly would, they would need these chairmen to help. Bush had proposed a $5 billion cut, to be achieved mostly by limiting payments to hospitals and doctors. Congress would not go along with anything that ambitious, but maybe a cut half that size was realistic. Earlier in the year, Panetta had spoken to Rostenkowski and Sasser had spoken to Bentsen. When, in early discussions among the negotiators, the budget chairmen suggested that Rostenkowski and Bentsen would not cut more than about $2 billion from Medicare, Darman and Brady apparently decided that this was inadequate.

In mid-March, Darman and Brady met with Rostenkowski, Bentsen, Rep. Bill Archer of Texas, Ways and Means' top Republican, and Sen. Bob Packwood of Oregon, Finance's top Republican. "You can do more than $2 billion," Darman told the Democrats. "We know you can." His logic seemed impeccable. Three of Medicare's cost-saving provisions were due to expire. If Congress chose merely to extend them, the provisions would bring in an unanticipated $1.8 billion in fiscal 1990. Presumably, Congress could easily do that and then look elsewhere to build upon those savings. "Wait a second," Rostenkowski countered. "The $1.8 billion aren't simple extensions"—not politically, anyway. Each was temporarily put into law as part of other deals. Powerful groups were awaiting their expirations and would fight any delays.

In early April, the negotiators agreed to seek a $2.7 billion cut in Medicare, assuming the $1.8 billion in expiring provisions were extended and another $900 million could be raised by limiting the reimbursements to doctors. But as with taxes, Rostenkowski and Bentsen had not agreed to the final figure. Whether they would ever enact the savings was questionable. Besides, by then, Panetta and Rostenkowski had cut a private deal. In the House budget resolution, which would mirror whatever deal the negotiators came up with, Ways and Means would only be *ordered* to make $2.3 billion in cuts. The panel would, by contrast, merely be *asked* to make another $400 million. Thus, if it did not find the $400 million, Ways and Means would not be breaking any budget rules.

■   ■   ■   ■

For the second, and last, week in Foley's office, discussion centered around defense, international aid, and day-to-day domestic programs. Domenici hoped to be ready. Unwilling to expose himself to later criticism for accepting a defense number lower than Bush's, he needed a signal from the White House. On Friday, April 7, he traveled to the Pentagon for a breakfast with Defense Secretary Richard B. Cheney in Cheney's huge office. Domenici was concerned, he told the secretary, about how a 1990 defense allocation that did not keep pace with inflation would affect the nation's security. Cheney acknowledged Domenici's point but said that, in developing his program, he was assuming that the negotiators would cut Bush's request. The defense secretary was not digging in for the Bush position. Instead, he was facing reality. Domenici had his signal. He was free to support a defense figure lower than Bush's.

Such a figure was a foregone conclusion. Besides, the White House seemed more interested in protecting international aid than in anything else. Earlier in the talks, Darman remarked offhandedly one morning that, in order to get a deal, negotiators just needed to agree on funds for defense and nondefense programs, as well as on a revenue-raising figure. When he returned for the afternoon meeting, Darman seemed taken aback. As he told the negotiators, while at the White House on other business after the morning meeting, Darman had been chastised by Bush and Baker for not mentioning international aid in his list of unfinished business. How those two had known of Darman's comments that morning was unclear. Whether, in fact, Darman was serious at all about what had happened at the White House was also unclear, although one participant in the budget negotiations said he was "oozing" sincerity as he told the story. Either way, Bush undoubtedly cared about international aid—enough to telephone Sasser about his concerns, and enough for Baker to meet individually with the negotiators as decisions were made in the last week.

On Monday, April 10, the negotiators began to exchange offers on how much to spend in each of the three main categories under discussion. Unlike for previous issues, where numbers were bandied about orally, the last week's offers were passed across the table on paper. Panetta proposed one set of numbers in the morning, while Sasser, Domenici, and Darman chipped in with separate counteroffers in the afternoon. Such bargaining continued the next day, with Sasser offering a proposal, prompting a verbal counteroffer from the Republicans and a counter to that from Sasser. By then, Darman and the Republicans were working as a team. After each offer was passed across the table, the Democrats went off to meet in one room, Darman and the Republicans to another. One side would give a little, then the other. The numbers edged closer together. The negotiators beamed with confidence.

Enough confidence, in fact, that they took a break to address other matters. Getting an agreement on the numbers was only half of the battle, as they all knew. What they needed was a way to enforce the deal, to ensure that the allocations called for in defense, international aid, and day-to-day domestic programs would be spent—no more, no less—that the cuts in entitlements would be made, that the revenues would be raised. The negotiators, after all, would have to impose their agreement on the executive departments and a Congress that were largely shut out of the talks. Getting others to go along would not be easy.

On the prior Saturday, April 8, the negotiators' top staffers had met all day to devise a list of rules, known as the written agreement, to ensure enforcement. Using the rules that accompanied the 1987 budget summit as a model, they suggested a three-page list of 13 rules that would accompany two pages of charts where the numbers would be displayed. For items on which they could not decide, disputed wording was set aside in brackets. The negotiators, they hoped, would quickly agree on noncontentious matters and debate the wording in dispute. They had no such luck, largely because of Darman. The OMB director has long exhibited a keen interest in the written word. In a 1986 interview with the *New York Times*, he had even argued, "In the end, all the substance and tactics come down to the drafting of words, whether you're talking about a law, a regulation, an order or a speech. My job frequently involves mediating about words. What it all gets down to often is somebody with a pen and paper."[6] In the Reagan years, the "somebody" was often Darman, whether it involved a presidential speech or a United States communique to other nations about economic policy.

He could not resist. When negotiators turned to the staffers' draft on April 11, Darman did not focus on the bracketed items. No, he wanted to survey every word. So he and the others started to read aloud from the beginning. Sentences were dissected, phrases torn apart and reassembled. One word was substituted for another. Punctuation was subject to debate. As morning or later sessions ended, the staff incorporated the agreed-upon changes into a new draft from which negotiators would resume their work. The process was long and tedious. The staff, for instance, had written a short sentence of introduction, stating that the agreement would meet the Gramm-Rudman target for 1990; Darman expanded it into four sentences and set it aside as a cover sheet. The OMB director haggled with the lawmakers, and the lawmakers with each other, over several of the 13 items below the statement. Democrats, for instance, insisted on an item under which the tax-writing committees would not press ahead on their $5.3 billion tax-hike bill without Bush's support for its contents; Rostenkowski had insisted on such a procedure. At Frenzel's urging, the negotiators expanded an item calling on the group to turn its attention next toward a bigger deficit-cutting deal.

After completing the written agreement on Thursday, April 13, the group resumed bargaining over defense, international aid, and day-to-day domestic spending. Beginning about 5:30 P.M., the two sides sent offers across the table. In between, each side met alone to consider what the other had proposed. The hour grew late. Foley ordered out for pizza, sending his driver to pick it up. Pizza was served where the negotiators worked. Pizza was consumed by staffers who entertained themselves by watching a Washington Capitals' hockey game while the principals worked. And pizza was given to the 15 or so reporters who were waiting outside, anticipating an agreement to write about for the next day's newspapers.

At Panetta's insistence, the Democrats sent the day's first offer, one calling for more domestic spending. Republicans moved toward the Democrats' domestic number, but asked that international aid money be protected in a separate category. It eventually was. Democrats returned with an offer to take the Republicans' defense number, in exchange for raising the domestic and international aid figures. Final details were ironed out with everyone at the table. As they finished, Darman turned to Sasser for a final bit of humor. "And I think we've even got money for Port Moresby," he joked. Negotiators reached agreement at about midnight, although Foley, who briefed reporters, pretended that no deal had been struck. The negotiators wanted to announce it the next day at the White House with Bush. Reporters were not fooled.

■   ■   ■   ■

The agreement was a sham. Negotiators claimed $5.7 billion in revenues from asset sales. They credited themselves with $1.8 billion by taking the postal service out of the budget—or "off-budget"—though such sleight-of-hand did not save the government any money. Negotiators agreed to shift $850 million in farm payments from 1990 into 1989, raising that year's deficit and having no long-term impact in terms of savings. Another $477 million in savings was derived from writing off food stamps that had been issued but never used; budget experts were particularly hard put to explain how that saved any money. Another $550 million in savings came from extending a law that limited federal retirees to 60 percent of their benefits in the first year, rather than 100 percent. Negotiators agreed to raise $2.7 billion in user fees, although nobody thought Congress would follow through. As for day-to-day domestic programs, spending on them was set at $181 billion, or just $300 million below the amount needed to keep pace with inflation.

The deal was a sham in the way that only a few Washington insiders understood. Fearing a backlash from conservatives that would threaten Congress's ability to implement the deal, the negotiators actually hid the size of the cut in defense, making it look like only $1.7 billion. (Actually, OMB's calculations showed that it totaled $5.2 billion.) That way, Bush and Republicans could sell the deal at the Pentagon and in Congress. Although one newsletter, *Inside the White House*, wrote about it, most reporters apparently did not see the chicanery. Barely a peep was heard from conservatives, who thought defense had come out well. Indeed, at the Rose Garden, House Republican Whip Newt Gingrich of Georgia described the deal as "very solid on defense; those who care about defense should be supportive of this agreement."

The agreement did not address the nation's long-term deficit problem. Even assuming that it were fully implemented—and that was highly unlikely—CBO pegged the deficit for fiscal 1991 at $130 billion; if so, Washington would have to find $56 billion in savings to cut the projected 1991 deficit to $74 billion and avoid Gramm-Rudman's across-the-board cuts. That Darman and the others would even strike this kind of deal was an affront to good government, according to business leaders and budget experts who understood it. It was an affront to at least one negotiator, too. "To tell you the truth," Frenzel recalled, "the bipartisan budget agreement was just at the very, very bottom end of acceptability, as far as I was concerned. I came very close to saying, 'I don't want to be a part of that,' because I thought it was not enough of a deficit reduction." Although he felt "obliged" to sign on when Bush did, Frenzel said, "I grumbled and cursed along the way."

Nevertheless, like the others, Frenzel viewed their pact as an important building block. They had agreed on *something*, and early in the year. As a result, Washington would not be consumed with a yearlong budget deadlock. With the players now trusting each other, they could move on to bigger and better things later in the year—in particular, a serious, long-term whack at the deficit. That spring, they hoped to begin meeting again to discuss the goal and to plot common strategy. It was a risky venture, fraught with political landmines, with no guarantee that Bush and Congress would even enact what they came up with. This time, the spending cuts would be deep and the tax increase high.

Such worries, however, would have to wait. By the spring, Bush had a more immediate problem. His proposal to beef up the savings and loan industry had run into a wall of early trouble. Democrats and some Republicans threatened to rewrite it. The administration, in turn, threatened to veto their handiwork. What they fought over, though, was not how best to handle the multi-billion-dollar problem. With Washington starving for cash, the battle was over who had the best idea for pushing the costs off into the future. The S&L battle showed how big of an impediment the deficit had become to rational policy making.

CHAPTER FIVE

"WE DO NOT LIVE IN A NORMAL WORLD"

As they met on May 16 with administration officials to discuss the savings and loan rescue legislation, more than a few House Republicans felt vulnerable. That morning, some of them had watched as television talk show host Phil Donahue devoted his program to the industry's problems. Rep. Joseph P. Kennedy II, a young Massachusetts Democrat, had capitalized on Donahue's interest. Appearing on the program, the son of former senator Robert F. Kennedy railed against the rich and mighty who, he suggested, had created the huge mess. He talked about the unfairness of asking "ordinary Americans" to bail out the industry's high-rolling gamblers. And he bragged about his vote against the legislation that was moving, slowly but steadily, through the Senate and House. Some of these Republicans thought it had been a rather demagogic performance.

But they could not ignore it. The crisis, later estimated to cost $300 billion or so over the next three decades to fix—at least half of which would come from taxpayers—took root under Reagan and was growing under Bush. Sure, there was plenty of blame to go around: the Democrats running Congress, regulators, S&L operators, and so on. But Republicans did not want to be left flat-footed. During the one-hour meeting in the Capitol, an idea was offered by Rep.

Bill McCollum of Florida who, like Kennedy, served on the House Banking Committee. It would sure help, he suggested, if Attorney General Richard L. Thornburgh would announce a prosecution or two of crooked S&L figures. That would show that the Bush administration was on the job. Sitting around a table, GOP leaders and other members nodded in agreement.

McCollum's political concerns were understandable. The S&L crisis, which engulfed Washington because of the government's commitment to back up to $100,000 of each depositor's funds in a federally insured institution, was an easy one on which an ambitious lawmaker could make political hay. Americans did not understand how the crisis started, how it had been allowed to explode in size, or how they got stuck with such a big tab. They wanted someone else to pay. Confusion ran rampant. "Why can't the government pay for these debts instead of the taxpayers?" one man asked on "Donahue," igniting applause from an audience of several hundred. "Well," Donahue replied, "because we are the government. It's going to be our money." His response prompted more confusion. When the show's panelists suggested that costs of the legislation represented an amount equal to $1,000 for every American taxpayer, some audience members seemed to think Uncle Sam was about to send them a bill for it. "How do they expect us taxpayers to work up $1,000 per taxpayer?" one asked. "I mean, where are we going to come up with this?" Another declared, "I don't have $1,000 in an S&L, and I don't have $1,000 in the bank. And I'd like to know what kind of job programs the Congress is going to come up with for those of us who are normal citizens and can't pay the $1,000." Between those cries came that of a woman who pointed at Steve Bartlett, a Texas Republican on the House Banking Committee and one of Donahue's guests, and said, "The issue is, I think, for Congressman Bartlett, whether we should continue to support people like you in Congress that's trying to screw the public."

It was "us"—the struggling, ignorant, malleable millions—against "them"—the rich and greedy who caused the problems. "Elena Hanggi—it's about time we hear an average person," Donahue said in one introduction. "Thank God for you, a real live average person. Let's hear it for her. You are former president of ACORN, and that acronym means Association for Organizations for Reform Now. ACORN is the largest low-income membership in the country.... And you step forward as a citizen and say what?" "I say," she answered, "that I am not willing to pay $1,000 of my tax money and $1,000 of my husband's tax money, and $1,000 of my mother-in-law's tax money to bail out not only people who have high-flying rides, but also people who benefited from the turning of the heads of regulators." A moment later, she added, "And we get to pick up the pieces, we the average taxpayers of America. And I say it's not fair. We didn't create the mess, we didn't benefit from the mess, and we shouldn't have to pay for the mess." "Right on!" Kennedy chimed in.

Donahue was not the only public figure to discover how angry Americans were. Three months earlier, David Brinkley opened a segment of "This Week," his Sunday morning television news program, by musing, "A common perception I hear around and read in the mail and so on among the American people is that officials and owners of the S&Ls are in trouble and, of course, are getting away with murder; that the taxpayers are going to send them away with money and then pick up the pieces." Other television and radio talk shows discussed the crisis, and the nation's leaders began to fear a public backlash against them. Guests on call-in shows described callers as furious, as feeling ambushed because nobody in the presidential campaign warned them about the problem.

Dukakis, however, had broached the subject nearly a year earlier. In a late September 1988 shot at Bush, he suggested that, as chairman of Reagan's task force on financial deregulation, Bush could have helped "head off" the crisis. "Mr. Bush," he said, "walked away from a ticking time bomb." Bush supporters fired back, blaming the Democrat-controlled Congress for not providing the $15 billion that Reagan requested in 1986 to beef up the Federal Savings and Loan Insurance Corporation (FSLIC), which insures thrift deposits. Dukakis quickly backed off, perhaps for an obvious reason. By then, the crisis was growing. Costs were skyrocketing. If he dwelled on the problem, reporters might ask Dukakis what he would do about it. What would he say? The Democratic candidate was having enough trouble combating the public's suspicions that he was itching to raise taxes. The last thing he needed was to highlight this upcoming expense.

Even after the election, nobody wanted to deal with the costs. The nation's leaders had their hands full with deficit cutting. But, if ignored, the savings and loan problem would only grow. More S&Ls, known as thrifts, were running into financial trouble. Those already in trouble were sinking deeper into debt. The more that happened, the more that Washington's liabilities rose. Without action, the situation could get out of hand. Worried depositors might decide to leave the thrifts. A "run" on deposits was not beyond the realm of possibility. And if thousands of depositors suddenly wanted their money, Washington would be hard-pressed to get it to them. A panic might ensue. Only public confidence that Washington stood behind the money had prevented such problems in the past. In cases where deposits were not federally insured, Americans had reacted differently. When, for instance, privately insured thrifts in Ohio and Maryland went bankrupt in 1985, depositors at other thrifts lost confidence in the private insurance funds. With depositors quickly withdrawing their money, state and federal officials jumped in to save the thrifts and avert a wider panic.

That was proof enough, if Washington needed any, that its own thrift deposit insurance system had to be saved. And by the summer of 1989, the White House and Congress had agreed on how. But their plan to undertake the most costly federal rescue ever—far exceeding those of, say, the Chrysler Corporation in 1979 and New York City in 1975—was not the best possible one, as participants openly admitted. It was more politically expedient than rational. It was shaped largely by the deficit problem and the unwillingness of officials to solve it with big tax hikes or spending cuts. Instead of facing the thrift problem themselves, this generation's leaders shifted most of the costs to the future (as if tomorrow's Americans had anything to do with it). Washington chose to borrow the money, repaying it and the interest costs over a period of 33 years. In doing so, the nation's leaders raised the total costs by many billions of dollars. Most took it in stride. They had grown so accustomed to heaping debt on future Americans that they were not fazed by it.

When they finished, Bush and Congress boasted that they had stayed loyal to Gramm-Rudman's annual deficit targets. Technically, they had. But to do so, they used the most shameless gadgetry. Rather than account for the costs directly, they set up a semipublic, semiprivate corporation to borrow $50 billion. Healthy thrifts would repay that principal; taxpayers would pay at least $150 billion in interest over the next 33 years. Because the corporation, not the government, would borrow most of the money, that amount would not show up in the budget books. But for the same reason, interest costs would probably be higher. In essence, policy makers decided that proclaiming loyalty to Gramm-Rudman's technical rules was more important than choosing the most cost-effective plan for thrifts. Unfortunately, because the rescue plan was so complicated, few Americans knew the solution would cost them billions more than was necessary. Many of those Americans had not even been born yet.

■　　　■　　　■　　　■

It was surprising, to say the least, that the savings and loan industry would cause such problems. Until the 1970s, the industry had been a financially steady one. A *Congressional Quarterly Weekly Report* in early 1989 traced its growth back to 1819 when the Bank of Savings in the City of New York, the nation's first mutual savings bank, was established. The first savings and loan, Oxford Provident Building Association, was set up twelve years later in Frankfort, Pennsylvania. Over the next two centuries, thrifts spread, groups that lobbied for them were set up in Washington, the industry won exemptions from various tax laws, and savings and loans were glorified in Frank Capra's 1946 classic, *It's a Wonderful Life*. As thrifts performed their traditional task of making loans for the American Dream of homeownership, their assets mounted.[1]

The problems, which began in the 1970s, arose from various economic changes that were exacerbated by legislative and regulatory blunders. First came the rise in interest rates in the late 1970s. Thrifts, which years earlier had loaned for 15-, 20-, and 30-year mortgages, found themselves paying higher rates on deposits than they received in loan repayments. And because Washington limited the rates of interest that thrifts could offer depositors, Americans shifted their funds en masse to money market accounts and mutual funds that offered higher rates. Washington responded by deregulating the industry. In 1980, to better enable thrifts to compete, it lifted the ceiling on interest rates that they could offer. At the same time, it raised the federal insurance on deposits from $40,000 to $100,000. Two years later, it let thrifts invest in new lines of business, with the idea that diversity would make for more profitability. States, which also regulated thrifts, let them make an even wider assortment of investments.

Unfortunately, the federal and state governments lacked the foresight to beef up supervision. Thrifts, particularly the state-regulated ones in Texas and California, engaged in risky, far-flung ventures with impunity. Because of federal deposit insurance, which even the state-regulated thrifts had, thrift operators had little incentive to be careful. As critics were fond of saying, many thrifts acted like their motto was, "Heads I win, tails the FSLIC loses." Depositors knew their money was safe and so had little reason to pressure the thrifts to stop. Indeed, thrifts were not gambling with depositors' funds. They were doing so with the government's funds. It was a system, as George F. Will suggested early in 1989, in which "profits remain private and the losses get socialized." As for federal regulators, they both contributed to the crisis and were victimized by it. On the one hand, they loosened their accounting standards to help thrifts overcome financial problems; that move let some dig deeper holes for themselves. On the other hand, when they tried to crack down forcefully on thrifts, their own staffs were too inexperienced and small in number.

Congressional delays in enacting rescue legislation only made matters worse. In mid-1986, Rep. Chalmers P. Wylie of Ohio, the House Banking Committee's senior Republican, introduced legislation developed by the Reagan administration and the Federal Home Loan Bank Board, which oversaw the FSLIC, to raise $15 billion by setting up a private corporation to sell bonds. Despite pleas by Edwin Gray, the bank board chairman, that the FSLIC must have the money, the legislation died later that year as the 99th Congress ended. A scaled-down form of success came in the 100th. In early January 1987, Wylie was joined by House Banking Committee chairman Fernand J. St Germain, a Rhode Island Democrat, in introducing a similar measure. When it was finally enacted in August, however, the legislation provided for just $10.8 billion.

That was hardly enough, as Americans would soon learn to their horror. In 1988, the thrift crisis was like an increasingly scary movie. As spring gave way to summer, and then to fall, estimates of how much the crisis would cost exploded. M. Danny Wall, the new bank board chairman, suggested in early summer that $22.7 billion would be enough. He raised that figure to $30.9 billion in early July, to $50 billion in October, and to $68.9 billion in November. Private experts raised their estimates as well, almost always keeping them higher than Wall's. As Frederick D. Wolf of the General Accounting Office, which also estimated the costs, explained the rising figures in late 1988, "Any time you open up one of these [thrift] institutions—and I'm using *open up* as in a can of worms—it turns out it is worse than anybody was thinking."[2] Wall talked about the need for a taxpayer contribution (to supplement whatever the healthy thrifts could give) as early as July, but lawmakers did not openly admit to such realities until the fall. By 1989, the crisis was growing by $10 to $20 million a day.

By the time Bush took office, the crisis had been transformed into a scandal, one that engulfed House Speaker Jim Wright, the nation's most powerful Democrat, other congressional Democrats, the industry's powerful lobby, thrift operators, major accounting firms, and other players. The tales of power and greed that came out were lurid enough to titillate even the most hardened observer. No longer was the crisis just one of errors and stupidity. Now it was one of stealing, of taking advantage of taxpayers who would be called upon to ante up. The public demanded retribution, revenge. The politicians would have to be sensitive to such emotion.

Wright, whose home state of Texas hosted probably the sleaziest, most costly thrift failures, put Democrats in an especially tough position. As attorney Richard J. Phelan told the House Committee on Standards of Official Conduct (known as the Ethics Committee), which hired him to probe Wright, the Speaker had pressured regulators to ease off on certain Texas thrift operators. In his dealings on behalf of two such operators, one of whom was treasurer of the Democratic Congressional Campaign Committee, Phelan reported that Wright went too far, violating House rules in the process. Gray, the former bank board chairman, said he believed Wright delayed House debate on legislation to beef up the FSLIC because of his unhappiness with the regulators. Even worse, according to Phelan, Wright told Gray over the telephone that one of his top regulators in Texas, H. Joe Selby, was a homosexual and had set up a ring of homosexual lawyers at various firms through which anyone who wanted to deal with the board had to go. Gray found nothing to confirm the charge. Nor did anyone else.

Other high-ranking Democratic lawmakers also were caught in compromising positions. In 1986, a year before he became the House majority whip, Rep. Tony Coelho of California received a $50,000 loan and special investment help from Thomas Spiegel, chief executive officer of the Columbia Savings and Loan Association of Beverly Hills, California, at a time when Spiegel was feuding with federal regulators. Facing a likely inquiry from the Ethics Committee, Coelho stunned his colleagues in May 1989 by announcing that he would resign. Nor were Senate Democrats immune from ethical problems. In April 1987, Majority Whip Alan Cranston of California, Riegle, the Banking Committee chairman, two other Senate Democrats, and a Senate Republican met with William Black, a bank board regulator in San Francisco, to question how the board was regulating Charles H. Keating, Jr.'s, Lincoln Savings and Loan of Irvine, California. The senators' actions, through which they were labeled "The Keating Five," prompted the Senate Ethics Committee to launch an investigation in 1989 and evoked predictions in Washington that one or more might eventually resign.

Even more questionable was the behavior of thrift operators. Between early 1984 and mid-1987, "misconduct" was uncovered in at least 168 of 210 insolvent thrifts, according to a 1988 report by the House Government Operations Committee. During that time period, the committee said, losses to FSLIC "from failed and insolvent institutions, where fraud or other misconduct was a contributing factor to, or a primary cause of, insolvency, will amount to an absolute minimum of $12 billion"—a figure that the panel called "very conservative."[3] In mid-1989, the Federal Deposit Insurance Corporation (FDIC), which was given a key role in the thrift cleanup, said possible criminal violations had occurred at almost half of the nearly 220 worst-case thrifts under its control.

More striking were the tales of individual thrift operators. With federal insurance backing depositors' funds, and with regulators giving them far more rein than was prudent, some operators engaged in the baldest of money-making shenanigans. They lived like feudal lords before their collective world collapsed. In Dallas, the *Wall Street Journal* reported, Western Savings Association increased its assets by 6,000 percent, closed loans "late at night with open-bar soirees," lent more to delinquent borrowers, and paid an executive a $500,000 bonus on the day federal regulators declared the thrift insolvent.[4] In Stephensville, Texas, according to *U.S. News & World Report*, Edwin T. McBirney III bought Sunbelt Savings for a mere $6 million and turned it into a $3.2 billion giant before regulators moved in. Until then, McBirney and his wife, Jamie, lived the good life. At the couple's 1984 Halloween party, she served lion, antelope, and pheasant, rented smoke machines, and provided Two Tons of Fun, a couple of disco performers, for entertainment. On Halloween in 1985, Mrs. McBirney "created a jungle in a warehouse, rented a live elephant and cast her husband as Bwana, complete with pith helmet and binoculars. That Christmas...the theme was, appropriately enough, a Russian winter, and waiters dressed as serfs served up the drinks."[5] Stanley E. Adams, owner of Lamar Savings Association in Austin, Texas, was the most imaginative operator of all. As a publicity stunt, the *Washington Post* reported, Adams filed an application with state regulators to open a branch office on the moon. The location? Cayley Crater in the Sea of Tranquility.[6]

Who was watching the store? The regulators were in a particularly difficult position, due to the regulatory structure in which they labored. At the top, in Washington, was the Federal Home Loan Bank Board, a three-member panel that supervised 12 district banks around the nation. A majority of board members at the district banks, however, were chosen by the S&Ls themselves. Each board, in turn, chose its own bank president and set his or her salary. The thrifts under its jurisdiction owned most stock in the district bank. So a bank president had to engage in two somewhat contradictory tasks: supervising the thrifts while keeping them happy as stockholders.

Relations between the regulators and the regulated were close, if not cozy. More than one crossed from one side to the other. As the industry's troubles mounted, some of those blamed for not regulating the thrifts forcefully enough went to work as lawyers for those troubled institutions. In January 1989, the *Wall Street Journal* reported that Thomas Vartanian, the Federal Home Loan Bank Board's former general counsel, had generated $12 million in billings as a Washington lawyer for his work on 55 mergers and acquisitions between thrifts. Others who switched from regulator to thrift client included Vartanian's old deputy, Patrick Doyle, his successor at the bank board, Norman Raiden, and at least seven former regulators who were working together at a law firm.[7]

Even when they were moved to act, the regulators worked under severe handicaps. For one thing, thrift examiners were ill prepared to deal with the new climate fostered by the financial deregulation of the early 1980s. For another, resources were inadequate, particularly at the district bank in Dallas. When that bank moved its operations from Little Rock, Arkansas, to Dallas in April 1983, only 11 of the 48 employees in the bank's division of supervision, most of them secretaries or low-level workers, moved with it. Of those 11, only 2 had ever worked as supervisory agents, and they were left with the truly ridiculous task of supervising the region's 480 savings and loans. Besides, the regulators in Little Rock had been three or four years behind in examining some thrifts, and recordkeeping was crude. Examiners were writing their reports in longhand, not on a computer.

In the late 1980s, whatever law enforcement actions were taken only added to the image of sleaziness. In May 1989, three former officials of Commodore Savings Association in Dallas, Texas, were convicted on charges in connection with making $135,000 in illegal campaign contributions. A month later, the former president of Vernon Savings & Loan Association of Dallas was charged with conspiring to make more than $50,000 in illegal campaign contributions to five lawmakers, including Wright. (A year earlier, a Vernon official had pleaded guilty to making "sexual payoffs" to other Vernon officials as part of another conspiracy.) Also in June 1989, two former officials of FirstSouth Savings and Loan of Pine Bluff, Arkansas, were indicted on charges of fraudulent management and conspiracy. In Louisiana, the FSLIC sued two former lawyers of New Orleans Federal Savings and Loan Association for $6.4 million in connection with loans made by the thrift.

Whether private examiners should have noticed some of the financial chicanery earlier was an open question. "Why did accountants throughout the nation fail to detect the shenanigans that triggered one of the biggest financial calamities this country has ever seen?" the *New York Times* asked in March 1989.[8] Others demanded an answer. By that spring, the Federal Home Loan Bank Board had sued 10 accounting firms that had audited failed thrifts, and it promised more lawsuits. Among the targets were three of the nation's "Big Eight" firms—Deloitte Haskins & Sells, Coopers & Lybrand, and Touche Ross & Co. This was not the first time that accounting firms had problems when financial institutions went bankrupt. Peat Marwick, which gave the Penn Square Bank of Oklahoma City, Oklahoma, a clean bill of health in 1982, faced $400 million in lawsuits when that bank failed just four months later. Shareholders of the Continental Illinois National Bank and Trust Company in Chicago took Ernst & Whinney to court for not warning them of dangers that led to its federal bailout in 1984. Grant Thornton paid an $80 million settlement because a partner admitted taking bribes to prepare false financial statements on E.S.M. Government Securities, Inc., of Fort Lauderdale, Florida, which failed in 1985.

While thrifts enjoyed great influence over the regulators back home, their lobbyists held sway in Capitol Hill's corridors, committee rooms, and offices. The industry's principal lobbying group, the U.S. League of Savings Institutions, was long viewed as one of Washington's strongest. It sprayed campaign contributions around generously, and its members could be energized quickly to call their local congressman about an issue. In July 1989, the *Washington Post* calculated that political action committees (PACs) associated with the industry had contributed $1.8 million for candidates to federal office in 1988, 80 percent of which went to incumbents. Savings and loan organizations also paid $218,000 to members of Congress during the prior three years for speeches, articles, and public appearances, 70 percent of which went to members of the House and Senate Banking Committees. Another $169,000 in campaign contributions came from executives of savings and loan institutions and others tied to the industry.[9] The big bucks apparently paid off. As Gray told the *Wall Street Journal* in early 1989, "When it came to thrift matters in the U.S. Congress, the U.S. League and many of its affiliates were the *de facto* government. What the league wanted, it got. What it did not want from Congress, it got killed."[10]

The very influence that worked so grandly for the industry came back to haunt it as the thrift crisis deepened. St Germain lost his seat in 1988 after three years of bad publicity about his close ties to certain thrifts and operators. In 1985, the *Wall Street Journal* reported on apparent conflicts of interest between St Germain's roles as a legislator and as an investor in a thrift, prompting an investigation by the House Ethics Committee and some snooping by the Justice Department.[11] The U.S. League was criticized in 1988 when newspapers reported on its annual convention, held in Honolulu at the same time that so many thrifts were losing money. "I am sure they have a lot of good, practical reasons for going to Hawaii," Rep. Bruce A. Morrison of Connecticut, a Democrat on the House Banking Committee, told the *New York Times*. "But it wouldn't have been a bad gesture if they had canceled their convention and moved it to a place less grand, maybe Hoboken."[12]

Early in 1989, lobbyists were further embarrassed at a Senate Banking Committee hearing when Gramm, the Texas Republican, quoted a 1987 letter in which the U.S. League called for just $5 billion to clean up the savings and loan mess. The league, trying to protect its healthy members against a big federal assessment to pay for the problem, said $5 billion would do the job. "If anyone has been irresponsible on this issue, it's the U.S. League," Gramm said. "You have no credibility here whatsoever," Sen. Richard Shelby, an Alabama Democrat, told lobbyists at the hearing. Looking back, Gray said the league's strategy was to delay action on an adequate plan so the problem would grow; at that point, taxpayers—and not healthy thrifts—would be called upon to pay the bills. "The league knew damn well that what they were telling the Congress was untrue," Gray told the House Banking Committee in early 1989. "The folks at the league told me this was the strategy—not once but on a number of occasions."

■   ■   ■   ■

When you added it all up—the high living, the fraud, the political ties—it did not make for a pretty picture, certainly not one for which Americans would willingly pay. If they could have, Americans surely would have let the thrifts die, sent the operators to jail, and thrown away the keys. But as Bush, Congress, the regulators, and others took great pains to explain, there was only one problem: the depositors. Washington, they stressed, was not "bailing out" the big boys, the high-rollers, the crooks, and the creeps. No, it was merely raising the money to ensure that innocent depositors did not lose their money. "Phil, let's be clear about this," Lawrence J. White, a member of the Federal Home Loan Bank Board, said on Donahue's show.

> It's awful, it's horrible.... But—and this is an important but—we aren't bailing out anyone, Phil. We aren't bailing out the owners, the stockholders, the managers. We're showing them the door when we close down those savings and loans. We're suing them to try to recover as much of the funds as possible. We're making recommendations to the local U.S. Attorneys to try to bring criminal indictment[s]. And the monies are going to pay the depositors who were told by the federal government, "Your money is good. Up to $100,000 [of] your money is good."

Congress sent the same message, hoping to make a taxpayer contribution palatable. "We cannot, in good conscience, accept the burdens that this bill puts on the taxpayer without actively pursuing every crook who stole from FSLIC with maximum criminal penalties and maximum recovery of ill-gotten gain," Sen. Christopher "Kit" Bond, a Missouri Republican, said while the Senate was debating its version of the thrift rescue bill in April 1989. Sen. Richard Bryan, a Nevada Democrat, added, "We must seek out and punish those that have committed wrongdoing in the management of these failed institutions. We must make every effort to recover assets diverted from S&Ls and place behind bars those who have caused losses as a consequence of their criminal behavior."

House members, debating their own bill in June, played on the same theme. "Now, in the news media we see stories that the legislation that we are about to pass is a bailout for crooked operators, which is not only insulting, but it does little to stabilize confidence in an essential industry," said Wylie.

". . . not one penny will go to pay off stockholders or management under this bill." Rep. David Price of North Carolina, a Democrat on the House Banking Committee, stressed, "None of this money will go to bail out the managers, owners, and investors of failed savings and loan associations. If these people have engaged in criminal behavior, they should be prosecuted and put into jail, and the bill provides increased penalties and more money for the Justice Department to pursue and investigate financial institution crime." Unfortunately, Thornburgh admitted early in the year that most of the money lost to fraudulent activity was lost for good. He was not even sure about recovering enough to offset the $50 million that Bush wanted to spend on increased prosecutions.

But if the taxpayers had to pay for the mess, a key question remained: Which taxpayers? That was a tricky matter from the start. The White House, laboring under its no-tax guidelines, discovered the sensitivities early. Days after Bush's inauguration, Brady offered an idea during a meeting with congressional leaders. What about a 25 cent fee that depositors would pay on every $100 of their federally insured deposits? The news leaked. A storm ensued. Democrats said it sure looked like a "duck"—that is, a tax. Others made jokes. "It's the reverse toaster theory," L. William Seidman, the FDIC chairman, smirked. "Instead of the bank giving you a toaster when you make a deposit, you give them one." Before long, the administration backed off the idea.

Who would pay? The question stirred on Capitol Hill in early 1989. The rich? The poor? Businessmen? Farmers? Northeasterners? Midwesterners? As the 101st Congress took shape, Rep. Lane Evans, the House's chairman of the Congressional Populist Caucus, identified the issue of "who would pay" as a potentially major one for 1989. Well-to-do investors had, in some cases, benefited greatly from the thrift industry's problems. With cash-starved thrifts offering excessively high yields on their savings accounts, these investors were able to plump $100,000 in more than one institution and, if the thrifts ran into trouble, rest comfortably with the knowledge that Washington stood behind their money. Now, Evans worried, was Washington going to turn around and dump the multi-billion dollar costs of rescuing the industry on middle- and lower-income Americans, perhaps in the form of higher taxes?

Ralph Nader, the consumer advocate, was worried about the same thing. Rather than just raise the question, as Evans and others had done, he provided an answer. To generate $10 billion, he proposed that income taxes on the nation's wealthiest 1 percent of individuals be raised by five percentage points. To garner another $10 billion, he suggested a 0.5 percent transaction tax on the sale of stock. Another $10 billion could be raised, he said, by imposing a 10 percent surtax on corporate income. If policy makers did not like those ideas, Nader said, they could try new excise taxes on junk bonds, leveraged buyouts, or luxury homes. In offering his wishlist of new soak-the-rich taxes, Nader was joined by Hanggi, the woman who had appeared on the raucous Donahue show.

Others stirred with regional concerns. Although deposits at all of the thrifts in question were federally insured, not all of the thrifts were federally regulated. Some states regulated thrifts by themselves, and it was the state-regulated ones that suffered some of the biggest losses. At the Northeast-Midwest Congressional Coalition—an organization of lawmakers from that region—members bristled at the idea that their constituents would pay as much for the thrift rescue as residents of states whose own regulators were at fault. "What we're doing," a staff member told me, "is bailing out the irresponsible actions of high-flyers in Texas, who were on an incredible speculative binge with funds that the taxpayer was responsible for insuring."

Why, the coalition asked, should residents of each state pay the same? Why not make some states pay more? Of $30.9 billion that Washington spent in 1988 to close or merge 205 insolvent thrifts, $23.3 billion involved state-regulated thrifts. Of that $23.3 billion, $16.7 billion involved such thrifts in Texas. Nor were the problems of Texas thrifts caused by general industry troubles or by economic problems linked to the 1986 drop in oil prices, the coalition argued. It was the regulators. So the coalition proposed that a state like Texas should contribute a kind of penalty tax for the troubles it caused. The tax would be levied based on the size of financial problems that the thrifts it regulated had brought. The states would be able to raise that money any way that they chose.

"Our effort will no doubt be attacked as an exercise in 'Texas bashing,'" the coalition wrote in a letter to House members. "We assure you that is not our intent." Other members probably would not have minded an attack on the Lone Star State. In the Northeast and Midwest, lawmakers recalled the attitude of Texans who, during the oil shortages, prospered from the explosion in oil prices and displayed bumper stickers that read "Let the Yankee Bastards Freeze in the Dark." During the Senate debate in April on a thrift rescue bill, Sen. David R. Durenberger, a Minnesota Republican, said, "It is not easy to explain to the hard-working citizens of my state who had to endure exploding energy prices in the early 1980s and then suffered through the economic depression and deflation of the mid-1980s that they must now ante up billions of dollars to bail out the speculators in the Southwest who profited from the expansive growth of just a few years ago."

■   ■   ■   ■

In the end, the coalition's ideas were largely ignored, as were Nader's. The plan that Bush unveiled in February 1989 was more politically palatable. Bush wanted to create a new corporation, the Resolution Financing Corporation (REFCORP), that would raise $50 billion by selling 30-year bonds. Proceeds would be used by a new institution, the Resolution Trust Corporation (RTC) that would, as its name implied, resolve the problems of troubled thrifts. Also contributing to the rescue would be thrifts and banks who would pay higher fees, the Federal Home Loan Bank Board, and other sources. Taxpayers, required to finance the interest costs associated with borrowing the $50 billion, would end up paying mightily. How much the whole thing would cost was hard to say.

Bush, in unveiling his plan February 6, first said $90 billion. Others scoffed, saying the costs would be much higher. Even the White House got into the act by revising its figures, first to $126 billion and then to $157 billion. Other estimates ranged from $200 billion by Sen. H. John Heinz, a Republican on the Senate Banking Committee; to $205 billion by CBO; to $285 billion by the General Accounting Office; to $335 billion by Rep. Henry Gonzalez, chairman of the House Banking Committee. Unfortunately, the experts tended to be measuring different things in different ways. Some opined only about what taxpayers would be charged, while others tallied up all costs. Some measured the costs only of the first decade, while others looked at all 33 years of the plan. Some adjusted tomorrow's dollars by factoring out inflation. Others did not. Also important were such unpredictable factors as interest rates on the borrowing and the level of new deposits acquired by the thrifts.

The $50 billion was no small sum, of course, but it barely caused a budgetary ripple. By proposing a semipublic, semiprivate corporation like REFCORP, the White House kept the money out of the budget—or "off-budget." That way, Washington could hold to its Gramm-Rudman schedule of annually declining deficits, and Bush could hold to his no-tax pledge. Such a maneuver, however, was not free. For the political gain of keeping some costs hidden, the White House had drafted a plan that would make the total costs of the thrift rescue much higher than they needed to be. Not everyone was enamored of the idea, which faced serious challenge in the months ahead. But Bush's approach had lots of precedence.

Indeed, corporations like this one were becoming more a rule than an exception in Washington. Government had grown much more complicated. No longer did Washington simply do things itself, in a straightforward way—whether it was building roads, offering health care, or providing for the poor. Increasingly, the nation's leaders found other roundabout ways. Washington interacted more with states and localities, often ordering that they—and not it—provide some services. So, too, did Washington order private businesses to provide certain benefits to employees. The federal government contracted out more for some services. Or, as in this case, it set up semiprivate corporations to do the job. The lines between the public and private sectors blurred.

By the 1980s, a new school of thought in political science arose to study the phenomenon. Donald F. Kettl, associate professor at Vanderbilt University, tabbed it "government by proxy."[13] Lester M. Salamon, director of Johns Hopkins University's Institute for Policy Studies, called it "third-party government."[14] Other experts worked in the Congressional Research Service, CBO, and elsewhere. The unofficial "dean" in this field was Harold Seidman, a former official with the Bureau of the Budget (OMB's predecessor) with a sense of humor and a flair for the English language. In 1988 he wrote:

> Several years ago, when I was teaching in Great Britain, I heard frequent references to strange organizations called quagos and quangos. A quago was a quasi-government organization and a quango was a quasi-nongovernment organization. No one was ever able to explain satisfactorily to me how one made the fine distinction between something that was quasi government and something that was quasi nongovernment. We have not been as imaginative as the British in inventing names, but we are now outdoing the British in creating our equivalent of quagos and quangos and blurring the traditional definitions of government and private. Developments in the last 20 years might make one suspect that the U.S. government is going quasi.

Who was in charge? Who was to blame if things went awry? The answers were unclear. The potential for trouble was obvious. Think back no further than the late 1980s, said the experts. From what did the Iran-Contra scandal of the late 1980s arise, if not a semiprivate operation designed to circumvent normal lines of authority? And from what was the

Challenger disaster of 1986 born, if not an arrangement in which the public sector contracted with business to produce material for its voyages? In the Iran-Contra case, Seidman wrote, "Congress professed to be shocked by the creation of the 'off-the-shelf' company to conduct government operations outside the law and the constitutional process. Yet in resorting to extra-constitutional measures to evade irksome laws and regulations, CIA director William Casey was adopting for his own purposes the model Congress itself had devised."[15]

One brand of corporation that had grown especially popular in recent years was known as the government-sponsored enterprise (GSE). So it was no surprise when Bush proposed one for his thrift rescue. Of the 10 GSEs in existence in 1988, some had been around quite awhile. The Federal National Mortgage Association ("Fannie Mae"), for instance, was established in 1938 to spur mortgage lending. But 5 of the 10 GSEs were set up in the late 1980s, for much the same reason that Bush and Congress eventually created an 11th—to take care of certain needs without increasing the budget deficit. In 1987, for instance, policy makers created a GSE in connection with its $10.8 billion measure for the FSLIC. Also that year, it set up a GSE to spur college construction and renovation loans. And in early 1988, Washington established three more GSEs to bail out the federal Farm Credit System.

The GSEs operated in a kind of budgetary never-never land. They all allocated or directed credit—loans, guarantees, and so on—to certain sectors of the economy, such as housing, agriculture, or education. Where private markets did not operate effectively, GSEs would venture. The GSEs all enjoyed a "special relationship" with the government; because Washington had set them up, investment bankers assumed that the government would step in if any of them ran into trouble. For that reason, they could borrow in the markets at interest rates just above those on Treasury securities. But even without the "special relationship," Washington would have had little choice but to rescue a struggling one. The GSEs were huge. By 1989, they had a combined $763 billion in outstanding loans; that figure represented an increase of more than 3,000 percent since 1970! As a result, a collapse by one or more GSE, just like a collapse by any of the nation's largest banks, could have set off a financial panic that would be hard to control. While a few White House and congressional aides and private experts fretted about the GSEs, most officials were content to let them flourish, apparently confident that nothing would go wrong.

The potential for trouble was obvious. To be effective, the GSEs had to perform a tricky balancing act. On one hand, their job was to allocate credit where private markets would not roam. Their targets would be those whose standing was considered too risky for banks and other lenders. On the other hand, if they issued too many loans to risky borrowers, they would wind up with huge numbers that would never be repaid. That, in essence, is what happened to the Farm Credit System. By the late 1980s, some lawmakers began to stir with concern. In early 1989, Ways and Means held hearings to learn more about GSEs. And yet, nobody expected Washington to do much except create more. Although officials might eventually have to bail out a troubled one, GSEs generally did not cause day-to-day problems. Most of all, they did not show up in the budget. Officials, then, could provide new benefits to voters and not worry about costs.

Or they could guarantee the benefits that they had previously conferred. Such was the case with federal deposit insurance, a benefit that was established in the 1930s so that Americans no longer had to fear the collapse of banks and thrifts. If a bank displayed the emblem of the FDIC, depositors by the 1980s could be sure that up to $100,000 of their money was safe. So, too, could those who put their money in savings and loans that wore the emblem of the FSLIC. While the FSLIC emblem assuaged the fears of Americans, it had ignited the worries of federal policy makers over the last decade as thrifts fell in record numbers. Suddenly Washington was being called on to cover those deposits. The FSLIC was running out of money. When the fund finally ran dry in the late

1980s, Washington had to stop closing thrifts altogether, a step that merely allowed the insolvent ones to lose even more money.

■   ■   ■   ■

Bush's plan to create another GSE received initial praise, but trouble was brewing. Congress soon was split into two factions. One liked the president's plan to put the corporation "off-budget." The other liked the corporation idea, but wanted to include its borrowing in the budget, or "on-budget." The dispute looked like a big one and, in the end, it almost threatened to block an agreement between Bush and Congress. But in the grand scheme of things, it was really trivial. Behind the verbal dueling lay a broad consensus: Washington would solve its thrift problems by borrowing money, rather than by raising taxes or cutting spending. "If one were sitting on the Moon, what is impressive is not the differences that are being articulated but the similarities," Rep. Jim Leach of Iowa, a Republican on the House Banking Committee, told the House in August before it passed the bill. "After all, we are talking about the same amount of money, the same long-term bonding technique." That consensus had its ethical drawbacks. Tomorrow's Americans were going to pay for a problem that arose over the prior decade—at a time when today's leaders ignored warning signs. Tomorrow's Americans had nothing to do with it. But just as Washington would not raise taxes or cut spending to rid itself of an old problem—the deficit—it would not do so when confronted with a new expense.

Not everyone went along willingly. Some lawmakers, objecting to the idea of borrowing, wanted Washington to pay for the thrift bill out of today's funds. Democratic efforts were shaded by partisanship; if Washington could not agree on enough spending cuts to pay for the thrift rescue, Bush would have to break his no-tax pledge. Thus, some Democrats wanted to force the issue. Reps. Kennedy and Morrison tried to offer an amendment to the House Banking Committee's thrift bill that called for raising most of the $50 billion through a tax hike. But Gonzalez, the committee chairman, ruled their motion out of order; tax changes, he said, must be left to Ways and Means. A similar, less detailed amendment by Rep. John J. LaFalce, a New York Democrat, met a similar fate. At Ways and Means, which contributed to the bill, members turned back three attempts by Florida Democrat Sam Gibbons to force a tax hike.

Gibbons surrendered, although he did not like what was happening. LaFalce would not. He carried his fight to the House floor. His amendment would have forced members to pay the $50 billion over three years and raise taxes or cut spending to do so. In June LaFalce told the House:

> Up until now, the debate in the media and in the Congress has focused on whether the costs of the S&L bailout should be off-budget or on-budget. Now, there is certainly some relevance to this debate.... But that is not the only issue.... What we would be doing, my colleagues, if we accept either of these two approaches, is saying, "There's a serious problem here. We must deal with it. We will deal with it, but we'll have our children and our grandchildren pay for it."

LaFalce's effort attracted a host of fascinating responses. Nobody questioned his logic. Nobody questioned the morality of his position. But he lost. His amendment was too direct. It raised too many politically troubling issues. "Sadly...we do not live in a normal world," said Rep. Thomas J. Downey, a New York Democrat.

> We live in a world where the president of the United States has said, "I don't want to see any tax increases." The consequences of adopting the amendment...would mean very simply that we would have to come up with $23 billion in additional revenue [in 1990], or we would have to cut spending by $23 billion [or accept the across-the-board cuts under Gramm-Rudman]. Now I say to my Republican friends, "None of you are beating down the door to raise $23 billion in new taxes, so that is not an option." I would say to my Democratic friends, "You clearly are not interested in seeing us open the door to further reductions in domestic spending."

In urging that LaFalce be defeated, Downey suggested that House members deal with "the world as we know it, and not the world that some would like to see us live in."

Rep. Jim Slattery, a Kansas Democrat, rose to challenge Downey.

> I would just observe that there is one fundamental point here, and that is, Are we going to pay today for the mistakes that were made in the last few years during the Reagan administration watch and during the watch of some of the members of this Congress? Are we going to pay for those mistakes now? Or are we going to borrow the money and spread it out over a long period of time? And, if we do it that way, it is going to cost us at least four or five times as much as it will if we pay now.

Downey, in turn, said of Slattery:

> The gentleman's refrain reminds me of the great Beatles song, "Let It Be." The only letting it be that we are going to let be is the fact that this House is unprepared to do what the gentleman would like us to do. The House is unprepared to pay for the bills today. The House is unprepared to cut the budget, as the gentleman would like to cut it.

It was, indeed, unprepared. LaFalce's effort failed, 256–171, ending talk of paying for the thrift mess without borrowing. No such effort was launched in the Senate, which finished work on its thrift bill in April. A few senators lamented the immorality of it. "Here we have a problem that for most people began approximately a decade ago and which we are now saying we, those who participated either by action or inaction, those who benefited directly or indirectly, those who went to the party, are not going to pay for the party," Sen. Bob Graham, a Florida Democrat, complained on April 17. "Those who are going to pay for the party are going to be our children and our grandchildren." Durenberger added two days later:

> At a time of huge federal budget deficits, when interest costs on the national debt continue to be the fastest growing part of the budget, it seems totally unreasonable that we have de-

veloped a financing package for this bailout that will pass the interest costs of this bailout onto our children and our children's children. I would have preferred that we paid for this package up front, right now, today.

The Senate did not act on such thoughts. The fix was in. Borrowing was easy. Doing otherwise would not be.

■　　　■　　　■　　　■

With that question answered, Bush and Congress fought over the best way to borrow. "Off-budget," the president and his allies said. "On-budget," some lawmakers countered. The issue was not as simple as the words. It involved not only the question of costs, which grew surprisingly controversial. It also involved some important political dueling, between the parties and within them. In the end, the fight went down to the wire, with dramatic speeches on the House floor just before Congress left for its August recess. Particularly striking were the terms of debate, largely shaped by the deficit and the law that was supposed to eliminate it.

If one were "sitting on the Moon," as Leach put it, he or she would have been struck by the all-encompassing role of Gramm-Rudman, the Rube Goldberg-type concoction that Washington created to force itself to cut the deficit. In this case (as well as in plenty of others), Gramm-Rudman inspired a host of fiscal shenanigans—and not the rational deficit-reduction plan of spending cuts or tax hikes that it was supposed to. Each side admitted that its idea to finance the thrift cleanup was a gimmick, a device to circumvent the law while pledging fealty to it. Although officials had created Gramm-Rudman, they acted as if it were imposed from the heavens, not to be tampered with even when logic dictated otherwise. They viewed it as a straitjacket.

One big challenge to Bush's bailout scheme came from Riegle. Instead of having an "off-budget" corporation borrow the money, he asked, why not let the Treasury borrow it? That would be cheaper. Federal borrowing is considered the safest around. Because nobody expects Washington to default on its obligations, its debt carries a lower rate of interest than any other. Under Bush's plan, Washington would not borrow the money; a private entity would. Interest costs would necessarily be a bit higher. Compared to Bush's, Riegle's idea was expected to save taxpayers (who would pay the interest costs) $4.5 billion or so over 33 years, according to various estimates. Of course, if the Treasury borrowed the money and its expenditure were counted in the budget, Washington would face a big problem—meeting Gramm-Rudman's targets. Riegle's solution was designed to exploit one of the law's big loopholes.

As we have said, Washington takes its last serious look at its Gramm-Rudman target on October 15—or 15 days after the fiscal year begins. OMB determines whether the deficit will fall below the target. If OMB says yes, across-the-board cuts are not triggered. At that point, attention shifts to the next year, which does not begin until the next October 1. As a result, between October 15 of one year and October 1 of the next, Washington can undertake new spending and not worry about across-the-board cuts. Riegle wanted to do just that. In early 1989, he suggested that Treasury borrow all $50 billion in that year—fiscal 1989. Washington could benefit from the interest rates accorded to Treasury debt and not fret about across-the-board cuts.

The administration fought back, with Brady leading the charge. No, he said, we cannot push all the borrowing into 1989. If we did, that year's deficit would swell to more than $200 billion. Investors, perhaps not understanding the chicanery involved, might get panicked about America's fiscal policy. Interest rates might rise. Just as important, Riegle's idea would set a bad precedent. Speaking in late March to business executives in Dallas, he said, "It is important that we do not make a mockery of Gramm-Rudman. It is not only the law of the land, it is the wheel horse of the fiscal discipline that will drive our deficit down. Meeting its deficit reduction targets is very important to the continued vitality of our economy." Riegle was not persuaded. A few days later, he unveiled the plan that, by then, everyone was expecting.

Riegle's initiative was turned back, but just barely. In support were several influential editorial pages. "Sen. Riegle's plan is better—and a lot cheaper," said the *Washington Post*.[16] The *New York Times* agreed, although it expressed a few reservations.[17] Even the *Wall Street Journal's* almost reflexively Republican editorial page gave Riegle's idea the nod over Bush's plan, saying, "By a very narrow margin, the Democrats may have the better of it."[18] But it was not enough. Brady threatened to recommend that Bush veto a measure like Riegle's. Darman sent word that, for technical reasons, OMB might not count all of the spending against 1989, but rather would spread it into future years, thus setting up a collision course with future Gramm-Rudman targets. The Senate Banking Committee defeated Riegle's plan, 11–10. The committee then sent its bill to the floor on a unanimous vote. Although Riegle dropped his plan at that point, Graham thought the chairman had had the right idea and pushed for it on the floor. He lost.

An on-budget approach had a lot more life in the House, where Rep. Willis D. Gradison, Jr., an Ohio Republican and one of Congress's most thoughtful members, was its chief advocate. A former chairman of the Federal Home Loan Bank Board's district bank in Cincinnati, Gradison had spent his life in the securities business. He understood financial issues as well as anyone on Capitol Hill. He was one of only 12 House members to vote against the $10.8 billion FSLIC measure in 1987 because he felt it was ill conceived and inadequate. In early 1989, he began to push for on-budget borrowing, although oddsmakers gave him little chance. By the spring, he had garnered the support of a House majority.

"The administration's financing proposal for the S&L bailout would impose unnecessary costs on the American people as well as on S&Ls," he said in a March 1, 1989 "Dear Colleague" letter to all House members, one of several he sent around that time. "These costs arise because of the off-budget design of the financing scheme." But unlike Riegle's plan to push the $50 billion into 1989, Gradison had another idea. He wanted Washington to simply set aside this $50 billion from its Gramm-Rudman calculations. Bush and Congress would ignore this spending when calculating whether they had met future deficit targets.

The White House did not think much more of Gradison's idea than it had of Riegle's, but Gradison had economic theory to buttress his own. Deficits matter, according to economists, because they raise federal borrowing needs. If so, then maybe this $50 billion was different. By beefing up its deposit insurance fund for thrifts, Washington was making good on an old obligation—to back up to $100,000 of each depositor's funds. Thus, the $50 billion did not, per se, create a new obligation, and according to some economists, there was reason to exempt it from Gramm-Rudman. "In short, the $50 billion of FSLIC payouts financed by new government borrowing does not increase aggregate demand or crowd out private investment," Feldstein, the former chairman of Reagan's Council of Economic Advisors, wrote March 1 in the *Wall Street Journal*, "It would be wrong therefore to count these payments in the Gramm-Rudman calculations and to adjust the desired path of taxes and spending to offset these payouts."[19] A Congressional Research Service report concluded similarly.

The administration was not persuaded. For much the same reason that it disliked Riegle's plan, it disliked Gradison's, which began to pick up Democratic support. Sure, taken by itself, an on-budget approach would attract lower interest rates than an off-budget plan, administration officials said. But, they added, that kind of thinking was shortsighted, if not naive. Gradison's idea might prove more expensive in the end, not less. Here's how: If Washington exempted any spending from Gramm-Rudman's calculations, foreign buyers of Treasury debt, on whom Washington relied so heavily, might grow nervous. They might not fully understand all the subtleties. All they would see is the deficit suddenly rising and Washington evading the targets. Perhaps they would cut their purchases, sending the market into a tizzy. To entice them back, or to entice others to replace them, interest rates might have to rise. If so, the increased costs could outweigh any savings assumed in Gradison's plan.

Markets are not *that* stupid, the on-budget advocates replied. After all, investors were sophisticated people. They could grasp complicated issues. Surely they knew Bush's plan was a gimmick, one designed only to hide federal obligations. If Washington acknowledged its obligations up front by putting them in the budget, investors might even react favorably, viewing the move as refreshingly honest. And so it went—the debate over how smart, or dumb, the markets were. At his private May 16 meeting with House Republicans, Brady even suggested a link between the 1987 stock market crash and Gramm-Rudman. The crash occurred, he noted, a month after Congress revised the law and, in doing so, delayed the date of a balanced budget. At about that time, Rep. Charles Schumer of New York, a House Banking Committee Democrat who advocated an on-budget plan, said of the White House's arguments, "If the markets are that bad, we ought to rethink the capitalist system."[20]

White House logic might have carried further if the markets had reacted adversely when Ways and Means, as part of the House's thrift bill, voted in May for an on-budget plan. The committee's vote came after Brady met privately with its Democrats but could not convince them to change their minds. Market reaction was barely identifiable. "The markets have registered their response to the committee's action, and it is just as one would expect—too small to identify if there is any," Gradison wrote in a Ways and Means report.[21] That month, Goldman Sachs & Co., the New York firm, issued a report that suggested the market would accept on-budget financing without an adverse reaction.

But the White House had other arguments and (as it noted somewhat indelicately) the power to veto a plan it did not like. What would set a worse precedent—Bush's plan or an on-budget alternative? The White House argued forcefully against the latter. If Congress could exempt this spending from the Gramm-Rudman targets, it might do so again. The distinction on economic grounds, as explained by Feldstein, between this exemption and other proposals for exemptions would be lost as lawmakers rushed to push their spending ideas through a more agreeable Congress. Gramm-Rudman would be destroyed, with its annual deficit targets existing in little more than name.

Critics, however, leveled the same argument against Bush's idea. Set up an off-budget corporation this time, with the costs kept out of the budget, and the temptation to do so again would be overpowering, they said. "The administration's insistence on this off-budget financing scheme," Rostenkowski told the House in August, "will be a precedent cited by many members of Congress as difficult budgetary issues present themselves in the future, such as financing the war on drugs, nuclear waste cleanup, and catastrophic health insurance." Similarly, Hollings said at the time, "You will have a drug czar proposing drug war bonds; you will have Admiral Truly proposing go-to-Mars bonds; you have all the other groups calling for bonds to clean up nuclear waste, provide child care, and so on, and then we really will have just given up the ghost." Which side was right? Perhaps both. As Panetta put it in a floor speech, "This is not a battle over which one sets a bad precedent. Frankly, both would set a bad precedent." Or, as Jake Garn of Utah, the Senate Banking Committee's senior Republican, said in a floor speech, "Both of them are turkeys."

The Democrats may not have bought Feldstein's rationale for exempting the thrift rescue from Gramm-Rudman. But the chance to save $4.5 billion—the lower interest costs associated with on-budget financing—was appealing. Democrats had been tagged as the party of wasteful spenders, as the bunch who mindlessly "threw money at problems" rather than considering less costly approaches. Here, courtesy of Bush, was a chance to level the same charge against Republicans. At Ways and Means, all Democrats lined up with Gradison and Raymond J. McGrath, a New York Republican, to send the on-budget approach to the House floor. House members overwhelmingly passed it in June.

Action moved to a House-Senate conference committee, with Brady still breathing fire over the on-budget plan, still threatening to recommend a presidential veto if Bush's off-budget plan was not accepted. A veto, the administration's allies noted, would send Congress back to the drawing board. Time would pass, with total costs rising by $10 to $20 million a day. The administration's message was ominous: On-budget advocates, hoping to save some money, would be costing Washington money each day through their stubbornness. But a *veto*? Skepticism abounded. After all, how would Bush justify such action? How would he counter the straightforward point that on-budget financing was probably less costly? And while Brady had insisted that he would recommend a veto, Bush had never said what *he* would do when faced with the decision. After some wrangling, the conference committee in late July adopted the House's on-budget approach, putting Bush in a "put up or shut up" position. He chose the former. "If the conference report is presented to me in its current form," Bush wrote in an August 3 letter to Michel, the House GOP leader, "I will veto the bill."

Senate Republicans, who controlled 45 of the chamber's 100 seats, could effectively enforce Bush's position. Because of Gramm-Rudman's technical rules, advocates of the on-budget plan would need 60 votes to even bring the conference committee's bill to the floor. Gramm, ever protective of the law bearing his name, had gathered 41 signatures on a letter vowing not to allow the Senate to consider a thrift rescue package if it included the House's on-budget plan. Bush's veto threat probably emboldened the signatories and others. When debate ended on August 3, Gramm carried the day, relying almost totally on Republican senators. The Democrats fell six votes short of bringing up the bill.

Back it went to the conference committee. Tensions ran high. Most members of each chamber wanted on-budget financing, but Bush did not. And not only could his large Republican minority in the Senate block just about any version of the bill, because of Gramm-Rudman, but he could also send it back to Capitol Hill himself by vetoing it. Would the administration compromise at all? Brady and Darman, representing Bush as the conference met on the evening of August 3, said they would. The White House did not want to exempt spending from next year's Gramm-Rudman target. But perhaps it would for 1989, as Riegle had long ago suggested. Brady offered $10 billion. Congress asked for $20 billion. The administration agreed. Congress, then, could put $20 billion on-budget in the current year, fiscal 1989, if it put $30 billion off-budget after that.

■   ■   ■   ■

What a deal! Everybody had a reason to be angry. If you wanted to avoid the off-budget scheme, you lost. If you wanted to avoid the on-budget scheme, you lost. If you wanted to avoid the precedent of loading spending into any year, after OMB issued its October 15 report, you lost. The administration pretended that it had protected Gramm-Rudman from attack, as did Gramm himself. In reality, the White House and Congress had exploited major loopholes in the law, just to avoid an *explicit* exemption from its annual deficit targets. The law was more important than the logic behind it. To ensure the vitality of Gramm-Rudman, which was set up to cut the deficit, the conference committee settled on a plan that would increase federal costs more than was necessary.

Nobody really cared for it. "That is not to the liking of any of us," Riegle told the Senate on August 4. "I certainly do not like the financing method or the compromise that we agreed to last night," said Garn. When the Senate passed the bill late that night, only a quarter of the senators were around; others, presumably, left early for vacation. Whether they would be able to stay away, though, was not immediately clear. If the House rejected the agreement, the conference would have to return to work again and send still another plan to the two chambers. Several influential House members were working toward that goal.

Earlier on August 4, Rostenkowski and Panetta joined two other powerful committee chairmen—Energy and Commerce's John D. Dingell and Government Operations' John

Conyers, Jr., both from Michigan—in circulating a letter in which they urged the House to reject the conference committee's plan. With $30 billion off-budget, they said, taxpayers would spend $3 billion more in interest costs than if all $50 billion were on-budget. When debate moved to the floor that night, some rank-and-file members complained that they had been "sold out" by the House conferees. But most House members probably just wanted to go home. Vacation awaited. And besides, if conferees went back to work, there was no telling what might happen next. For one to believe that the bill would improve, joked Barney Frank, a Massachusetts Democrat, one needed to "have faith in the U.S. Senate. So every member who believes that those members can make a good bill better by trusting in the resolve and courage and conviction of the U.S. Senate, those members should vote no and pray." The House voted yes, 201–175. Bush signed the bill on August 9.

Nobody could be sure what the whole thing would cost, but $300 billion over 33 years was not an unreasonably high estimate. If anything, it might have been too low. If interest rates were higher than the White House estimated for the next three years (when the $30 billion in off-budget bonds would be sold), borrowing costs could rise by at least several billion dollars. If deposits in savings and loan institutions did not increase as the administration thought they would, taxpayers would have to offset a shortfall in thrift insurance premiums. The administration's estimate that deposits would increase 7 percent a year would not have been unreasonable at another time. But, because of the bad publicity surrounding thrifts, depositors in late 1988 and early 1989 had actually been draining funds from the institutions in record numbers. Whether they would reverse course was an open question.

The legislation left sour tastes and a feeling on Capitol Hill that the White House had pushed the off-budget issue a bit too hard. Even Republicans complained. Aside from that issue, Wylie said, "The administration got at least 90 percent of what it wanted in this bill."[22] The political wounds would heal. But memories would linger. This battle added to a growing list of complaints from key lawmakers about Bush's fiscal gamesmanship. The warm White House-congressional relations, on which Darman was counting so heavily for a major deficit-cutting agreement in the fall, were turning quite chilly. Chances for the "Big Deal" began to look bleak. It is to this chill in relations that we now turn.

CHAPTER SIX

"SHOT AND WOUNDED AND BANDAGED"

Panetta was sitting in his office in early September, musing about the five months since he and the other negotiators had heard Bush speak so glowingly in the Rose Garden about their budget agreement. Back then, despite that deal's obvious shortcomings, the negotiators had hoped they could do something more significant about the deficit in Stage II, later in the year. But by late August, even Darman, who had been the group's most outwardly optimistic member, conceded that the chances of that happening were slipping away. When I asked Panetta about Darman's remarks, he smiled knowingly, as if thinking the OMB director had finally learned something that those on Capitol Hill had long known.

"It's funny," Panetta said,

> because I kept telling Darman about the concerns about, you know, that you can't separate these two worlds, that the world of the day-to-day battles, the day-to-day decisions, the fights over capital gains, or the fight over this or the fight over that issue ... that ultimately, you can't just isolate that and pretend that, "oh, well, you know, that's kind of the day-to-day world and now, let's go into a room and develop this bolder package [to cut the deficit]." Those two come together. I mean, they are in fact one. And I kept saying to him, "With all these other

169

battles on reconciliation, and getting our appropriations bills through, getting the enforcement done, fighting over whatever revenue package is part of the reconciliation bill." Those are going to create feelings, they're going to create emotions. This is a human process.

As Darman. kept up his optimistic talk into the summer, Panetta said he asked him, "When do you assume that somehow we're going to be able to suddenly step aside into some kind of 'Cloud 9' and ram up this other package and then bring it back and say, 'Hey, guys, we've come back'? Everybody's bloody on the battlefield. And guys have been shot and wounded and bandaged—suddenly say to them, 'Hey, we've got a whole new war for you.'"

Perhaps Darman's approach was naive to begin with, although few had ever suggested that this brilliant, shrewd public servant was naive about politics. But between April and Labor Day, the "spirit of cooperation" that Darman had insisted was the key to more deficit cutting in 1989 grew largely irrelevant, as the pitched battles over this or that issue separated the parties and soured relations among important leaders. To be sure, the negotiators had wanted to press forward, and they shared a sense of how and when to come together on a big deficit-cutting deal. They all knew what such a deal would entail—a sizable tax increase, limits on the growth of entitlements, and cuts in defense and day-to-day domestic programs. But they could not proceed. For all their knowledge of the budget and their power in the White House and Congress, these were not independent operators. They were, instead, members of competing teams. And despite the long-term incentives on all sides to solve the deficit problem, short-term political concerns precluded the bipartisanship that such an effort would have required.

By Labor Day, Bush had long ago finished whatever honeymoon the Democrat-controlled Congress would give to him as a new president, and they proceeded to fight over not only the savings and loan legislation, but also capital gains tax rates and various spending initiatives. On Capitol Hill, meanwhile, Democrats and Republicans suffered through a bitter

year of struggle, propelled partly by historical antagonisms
and partly by a new concern for ethics. Indeed, the rank and
file of both parties seemed less comfortable with any "spirit of
cooperation" with their adversaries. Many Democrats urged
the party to more openly return to its philosophical roots
and draw a clearer distinction between it and the Republican
party. So, too, did many Republicans hope to sharpen their
differences with Democrats.

■　　　　■　　　　■　　　　■

That Darman's hopes for the "Big Deal" were not realized probably did not surprise many observers in Washington. For most of 1989, policy makers had wondered how he
planned to fulfill this rather immodest goal. "What's Darman
up to now?" a newsletter asked in a front-page headline in
mid-June.[1] Others had been asking the same question for
months. If Darman was the strategist everyone said he was,
surely he must have a plan. What was the plan? How did he
hope to steer the political process from the small fiscal 1990
agreement to a bigger one for fiscal 1991 and beyond? Darman himself would not answer many questions about it, even
in private meetings. Those who asked went away frustrated.

On April 18, four days after the Rose Garden ceremony,
Darman met privately with Republican members of the House
Budget Committee. Gradison, who served as the House GOP
leadership's representative on the committee, asked the first
question of Darman: "What's the next step?" The OMB director replied vigorously. "You want me to tell you I've got a plan?
I don't. We're taking this one step at a time. We hope to get to
the next step." Senate Budget Committee Republicans were
no more successful in ferreting out Darman's "plan." A week
earlier, Bond, the Missouri Republican, had asked Darman a
similar question over the phone. A colleague later asked if
Bond had gotten an answer. He had not.

"One step at a time," as Darman put it. Maybe he did
not have a plan after all. Maybe he had many: Plan A for
one situation, Plan B for another, and so on. Meeting with
reporters in late August, Darman likened his plight to that

of a football kickoff returner at the 8 yard line—focused on the other team's end zone, determined to use his blockers as best he can, but unable to predict where he will run until the play unfolds.

> You say, "What are you going to do if, when you get to the 30, there are seven guys standing on the right hand side of the field?" Well, chances are good your answer would be, "I'd go left." But you don't know what you will have done between the 8 and the 30. And you don't know whether they're really going to be out there or not. To some extent, you know you're trying to get to that end. And you know there's only 11 players, or supposed to be 11, on their side. And there's 10 others on yours. And you know a bunch of rules. And some things are predictable. If a guy goes down, how long it is before he gets back up. And how fast the average person can run. And what happens if you go in that angle versus that. You can figure all of these things. But ... there isn't a broken field runner, a successful one, alive who can tell you reliably exactly what path he's going to follow from the 8 to, if all goes well, the other end zone.

After a chuckle, he drew another telling analogy:

> When I was a kid, my father told me about a guy ... maybe some of you know him. I think he's in the Hall of Fame. A famous football player named Charlie Trippi. Anybody know of Charlie Trippi? I don't either. Well, we'll have to look him up. But at any rate, Charlie Trippi was supposedly a great punt returner. And my father said that you never, ever knew exactly what pattern he was going to run in, except for one absolute rule he always had—that the first two steps should be forward. Well, it's a rule worth thinking about. I start with a prejudice in favor of steps that are forward, if not even an absolute commitment.

Whether or not Darman had mapped out a detailed strategy for deficit cutting and was hiding it from everyone was unclear. But surely he and the key players on Capitol Hill were not merely resorting to the instinctive manner of the broken field runner. Privately, Darman and the congressional negotiators met formally and informally, together and one-on-one, to form a strategy to get to Stage II and craft the Big Deal.

The fiscal arithmetic was compelling enough. CBO, as we have said, estimated that spring that even in the very far-fetched event that Congress fully implemented April's agreement, the fiscal 1991 deficit would be $130 billion. (In the summer, it raised that figure to nearly $140 billion.) Even OMB, assuming a healthier economy in 1991 than CBO did, thought the deficit would hit $90 billion. Under Gramm-Rudman, Washington could avoid across-the-board spending cuts only if it reduced that year's projected deficit to $74 billion. So, in CBO's view, the White House and Congress would need to find at least $56 billion in tax hikes, spending cuts, or both. The two branches had fought bitterly over much smaller deficit-cutting tasks all through the 1980s.

Each side had political incentives as well. Bush had to present his 1991 budget in January 1990. Absent a deal with Congress, Bush would have to show how he alone would recommend reaching the Gramm-Rudman target. (In fact, Gramm-Rudman forced the president to show how to reduce the deficit to $64 billion.) If Bush planned, as he had said, not to tolerate future defense levels that did not keep pace with inflation, he would have two ugly choices: to cut deeply into domestic spending programs, thus clashing with his "kinder, gentler" outlook, or to raise taxes. However, if he made the Big Deal with Congress in late 1989, he could incorporate its major decisions on tax and spending levels into his 1991 budget. That way, Democrats would share blame for whatever politically tough steps he outlined.

Democratic incentives may have been even larger. The president only *proposes* a budget. Congress has to *implement* one with tax and spending bills. Although Democrats might enjoy bashing Bush for the "meanness" or "cruelty" of whatever spending cuts he proposed, they would have to reply. As Darman, predicting Democratic interest in the Big Deal, told me in July, "the ball will be in their court." Sasser, with whom I also spoke in July, agreed: "We could have a lot of fun for about three months beating up on [Bush's budget]. But then, we've got to sit down and put together a budget." If the Democrats met Gramm-Rudman's target by cutting defense, Bush could accuse them of "weakness." If they cut domestic programs, they would anger their own constituencies in education, housing, and so on. If they called for a tax hike, Bush and the congressional Republicans would no doubt lambaste them for practicing the old tax-and-spend liberalism. But whether rank-and-file Democrats recognized the political dynamics back in mid-1989 was not clear. As Sasser put it, "Some of these fellas have not really thought it through. And they have forgotten those all-night sessions when we wrestled over the budget over here for a number of years. And they've forgotten how all legislation was delayed, as we fought over miniscule budget matters. And," he noted, "they can be reminded of that."

Whatever the incentives, though, the Republican president and the Democratic-controlled Congress would not ante up the needed tax hikes and spending cuts in late 1989 unless they felt *forced* into it. Elected officials tend to focus on their immediate futures—today's battle, tomorrow's headlines. If they could set aside the deficit problem for another day, they were inclined to do so. After all, the Big Deal entailed serious deficit cutting, not more of April's gimmickry. The prospect of bitter White House-congressional battles in 1990 to meet Gramm-Rudman's next target was not, by itself, enough to spur the Big Deal in late 1989. With the public sure to oppose whatever they tried, policy makers needed a rationale by which to explain their actions. They had to portray themselves as impelled by crisis, even by a crisis of their own making.

■   ■   ■   ■

As for the mechanics of manufacturing a crisis, two options beckoned. The first was, in effect, to nullify the April agreement for fiscal 1990. In July, OMB had to revise its deficit projection for 1990 and determine whether, based on updated economic assumptions and enacted legislation, Washington was likely to cut the deficit to below $110 billion and thus avoid across-the-board cuts. If OMB declared that legislative action arising from April's deal was not adequate to do that, Washington presumably would have to take further deficit-cutting steps. At that time, the nation's leaders could decide to confront not only the immediate problem for 1990 but also the larger one for 1991 and beyond. Darman, as we have said, pledged early in the year that there would be "no surprises"—that, if implemented, he would ensure that April's agreement was sufficient. But perhaps he and key lawmakers would now decide that a "surprise" was in their interests—if they sprang it on everyone else. OMB would simply have to dampen its economic outlook a little bit. Although OMB was supposed to survey the economy objectively, most of Washington's policy-making community thought the agency manipulated its projections for political reasons anyway.

The negotiators rejected this option. For one thing, OMB had scant data at its disposal to explain why it dampened its outlook; though not performing as robustly as OMB projected in February, the economy was humming along. For a second thing, Darman had essentially conceded that the Big Deal would include a tax hike, if just to entice Democrats on board. But, he told the negotiators, Bush certainly could not agree to one in his first budget. Fiscal 1990 had to be kept apart from later years, not merged in such a way that Bush would end up breaking his no-tax pledge for that year. For a third thing, the congressional budget leaders had told their rank-and-file colleagues that April's deal was sufficient to meet Gramm-Rudman's 1990 target. Numerous congressional committees knew how much they had to cut from spending programs or raise in revenues. Those that followed through would feel they had done their part. Budget leaders did not want to ask for more until they had fashioned a separate deal for 1991. Otherwise, the committees might balk.

So Darman and the congressional players focused on Washington's need to raise the nation's debt ceiling. Debt limit bills are strange pieces of legislation. Because Washington sets limits on the amount of outstanding federal debt, it must vote to raise the limit on occasion as the debt grows. In doing so, the nation's leaders are merely agreeing to pay the bills they have previously rung up through tax and spending measures. It's akin to a family formally deciding to make the mortgage payments on its house. The nation, of course, must pay. If it didn't pay interest on Treasury securities that came due, the markets would tumble into panic. No longer would investors view U.S. debt as unimpeachably safe.

Unfortunately, few Americans understand debt limit bills, if letters that reach congressional offices are any indication. Most apparently think that by voting to raise the debt limit, elected officials are voting for more deficit spending in the future. Because of such confusion, votes in favor of debt limit bills are considered politically dangerous. Opponents chastise incumbents for them, saying they demonstrate a propensity for fiscal recklessness. "If you do the responsible thing and pay the bill that previous actions of the Congress totaled up, you're going to take the inevitable flak," Rep. Les AuCoin, an Oregon Democrat, told me in July. "That is the oldest political game in town. That shows up in campaign literature all the time."

Because they must be passed, debt limit bills are considered the "last train out of the station"; that is, lawmakers try to affix their pet proposals to them. In particular, the debt bills tend to attract proposals to change the budget process. Both versions of Gramm-Rudman were attached to such bills. By voting for Gramm-Rudman, lawmakers could say that although they had agreed to raise the debt limit, they also supported legislation that would force Washington to soon balance its budget. In mid-1989, the Treasury Department asked Congress to raise the debt limit to more than $3 trillion—more than three times the level of debt as Reagan took office in 1981. To vote for such a limit, many lawmakers thought they would need to link the debt limit bill with other proposals, such as a further change in the budget process, to make it politically palatable. Another option was to attach a Big Deal that would eliminate the deficit altogether.

This is what Darman, Panetta, Sasser, and the other key players were thinking. Here was the plan: Before beginning its month-long recess in early August, Congress would pass a short-term increase in the debt limit to cover the nation's borrowing needs until sometime in the fall. Rank-and-file members would not offer any pet proposals, so no debates on controversial ideas would delay the recess. In exchange, congressional leaders would assure lawmakers of the chance to offer their proposals when, in the fall, Congress considered a long-term debt limit increase. Meanwhile, with fiscal 1990 matters wrapped up by early fall, Darman and an expanded group of congressional negotiators would devise the Big Deal, which, in turn, would be affixed to the debt limit bill. The rank and file, however reluctantly, would adopt the tax hikes and spending cuts to put the deficit problem behind them for good.

To make the Big Deal work, Rostenkowski, Bentsen, Archer, and Packwood would have to participate in crafting it. The House Ways and Means and Senate Finance Committees had jurisdiction over too much of the fiscal landscape for them to be excluded. Chairmen and senior Republicans on the House and Senate Appropriations Committees held sway over enough other spending to be included. Foley, who became the House speaker in early June when Wright resigned, expressed interest in staying in the negotiating group. Gephardt, who succeeded Foley as majority leader, might want to join. Mitchell might, too. If Foley, Gephardt, and Mitchell partook, GOP leaders Michel and Dole would insist on participating.

Establishing a group of appropriate size was a ticklish proposition. On the one hand, you needed all of the key players on Capitol Hill; a deal was only worth making if Congress would implement it. If powerful committee chairmen and senior Republicans were left out of the room while key decisions were made, they would not embrace the agreement without reservation. The budget chairmen and senior Republicans, for instance, could agree to raise $10 billion by boosting the federal tax on gasoline, but it was Rostenkowski and Bentsen who knew whether or not they could muster the votes in Ways and Means and Finance for such a move. The same was true for cuts in major domestic discretionary programs, over which the appropriators ruled. On the other hand, a negotiating group that was too big would quickly become unwieldy. Egos would clash. Scheduling conflicts would force delays, as participants left for hours and then needed a recap of discussions while they were gone. Talks would drag on and decisions would prove elusive. The 1987 summit—which included the same type of cast, with a few exceptions—suffered from such problems. Even its modest deficit-cutting agreement was produced only after an agonizing four weeks.

Whether such a group would assemble at all was problematic. The administration sent a few encouraging signs of interest. At a White House meeting May 16 with congressional leaders, Bush urged Darman and Brady to soon begin discussions with Congress's key players to iron out a 1991 plan. On the question of tax hikes, which Democrats said was the key to success, Bush showed a new openness. Rather than rule them out for 1991, as he had for 1990, he and his top aides were much cagier. Sure, they said, Bush did not *want* to raise taxes. But whether or not he would agree to, under certain circumstances, was another question. At that meeting, Bush did not respond when Democrats brought up the issue. Later, White House spokesman Marlin Fitzwater said of Bush, "The commitment is that he'll do everything possible not to raise taxes in any year ... but we take the budget one year at a time." Nor would Brady or Darman publicly rule out a tax increase—when Brady testified in July to the Joint Economic Committee, when Darman went before the House Budget Committee that month, or when Darman met with reporters in late August.

Privately, Darman seemed to open the tax-hike door a bit wider. At his and Panetta's suggestion, the group that negotiated April's agreement—minus Brady and Domenici—met on May 31 for breakfast in Foley's office. They spoke in general terms about the deficit numbers facing them for 1991 and about how they could craft the Big Deal. With discussion centering on packages of perhaps $40 or $50 billion in savings each year, Democrats suggested that half would come from spending cuts, the other half from tax hikes. Rather than opposing that notion, Darman seemed to accept it. He probed for ways to put a deal together, rather than reconfiguring its components. Democrats were not surprised. Despite his public duel over taxes with Sasser in March, he had indicated to the Democrats that, to get the Big Deal, he would ask Bush to accept a tax hike.

Two months later, Darman seemed to lay the public relations groundwork for tax increases and spending cuts. In a July 20 speech at the National Press Club, he chastised Americans for "now-now-ism," his label for "cultural shortsightedness, our obsession with the here and now, our reluctance adequately to address the future," of which, he said, the deficit was a symptom. "In our public policy—and, to some degree, in our private behavior—we consume today as if there were no tomorrow," Darman said. "We attend too little to the issues of investment necessary to make tomorrow brighter. Like the spoiled fifties child in the recently revived commercial, we seem on the verge of a collective now-now scream: 'I want my Maypo; I want it *nowwwwww!*' " Surely, a Big Deal would help turn America's fiscal policy away from such evils.

Although the negotiators held no more formal get-togethers as a group before Congress recessed in August, Darman visited and phoned the key players from time to time, hoping to keep the lines of communication open. Asked about his informal conversations with Darman, Sasser said in July, "It's kind of like you've seen two boys in the school yard that everybody's egging on to have a fight. One's afraid to fight and the other one's glad of it. That's kind of the way we are with the administration. We sort of circle each other, everybody trying to figure out how we're going to deal with this problem without getting hurt too badly."

The Democrats also were dueling among themselves, whether or not they knew it. Had talks on the Big Deal ensued, Sasser and Panetta would have begun with different views about them. While the two chairmen talked about putting everything "on the table," they differed over what that meant. Panetta's list of items was longer than Sasser's in at least one important respect. Panetta thought that annual cost-of-living adjustments (COLAs) for Social Security should be a target for cuts. When I asked Sasser about Social Security in July, he forcefully ruled out such cuts. The only thing he would consider, he said, was raising the current tax on Social Security benefits for the more well-to-do:

> **Question:** Are there spending cuts that would be as politically difficult for the Democrats to accept as a tax increase would be for Bush?
>
> **Sasser:** Oh, sure. Social Security.
>
> **Question:** It's that rough?
>
> **Sasser:** Oh, yeah. It's rougher.
>
> **Question:** It's rougher?
>
> **Sasser:** Yeah.
>
> **Question:** Can you put it on the table?
>
> **Sasser:** We're not going to put Social Security on the table.
>
> **Question:** No matter what?
>
> **Sasser:** No matter what.
>
> **Question:** Even if taxes are on the table?
>
> **Sasser:** Look, we think it's unfair to put Social Security on the table. I mean, that goes right to the very heart of what Democratic philosophy is. We're not going to put Social Security on the table. Period. Exclamation point. And just let me say, they [the administration] don't want to put it on the table either.

On the Republican side, meanwhile, Domenici had doubts about the very idea of a Big Deal. You could hardly blame him. As Senate Budget Committee chairman from 1981 to 1986, he was in the thick of some of the ugliest, most partisan battles of the Reagan years. A deficit hawk during that period, he was repeatedly rebuffed in efforts to construct earlier versions of the deal. He did not want another fruitless endeavor. What he understood very well was that fiscal affairs could not be divorced from the day's larger politics. In a June 9 meeting with Bush, which Domenici requested, he urged the president to move cautiously on the Big Deal for that very reason. Just as Bush had to actively support any Big Deal that was drafted, Bush needed assurances that Democratic leaders would. If Bush planned to accept tax hikes, Democrats had to accept sizable limits on entitlements. Both sides also had to ensure that the deal was enacted: Bush had to guarantee GOP votes on Capitol Hill; Foley, in particular, had to do the same with Democratic votes. By choosing to do so, Domenici cautioned, Bush and Foley would be risking their political futures. Domenici suggested that Bush meet with Foley to feel him out. Bush offered no hints about his thinking, telling Domenici that he understood the message and thanking him for it. (Nor did Bush offer more when Frenzel told him, in a private meeting over the summer, that a Big Deal would have to include tax hikes.)

Domenici was especially keyed in to political matters. As he had told Darman in a private meeting a week earlier, with his reelection coming up in 1990, he planned to spend the second half of 1989 concentrating on homestate business. At the time, Domenici was concerned about a potentially tough race against Rep. Bill Richardson, a New Mexico Democrat; Richardson later decided not to challenge the senator. Other congressional negotiators may have been less concerned with their own reelections, but they, too, had political matters to attend to. The more those matters impinged on them, the less freedom the negotiators would have to orchestrate the Big Deal. As the months passed, these concerns rose in importance, clouding hopes for a deal. By August, when lawmakers trudged home for vacation, key players talked not about *when* they would restart their talks, but *if* they would.

■　　　　■　　　　■　　　　■

Early troubles cropped up at the budget committees. Members of both panels were frustrated by the closed-door negotiations that led to April's agreement, and Democrats in particular were more than a little angry at their chairmen. Even Rep. Charles Schumer of New York, who shared a Washington townhouse with Panetta and two other House Democrats, quipped sarcastically at a House-Senate conference in May on the fiscal 1990 budget resolution, "We have been thanking the chairmen of both [budget] committees and the ranking minorities. On behalf of the rest of the Budget Committee members who did very little, we want to thank the four of you for doing the whole budget." Like Schumer, the other Democrats had joined the budget committees to help draft budget resolutions. Although Panetta and Sasser kept them abreast of events while the talks were occurring, the rank-and-file Democrats had little influence over decisions. When the deal was signed for 1990, these Democrats made it clear that, for 1991 and beyond, they wanted to play larger roles.

In a sense, Panetta and Sasser were happy to oblige. Because they did not help draft it, other lawmakers harshly criticized the April deal and the budget resolution that flowed from it. "This agreement is pure sham and it's the worst charade," Hollings said in April. Asked why he opposed the deal, Rep. Lee H. Hamilton, an Indiana Democrat and chairman of the Joint Economic Committee, told NBC's "Meet the Press" in May, "Look, we've got to stop playing these games, which we are doing with the budget today." Nor had the budget players gotten much support from congressional leaders, who praised the pact in only the most guarded terms. Yes, they complimented their underlings for crafting a deal. But details were another matter. "Not an heroic agreement"—that's the way Wright described it. Mitchell added, "Very hard choices lie ahead. Much sterner measures will be required in the future."

The press was equally unkind, whether in one-on-one interviews with the negotiators or in pointed writings. Darman, in an April 16 interview on ABC's "This Week with David Brinkley," said of the agreement, "What we've done here is, basically, with the first batter up in the first inning, hit a double. Some people are saying, you should have hit a grand slam home run. You can't hit a grand slam home run until you at least have a few people on." A moment later, George F. Will answered, "A more precise analogy might be that you're trying to steal first base." The print media was equally critical. "Let's not beat around the Bush," declared the *Washing-*

ton Post's economics columnist, Hobart Rowen. "The Administration's deal on the budget with Democratic congressional leaders is a fraud."[2] The editorial page of Rowen's newspaper wrote, "In neither party nor branch is there the economic leadership the country needs."[3] Under the headline, "Phantom of the Rose Garden," the *New York Times* remarked that "the vision of the Rose Garden was little more than a phantom. The budget dilemma remains."[4]

Major regional papers slammed the deal as well. "For some strange reason, it took negotiators for Congress and the White House more than a month to script the vague, $1.2 trillion budget plan that they unveiled Friday," the *Philadelphia Inquirer* editorialized. "Any good PR firm or fiction writer could have produced it overnight."[5] The *Chicago Tribune* wrote of Bush, "He called it a 'first manageable step,' but it was more like a tiptoe, hurting no one and leaving no visible footprint."[6] The weekly news magazines left little doubt what they thought. *Time*, in a hard-hitting account, said, " 'Rose Garden Rubbish.' Up to now that richly evocative phrase has been used exclusively to describe what political lexicographer William Safire calls the 'supposedly ad-lib remarks made by the President on minor occasions.' But that was before George Bush and a phalanx of congressional leaders strolled into the Rose Garden last Friday morning to announce that they had hammered out the 1990 budget concordat."[7] To Mitchell's comment that "this is no small accomplishment," *Newsweek* replied in its account, "It was no major accomplishment either."[8]

Reading all this, Panetta felt that he was being unfairly criticized. After all, he and Sasser were just two of the many Democrats who had urged Bush and his top aides to help fashion a Big Deal in his first few months. That way, Bush could capitalize on the broad public support that a new president's honeymoon almost ensures, and he could free his presidency of the deficit problem. But no, Bush decided, he could not break his no-tax pledge that soon. Now, with Bush having guaranteed that an early agreement would be modest at best,

Panetta and the others were criticized for what they had accomplished. When I asked him about that in late May, Panetta answered strongly:

> The problem is, from the academic's perspective, taxes should be raised. But the reality here is that you couldn't find a vote for a tax, wherever you looked, outside of maybe a handful of people that would vote for taxes. It was clear that that was not going to happen. You always have to ask the academic, "Now what, wiseguy? You haven't got the votes to pass taxes. You haven't got a president who's going to support taxes. What would you like us to do now?"

"Now what, wiseguy?" Panetta wanted to ask his committee the same question. If his members thought they could do better on the deficit problem, he would give them a chance. He and Frenzel organized a series of weekly, two-hour meetings in order for the committee's Democrats and Republicans to discuss—together—various options for devising the Big Deal. The staff, they said, would brief members for an hour on a general topic—entitlements, defense, and so on—and members then would meet privately for an hour to form a consensus on what to recommend in that area. Sasser organized a series of meetings with his Democratic members, though they were designed to be less structured than those of the House committee. Sasser planned to brief members on the general fiscal outlook or on more specific topics and to ask members for their thoughts. Domenici, feeling the heat of his GOP members for their exclusion from the fiscal 1990 deliberations, organized a meeting with Darman in mid-July so they could offer input on how the White House and congressional players should proceed on the 1991 problem.

The meetings, however, did not live up to expectations. On the House side, turnout for the seven sessions was low, with 6 to 10 of the 33 rank-and-file members joining Panetta and Frenzel each week. As a result, the chairman and senior Republican scrapped plans for the one-hour sessions among lawmakers. (They held just one—on retirement programs.) With few members around, the committee could hardly form a consensus on ticklish issues. Panetta later said the poor attendance did not surprise him. Some members were busy, while others did not want to risk association with the tough choices being discussed. Nevertheless, he said, the sessions would give him leverage with his members as he approached talks on the Big Deal. What he would tell them, Panetta said, was, "We went through this process. Now's the time to come together. Don't give me the bullshit that you haven't had the opportunity to be briefed on this stuff." On the Senate side, attendance was better in the Democratic meetings. But in these, too, members made little progress in forming a consensus. As Sasser put it in July, "If you listen to all the divergent voices, it can be confusing." As for Domenici's session between his members and Darman, that was dominated by talk about problems in implementing the 1990 deal, not what to do for 1991.

For the negotiators, cutting the Big Deal was one thing. Selling it to Congress might be another. Sure, in theory, most members wanted the deficit to go away. But theory was never the problem. Rather, it was the tax hikes and spending cuts needed to translate theory into reality. Every lawmaker, with hometown interests and philosophical predispositions, had his or her own ideas. For the Big Deal to work, each had to accept some bitter medicine. The farm state senator had to understand that farm programs would be cut, and the urban lawmaker had to accept the same for things like mass transit aid. The White House and Congress had to understand that taxes would rise for business and individuals. Would lawmakers go along? As early as May, Panetta expressed doubt. "I'm always skeptical about that, because I've heard it for so long," he told me. "From a political point of view, the easiest thing for a member is to castigate the budget resolution or whatever deal is on the table, and say that much more could be done, vote no on the deal and then not have to vote on a tougher package. It's when you confront members with a vote on a tougher package that will really determine whether members are serious about the bolder step. And as I said, all of us are waiting to see what is going to happen."

By continuing its steady growth, the economy provided little impetus for action. For awhile, trends had suggested otherwise. In spring and early summer, figures pointed toward a recession in the near future. The index of leading indicators, which attempts to gauge the economic outlook, fell in March by the largest amount since the previous summer. May's index, in turn, suffered its biggest drop since November 1987. The economy itself grew slowly in the first quarter of 1989, if one discounted for the farm sector's one-time rebound from the 1988 drought. Unemployment, meanwhile, ticked up to 5.3 percent, from 5.2 percent, in June. Consumer spending slowed in March and fell in May. Construction spending fell in June to its lowest level in eight months. Housing starts plummeted for the fourth straight month in May, while sales of new homes suffered a second consecutive decline in March. Factory orders hit their lowest level in eight months in July, the same month that orders for machine tools and durable goods also declined.

In the spring, half of the 50 economists surveyed by *Blue Chip Economic Forecasters* predicted that a recession would occur in late 1989 or early 1990. In July, 38 economists surveyed by the *Wall Street Journal* were just a bit more optimistic, predicting no recession for at least a year but only sluggish growth. With inflation hovering around 5 percent, more commentators began to warn of "stagflation"—that crippling combination of slow growth and inflation that plagued the 1970s. By summer, the White House was worried enough to publicly criticize the Fed for not loosening its grip on monetary policy. "If we do have a recession," Darman told a questioner August 14 on NBC's "Meet the Press," "I think it will be because [the Fed] erred on the side of caution." Bush, two days later, described himself as "very comfortable" with Darman's remarks. Greenspan was not oblivious to the economic trends. In his semiannual review of monetary policy, he told a House Banking Committee subcommittee in July that "the balance of risks" had shifted away from inflation and toward recession."

As Labor Day approached, however, Greenspan began to look like a miracle worker. The Fed, having sent interest rates up earlier in the year, apparently slowed the economy enough to keep inflation in check. By June, as fears of recession spread, the Fed loosened monetary policy to cut interest rates, jump-starting the economy while inflation remained moderate. Early that month, it let the federal funds rate fall for the first time in 15 months. Banks, anticipating the Fed's action, had begun to drop the prime rate a few days earlier; it fell from 11.5 percent to 11 percent in early June, and to 10.5 percent at different banks throughout July. Over the same period, the Veterans Affairs Department cut its rate on home loans from 10.5 percent to 10 percent and then to 9.5 percent. By August, mortgage rates had fallen to their lowest levels in two years, and many owners of old mortgages refinanced them.

Greenspan's medicine apparently worked. Sales of new homes, after rising in April, May, and June, surged 14.4 percent in July, their biggest increase in nearly three years; construction of new homes rose that month as well. Consumer spending rose in July, and the index of leading indicators edged up a bit. Unemployment dipped by 0.1 points that month and again in August to settle at 5.1 percent. Commentators increasingly predicted the "soft landing" of moderate growth and moderate inflation—as opposed to the "hard landing" of recession or surging inflation—for which everyone hoped. A few big-name experts even suggested there might be no landing. David D. Hale, chief economist for Kemper Financial Services in Chicago, coined the phrase "soft takeoff." Stephen S. Roach, senior economist at Morgan Stanley & Co. Inc., in New York, said, "The wheels haven't hit the runway."[9]

Good economic news was bad political news for the deficit hawks. Nevertheless, Darman remained optimistic. He cautioned me in July:

> I don't think we should be trying to solve this problem based on the state of the economy. And I don't think we should be looking towards solving it by using an economic crisis as the forcing mechanism. I'm naive enough, or hopeful enough, depending on your perspective, to wish, to some degree to think, that we can address this problem on the merits because it requires our constructive attention, not because the economy is

at the moment either strong or not so strong or because a financial market is doing one thing or another on a given day.

When I pressed on, he said:

People in the political system can decide to do the right thing from time to time independently of crises. The political system, we tend to be excessively cynical about it. You know, most of our foreign policy, for which the Congress takes all kinds of action, is oriented toward the prevention of future crises or the expansion of some favorable state of affairs, not necessarily the response to some present crisis. I mean, take the whole investment in strategic arms. That isn't in response to a crisis. That's prudent investment to prevent an adverse outcome. So the system's not incapable of taking rational action in the absence of crisis. It's not incapable. I grant you that it needs prodding from one source or another from time to time. No doubt about that. Absolutely no doubt about that. But I don't think we should jump from that observation, which is correct, to the conclusion that would be utterly cynical, that only in an extreme crisis can the American democratic system respond.

Maybe so. But a healthy economy served as one more excuse for the White House and Congress to avoid the pain of deficit cutting. Sasser expressed concerns about the former, and Panetta worried about the latter.

Sasser told me in July, "There may be a thought on the part of the administration, with the economy continuing to hold up and with revenues outrunning their expectations, and with interest rates coming down, that it's going to be easier to meet the targets, and perhaps we're not as important to the equation as we were a few weeks ago—that is, the Congress." In September, Panetta said of Congress, "By virtue of the economy continuing to look like it's perking along ... combined with the ability to slip by on [fiscal] 1990, I think lessen the pressure to face up to the tough choices. I'm not getting the pressure of the deficit playing very much of a role now."

Signs of apathy abounded throughout Congress. Rep. Timothy J. Penny, a young House Democrat from Minnesota, had been active in past efforts to force lawmakers to cut the deficit more than most were inclined to do. In July, he organized a meeting in his office with a handful of like-minded House members, including Texas Democrat Charles W. Stenholm, to discuss how to force such deficit cutting later in the year when Congress debated the long-term debt limit bill. They decided not to try. The economy's continued health had lessened the interest of others, according to Stenholm. "You keep talking about something bad going to happen [to the economy], and it never does," he explained a week later.

Besides, the rank and file were balking at implementing even April's modest agreement. Two competing theories about this problem were popular in Washington. One held that because April's deal was so modest, lawmakers felt no incentive to implement it. Even modest spending cuts would ·anger powerful interest groups in town. And because the deal was so small, it would make little progress toward reducing the deficit. Only with the Big Deal would lawmakers view the endeavor as worthwhile. Then they would accept the needed spending cuts and tax hikes because, by doing so, they would solve the deficit problem. The second theory took a decidedly more pessimistic view. According to this line, if lawmakers would not implement April's deal, they would balk even more if asked to enact a bigger one. Calls for the Big Deal served as a convenient smokescreen. Lawmakers did not want *any* spending cuts or tax hikes.

In any case, some committees were reluctant to do much until they saw how the Ways and Means and Finance panels were progressing. Of the nearly $14 billion in reconciliation savings (revenue increases or entitlement cuts), $8 billion came under the jurisdiction of those panels: $5.3 billion in taxes, $2.3 billion in Medicare cuts, and at least $0.4 billion by any method that the committees chose. If those committees did not do their work, others would not feel inclined to do so. All eyes turned to the panels and their chairmen. Meanwhile, because the Constitution requires that tax bills originate in the House, Bentsen chose to let Rostenkowski push a bill through his committee before he did so at Finance. As Bentsen waited, other Senate committees moved slowly. House committees moved slowly as well, waiting for Ways and Means. Attention focused on the Democratic chairman from Illinois.

But Rostenkowski was forced to proceed more slowly than he had wanted. Committees were ordered to send their handiwork to the Budget Committees by July 15. While Ways and Means finished its Medicare changes by then, the deadline passed with the panel mired in controversy over its tax portion. Fierce battles broke out between the White House and Democratic leaders, as well as among Democrats, over whether to cut the tax rate on capital gains. Meanwhile, an outcry from senior citizens forced Ways and Means to consider changing the catastrophic health insurance program, for which many older Americans had begun to pay taxes. Progress was further delayed when the attention of key Ways and Means members shifted to the thrift rescue bill. When Congress left for vacation in August, the committee still had not finished the tax bill. The longer that took in September, the longer Congress would have to wait before taking up its reconciliation bill. As April's negotiators recognized, time was eating away at chances for the Big Deal.

"What has developed in the way that reduces the chances of satisfactorily negotiating something in this calendar year is the way in which this has stretched out in time," Darman told reporters in late August. As he anticipated Congress's return on September 6, the OMB director recognized the huge amount of work left to implement the April deal. Ways and Means had to finish; the House had to pass the reconciliation bill; the Finance Committee had to draft its tax bill and Medicare cuts; the Senate had to pass its own reconciliation bill; a House-Senate conference had to iron out a compromise between the two reconciliation bills for final approval by Congress. On another front, while the House had passed all 13 of its appropriations bills in a mad dash before the recess, the Senate passed just four of its own. The Senate had to finish, so 13 conferences could draft final measures. All that work likely would occupy Washington's time at least well into October.

Until Congress finished, the key players would be too busy to think about the Big Deal. Foley, Mitchell, Michel, and Dole would be managing all of this activity, working out deals among the rank and file on such items as who would offer what amendment to what bill. Panetta, Sasser, Frenzel, and Domenici would be monitoring the reconciliation and appropriations bills and perhaps fighting provisions that violated April's deal or Congress's budget rules. Rostenkowski, Bentsen, Archer, and Packwood would be busy with their own conferences, as would both Appropriations Committees' chairmen and top Republicans. Once all that was done—or concurrently, if it dragged on—attention would turn to the debt limit bill, where the rank and file promised a host of amendments to change the budget process. Once more, party leaders and the key budget players would be in the thick of hot battles. More and more lawmakers, who once hoped to finish their year in Washington by Thanksgiving, talked about staying around until just before Christmas.

Time was not the only enemy. None of these bills held the promise of easy resolution. As opposing sides dug in and battles heated up, tempers would fray. Personal relations would sour. When asked about prospects for the Big Deal, Darman spoke to that very point in late August when he said:

> There's nothing physical or logistical or analytical that would be a constraint that would prevent getting the job done. It's going to depend on mood, attitude, spirit, and for those who might wish not to do this, the fact that there is much less time gives them a better excuse to say, "No, well, let's just wait, there's not enough time." They wouldn't have had that excuse had we been able, as I'd originally hoped, to get this thing [fiscal 1990 legislation] wrapped up when backing up against the August recess.

Darman probably was not surprised. At the May 31 breakfast in his office, Foley warned that political "exhaustion" in implementing the April deal might preclude more deficit cutting in 1989. After April, Panetta had warned Darman more than once about the same thing.

■   ■   ■   ■

Pitched battles were already under way, and not just on the fiscal front. Despite Bush's "offered hand" of January, interparty relations deteriorated rapidly in the first half of 1989. At least some problems were beyond Bush's power to prevent. Republicans in the House had long-standing complaints about how Democrats ran the place: that Republicans were not given enough seats on committees, could not offer enough amendments when key bills reached the floor, and so on. But their frustration may have reached unprecedented levels on October 29, 1987, when Wright, having lost a close and embarrassing vote on a deficit-cutting bill, twisted House rules to schedule another vote that day on an altered version of the bill. About to lose by one vote on this second attempt, Wright held the vote open for an unusually long time as he waited for someone to switch sides. Eventually, Jim Chapman, another Texas Democrat, did so. Republicans were outraged; even some Democrats were mortified. Cheney, then the House Republican Whip and normally a mild-mannered intellectual, used an interview the next day with my *National Journal* colleague, James A. Barnes, to lash out at Wright as a "heavy-handed son of a bitch."[10] Barnes had not even asked about Wright. Cheney volunteered his feelings, obviously hoping that Barnes would print the remarks so that Wright would see them. In an article for *Public Opinion* magazine in early 1989, before Bush nominated him as Defense Secretary, Cheney referred to October 29, 1987, as "Black Thursday."[11]

As a group, House Republicans had grown more confrontational. "Our people are ready to go to war," Edwards, the newly elected chairman of the House Republican Policy Committee, told *Congressional Quarterly Weekly Report* in late 1988.[12] In a speech to his GOP colleagues at that time, he said, "Let me be very clear. I did not run for chairman of the Policy Committee in order to preside over a lot of talk while the Democrats write the congressional agenda and attempt to force it down the throats of the American people." With presidential candidate Jack F. Kemp's retirement from the House leaving a vacancy in their leadership, Republicans chose a younger, more conservative, and more combative team than it had before. Even Michel, who used to golf on occasion with O'Neill and who seemed uncomfortable in blatantly partisan brawls, adopted a tougher stance in his dealings with Democrats. Back in December, in an unusually strident speech to his Republicans, he called on Democrats to join him in naming a task force to look at reforms in House ethics rules and campaign finance laws. When Foley assumed the speakership on June 6, Michel used the occasion to launch a stinging broadside against Democrats for their 35-year grip on the House. GOP campaign operatives also promised to be more aggressive. Reagan's political aide, Edward J. Rollins, was picked in February to serve as cochairman of the National Republican Congressional Committee, where he vowed to pump fresh blood into the operation.

Perhaps the most symbolic change came after Bush picked Cheney for the Pentagon in March. Two candidates sought to succeed him as whip: Edward R. Madigan of Illinois, a seasoned, respected inside player who was supported by Michel; and Gingrich, a young, brash, very aggressive, and very partisan right-winger. Gingrich squeaked out a two-vote victory, drawing surprising support from moderates who, it seemed, were as fed up with Democratic control as were the upstart conservatives. Gingrich had virtually declared war on Democrats, had spoken out against what he said was a systemic corruption evident in the majority's brand of House control, and had filed the complaint before the House Ethics Committee that eventually led to Wright's downfall. In 1984, he had enraged O'Neill by using C-SPAN's live coverage of the House to quote extensively from the speeches of Democrats who, he said, "give the benefit of every doubt to the Communists and doubt every benefit of your own nation." Because C-SPAN's cameras were focused solely on whoever was talking, viewers did not know that Gingrich was speaking to a virtually empty chamber. (After the episode, O'Neill ordered that the cameras show more of the House.) After Wright resigned in the wake of Phelan's report to the Ethics Committee, Gingrich spoke of targeting about 10 more Democrats for attack.

While virtually every Democrat respected Foley, some wondered whether he was ill equipped to deal with the new GOP team. He was, after all, a smooth conciliator, one more comfortable with negotiation than with political warfare. O'Neill supposedly once said that Foley sees three sides of every issue. Whether the political environment called for such open-mindedness was questionable. Foley himself was the subject of a vicious rumor in Washington that spring that he was a homosexual. Where the rumor started was unclear, but Republicans wasted little time in exploiting it. As he assumed the speakership, the Republican National Committee issued a nasty release that compared Foley's voting record to that of Barney Frank, the openly homosexual Massachusetts Democrat. Entitled "Tom Foley: Out of the Liberal Closet," the release was a blatant effort to link Foley with homosexuality. In an obviously uncomfortable exercise, Foley publicly denied that he was a homosexual.

To suspicious Democrats, Bush and his GOP colleagues seemed to be playing the "good cop, bad cop" act. Bush preached cooperation, bipartisanship, and trust. He fashioned deals with Democrats. Republicans on Capitol Hill and at the campaign committees meanwhile launched partisan smoke-bombs from the back benches. For example, as the White House offered its hand in early 1989, Rollins had already decided to use Wright's troubles to attack Democrats in the 1990 elections. As the White House worked to fashion April's budget deal, Rollins made it clear that at election time he would blame Democrats for any taxes it included. After the RNC released its memo about Foley, Bush called it "disgusting," but RNC chairman Lee Atwater disavowed it only after pressure mounted.

Whatever his public demeanor, Foley understood the threats posed by GOP broadsides. At the May 31 breakfast, he warned Darman that such harsh attacks could not be viewed in isolation. However much they trusted Darman, Democrats could hardly work with him in the face of Republican attacks on their sexual proclivities or political leanings. If the attacks continued, Foley said, they would threaten chances for the Big Deal. The budget chairmen agreed. As Panetta told me later that day, "You've got major turmoil going on in the House, a kind of Mafialike war going on between who is shooting whose leadership. And that obviously is feeding the partisan flames on both sides. If that kind of thing continues, it's not going to be easy to kind of move members on either side to say, 'Well, OK, we're playing this one game over here, but let's do serious things, and statesmanlike things, over here.'" Or, as Sasser said in July, "You can't operate one day with a white-hat guy, and the next day have somebody put on a black hat and come and hit you across the head with a two-by-four, and then get together with the white-hat guy the next day and not have your head hurting."

Foley was undoubtedly thinking a lot about his party mates, for they were a nervous bunch. Though in charge of the House and Senate, Democrats resembled a besieged minority that spent most of its time peering back in anticipation of the next attack. They were slow to respond to the Republicans, as if unsure of what to say. In mid-1989, Bush was riding high in public opinion polls, with approval ratings that approached those that John F. Kennedy enjoyed at this stage of his presidency. Meanwhile, some Democrats wondered how solid their grip on Congress was. The institution was facing a torrent of adverse publicity; because they controlled both chambers, Democrats had more to lose if voters decided it was time to "throw the bums out." A few particularly hard-hitting shots came from the media. On May 13, the *New York Times* and *Washington Post* both ran stories about Congress's slow start in 1989. Six days later, as Republicans complained about the inaction, the House Democratic Study Group issued a report that defended the 101st Congress, saying it had been less active than some of its predecessors but more active than others. It blamed the White House for many delays, saying

Bush's slow pace in choosing top aides made it hard for some committees to find an administration official to deal with.

In probably the harshest media attack of all, *Newsweek* ran a cover story in late April that described "CongressWorld ... a fortress of unreality, its drawbridges only barely connected to life beyond the moat." Although the story served to cool relations between lawmakers and the media, its most damning material came from lawmakers themselves. Rep. Pat Schroeder, a Colorado Democrat, said of Congress's unwillingness to make hard decisions, "Everybody here checks their spines in the cloakroom." Although it did not quote him directly, *Newsweek* used a story that it said Sen. Jake Garn, a Utah Republican, often tells. After Garn donated a kidney to his daughter, another senator complimented him on the Senate floor for the publicity it engendered. "You got *great* coverage," the other senator said. Garn wryly suggested that this senator might top it by trying a heart transplant.[13]

Although members grumbled about *Newsweek*'s story, which they viewed as one-sided, its focus on congressional lifestyles and ethics seemed appropriate for the times. Congress spent more energy worrying about those things than anything else in early 1989, providing critics with a bundle of ammunition. First came the pay raise fiasco, when a carefully crafted strategy to boost the salaries of most members from $89,500 to $135,000 collapsed in February in the face of public pressure. Next came Congress's preoccupation with personal ethics, occasioned by Wright's troubles. Suddenly, all members wondered whether the "rules of the game" by which they had handled their jobs would pass muster in this environment. Now no indiscretion was too small to worry about, no mistake too easily explainable if seized on by an opponent. Small gifts that lawmakers ordinarily would have accepted from lobbyists without much thought now became matters of potential trouble. Not only did they refuse to accept new gifts, but some members returned old ones. The public hardly differentiated the troubled Wright from his colleagues. A *Washington Post*/ABC News Poll in late May found that 4 out of 10 Americans believed many members were guilty of similarly serious violations as those with which Wright was charged. More than half thought that lawmakers "make a lot of money by using public office improperly." Three fourths of Americans said lawmakers would lie to help themselves politically and favor special interests over those of the public.[14] With so much scrutiny of Congress, its members became gripped by a bunker mentality that replaced the usual air of cordiality and easy conversation between and within the parties.

Ethical concerns engulfed the Senate, too, as Democrats, in an extraordinary rebuff to a new president and to one of their former colleagues, voted mainly along party lines to reject former Sen. John Tower for the Pentagon. The issue was not Tower's knowledge of defense matters; he had been chairman of the Senate Armed Services Committee. Rather, the debate was about Tower's alleged drinking, womanizing, and ties to the defense industry. A hotly debated issue was whether Tower's tendency to consume large quantities of alcohol in the 1970s, to which he admitted, continued into the 1980s, despite his protests to the contrary. Tower's defeat probably gave Bush as much reason to question Democratic motives as his "good cop, bad cop" routine had given Democrats to question his.

Whether the Democrats would be able to block presidential appointments much longer was an open question. Although Democrats held a 55–45 margin of control in the Senate, Republicans began to talk about recapturing the Senate in 1990. As 1989 wore on, the GOP had reason for optimism. Several of the Democrats' most attractive candidates for key races chose not to run, including former Vice President Mondale of Minnesota, Reps. Ben Nighthorse Campbell and David E. Skaggs of Colorado, Reps. Lee H. Hamilton and Jim Jontz of Indiana, Texas Agriculture Commissioner Jim Hightower, and Rep. Tim Johnson of South Dakota. Meanwhile, incumbents Tom Harkin of Iowa, Paul Simon of Illinois, Levin of Michigan, Max Baucus of Montana, Howell Heflin of Alabama, and Claiborne Pell of Rhode Island faced possibly troublesome races. Even if Republicans won just a few seats but fell short of control, they would be in position to assume it in 1992 when battles for 34 seats included 20 occupied by Democrats. More surprising were the murmurings of fear in the House. Democrats suspected that the GOP, through its campaign committees and harsh attacks, was laying the groundwork for taking over in the 1990s and that Democrats were not putting up much of a fight.

■   ■   ■   ■

But as the year wore on, evidence of a new partisan militancy arose within Democratic ranks. More Democrats decided that, yes, one had to fight fire with fire. Writing on the *New York Times*' op-ed page in late April, House Democrat Bill Alexander of Arkansas issued this warning to his colleagues:

> I have a message for Democrats based on my baptism by political fire in Southern politics: Answer Rep. Newt Gingrich's attacks upon our party or be prepared to lose again and again. . . . Democrats have faltered because they have remained silent far too often in the face of the partisan Republican onslaught. People expect a person to stand up for himself if he is attacked."[15]

Alexander filed a complaint against Gingrich with the Ethics Committee, raising questions about a financial arrangement that the latter used to promote a book. The committee hired Phelan's law firm to investigate.

The Democrats' political militancy matched a similar evolution in their fiscal thinking. Absent from the White House and searching for a proper way to deal with that fact, the Democrats, particularly in the House, were split into two schools of thought. Foley, Panetta, Rostenkowski, and others were leaders of a "governance" wing. In their view, they were elected to serve, to make the political system work as well as it could. Although Bush was a Republican, these Democrats preached the gospel of cooperation and negotiation with him. They worked to reach Gramm-Rudman's annual deficit targets in an orderly way and to pass budget resolutions and spending bills according to Congress's timetable. With not only their constituents looking on but the markets as well, these Democrats hoped to display Congress as a smoothly run legislative machine. If the machinery broke down with the White House and Congress at war over fiscal policy, they worried that Democratic lawmakers would share political blame with Bush.

Opposed to that group was a "partisan" wing, represented heavily by the liberal Democratic Study Group and such shrewd House members as David R. Obey of Wisconsin. This wing had long ago tired of "bipartisanship," "the spirit of cooperation," and the governance wing's other high-minded phrases. With Bush setting the parameters for fiscal policy by opposing tax hikes and defense cuts, these Democrats viewed White House-congressional negotiations as counterproductive to their party's interests. Only if they challenged Bush more effectively could they reduce the deficit on their *own* terms, not the president's. As one example, the "partisan" wing was far more willing to let Gramm-Rudman's across-the-board spending cuts take effect. Not only did this wing not think voters would blame them—as individual members—for the temporary chaos in Washington that such cuts might generate. These members also thought the cuts would present Bush with the Hobson's choice of accepting much lower defense levels or proposing a tax hike to restore the money.

The more that bipartisanship worked—with the deficit falling and Democrats not suffering politically—the more that the governance wing would prosper. But April's deal was too small for Democrats to claim much progress. And in the eyes of some, political costs were high. Deals like this put all parties on record *for* the same things and *against* the same things. That's OK for the GOP, which ran the White House. It was not necessarily so for Democrats, who had won the presidency only once in 20 years. "In a process that blurs distinctions between the two parties ... George Wallace will be right [in saying], 'There's not a dime's worth of difference between them,' " AuCoin told me in July. "Where are our values, if they're not reflected in where we choose to put money, and where we choose to take it away?" Many Democrats argued

against future deals. Rep. George Miller of California con-
vened meetings of several Democrats, including AuCoin, to
find ways to sharpen distinctions between the parties. They
offered amendments to spending bills that would force lawmakers to choose between competing interests. One would
have shifted funds from Star Wars to antidrug efforts. Another would have transferred money from the proposed space
station to veterans' and other programs. Both were defeated,
but the Democrats were pleased; Republicans opposed each
in bulk, demonstrating their greater interest in defense and
space than in social spending.

At the same time, administration actions raised doubts
about its commitment to April's deal. The most controversial
occurred at the Pentagon where Cheney, struggling to trim
defense spending to comply with the deal, opted for a little sleight-of-hand. To "save" $2.9 billion, he shifted the first
pay date for military personnel from October 1 to September 29. In doing so, he moved the date from fiscal 1990 to
1989. Democrats and some Republicans cried foul, and not
only because they were truly offended by such shenanigans.
They understood the political ramifications. If Cheney could
get away with that, everyone would want to. To avoid real
cuts in programs for education, science, space, or anything
else, lawmakers would propose that Congress shift spending
from one year to the next. Testifying before the House Budget Committee in July, Darman tried to distinguish between
Cheney's maneuver, which he insisted he did not know about
beforehand, and pay shifts that lawmakers contemplated to
save money in domestic programs. "Our firm policy is no new
pay shifts," Darman said, evoking raised eyebrows from lawmakers and aides, "and, as you know, the defense pay shift is
an old pay shift." Defense secretaries, he said, had legal authority to move pay dates that other cabinet secretaries did
not. "It does not extend to other parts of the government," he
said, "with, I believe, the exception of VA pension payments."

Whether Cheney had the authority or not, though, was
of little political consequence. Panetta replied:

No matter how you justify an exception for Defense if, in fact, that exception is created, it makes it very difficult to fight pay shifts with regard to other agencies.... I frankly cannot face these other chairmen of [Appropriations Committee] subcommittees and argue against a pay shift in their areas when they will, in turn, point to defense and say that a pay shift has been permitted there. That is a weakness and it is hurting us, but we intend to be as consistent as possible with regard to this issue.... The argument I am running up against is they feel that Secretary Cheney and the administration, by virtue of this pay shift, have violated the budget agreement.

Frenzel expressed similar concerns. "I am glad you are trying to close the barn door after the biggest horse escapes," he told Darman, "and I hope that we will be able to keep the barn door closed."

Other White House actions spread ill will among Democrats. Bush's June 27 call for a constitutional amendment to protect the flag, after the Supreme Court ruled that flag burning was protected by the First Amendment, infuriated many. Although he denied partisan motives, Bush's response to the court's decision reminded Democrats of how he had used the flag issue against Dukakis. Democrats were again in a politically untenable position. Although many viewed an amendment as mischievous, if not irresponsible, they did not want to appear to be less patriotic than Bush. To address such concerns, they pushed for a new law to protect the flag, hoping the public would find that acceptable.

At about that time, Democratic anger was bubbling over another White House tactic. From time to time, Bush proposed new programs but did not specify how to finance them. Each announcement brought a burst of good publicity in newspapers, on the evening news, and so on. If deficit constraints blocked these ideas from coming to fruition, Democrats feared that, because they controlled Congress where spending decisions are made, they would be blamed. Bush had put the Democrats in an impossible situation. If they said nothing, he could continue to make grand pronouncements with impunity; if they complained, they risked looking like naysayers. Whatever the risks, when Bush proposed a long-range "mission to Mars" on July 20—the 20th anniversary of the moon landing—Democrats could sit still no more. Sasser called Panetta to suggest that they hold ᴗ news conference. Others Democrats held their own.

Speaking from the Senate Radio and TV Gallery, Panetta sketched out the pattern. "The first address to the Congress by the president, President Bush, was a series of very interesting proposals for a 'kinder and gentler' America on a number of issues. Not one word of sacrifice. Not one word about how we were going to pay for them." After that February 9 speech, Panetta noted, came proposals to fight crime, crack down on drugs, provide loans to Hungary and Poland, and, finally, go to Mars. "It's a series of those things that I think are raising false hopes and false expectations on the part of the American people, when we should be telling them, 'Now is the time for a tremendous amount of sacrifice in order to try to restore the resources we need in order to meet some of these priorities.' " Two weeks later, Panetta listed the price tags of Bush's proposals and other needs in a *Washington Post* op-ed piece: "$70 billion for the B-2; $69 billion for Star Wars; a five-year overall defense program that exceeds projected funding levels by $140 billion; $400 billion to go to Mars; $6 billion for the Superconducting Super Collider; $2.4 billion in 1990 to fight drugs and crime. Now add a couple billion more for education and Head Start and $145 million in aid to Poland and Hungary. Then add $150 billion in federal bailout costs for the S&L industry and another $150 billion to clean up our defense nuclear manufacturing facilities."[16] At another news conference, Gephardt said simply about the Mars proposal, "There's no such thing as a free launch."

The contrast between presidential rhetoric and fiscal reality seemed especially galling to Panetta and Sasser. At that time, both were engaged in tough battles to enforce the April deal. Panetta, in particular, was diligently challenging appropriations bills, as they came before the House, that did not strictly conform to it. In Panetta's words, by "creating images of a rich bounty of funds," Bush was making his job that much harder. Why should the average lawmaker not want to spend more for this or that when the president suggested that sacrifice was not necessary? After his news conference, I approached Panetta to see how angry he really was. When I asked, he blew up: "I'm over there, playing chief cop ... kicking the shit out of guys based on the fact that they can't find enough money even to deal with the stuff that's on the [House] floor right now. You know, they're struggling to find a few cents here, a few cents there, and then suddenly ... you've got this whole new promise about some dramatic new program."

■   ■   ■   ■

Panetta's anger was revealing. As we sat in his office in early September, I asked how events since April had affected chances for the Big Deal in the fall. Reviewing Bush's "black box" of February, his later pronouncements of new programs, and his unwillingness to specify how to pay for any of them, Panetta said:

> Democrats, I think now, the Speaker [Foley] reflects this, are concerned that we're getting set up. So that if, in fact, we were to ever put any taxes into [the Big Deal], the president would use the argument that somehow that was the fault of the Democrats. And if, in fact, you put together a package that, let's say, includes taxes which we get the blame for, includes budget [process] reforms which don't do anything for Democrats, and then, let's say, includes some cuts in entitlement programs, which are our constituency, which we would also be blamed for, then I begin to wonder, what do Democrats get out of that kind of agreement?

There it was—the very distrust that April's negotiators had pledged to avoid. *Cooperation, bipartisanship, trust*—the bywords by which Darman and Congress's budget players had pledged to work together—seemed like distant memories. They were replaced by a wide-eyed wariness, an uncertainty as to what the other side really hoped to achieve. Not that any of this was surprising. Fiscal policy was not made in a vacuum. It was, rather, the outgrowth of overriding political forces, none of which could be wholly controlled by a handful of individuals, albeit important ones, who wanted a Big Deal. Darman, Brady, Panetta, Sasser, Foley, Frenzel, Domenici: however high-minded their goal, when it came to fiscal policy, they were political animals, answerable to their party and its members, both superiors and subordinates. As the parties moved apart, so did these individuals.

Nothing moved the parties further apart than their months of battle over capital gains. Before it ended, the fight embarrassed the House's Democratic leaders, raised questions about whether Rostenkowski's friendship with Bush had skewed his political judgment, and prompted a "bidding war" of tax breaks in which Democrats and Republicans competed for the love of middle- and upper-income voters. More importantly for this story, the battle took on a symbolic value. For the White House, it offered a chance to push a key campaign pledge to enactment. For the Democrats, it prompted deep suspicion about whether Bush really cared about cutting the deficit and, if so, whether he would be willing to accept a tax increase as part of the Big Deal.

CHAPTER SEVEN

THE HOLY GRAIL

Bush's powerful friend on Capitol Hill had some bad news for him. "I personally will strongly resist any efforts to undo tax reform, including the return to a preferential tax rate for capital gains," Rostenkowski said in a speech to the National Press Club on February 9, just hours before Bush sent Congress his 1990 budget proposals, which included the long-awaited capital gains cut. "I'm not about to tell the wage earners in Chicago that they should pay a higher tax rate than stockbrokers."

Nor did his rhetoric soften much over the next few months. "We are talking about helping the rich here," Rostenkowski said in Chicago in March. "We're talking about a benefit for the richest 5 percent of taxpayers that will allegedly somehow help the other 95 percent. On its face, it's an argument that defies logic. It's as if someone had suggested that the law of gravity be repealed." By May, he still seemed unmovable. Expressing concern about "a system that taxes money made by hard labor at a higher rate than money made by the clever manipulation of capital," he outlined other complaints about a capital gains cut: that it would cause the deficit to swell; skew investment decisions needlessly toward certain ventures and away from others; not produce the investment in new businesses that advocates claimed; and generate congressional interest in raising tax rates on the wealthy, which would destroy the structure of the 1986 Tax Reform Act. Bush's proposal seemed dead. If opposed by Rostenkowski, Congress's most powerful taxwriter, Bush had few options for moving it along. As Darman later recalled, pundits early in the year put the odds against Bush's proposal at 100–1.

Had they known what was happening in private, the pundits would have raised those odds. At a White House meeting in mid-April, the chairman offered to get Bush a one-year cut in the capital gains rate to help his friend meet Gramm-Rudman's target for 1990 without breaking his no-tax pledge. A cut like that, experts said, would *raise* revenues for a short time as investors cashed in assets to take advantage of the lower rate. And, as long as the rate cut expired after a year, it presumably would not threaten the landmark tax reform law that Rostenkowski worked so hard to bring about. Of course, a horse trader like Rostenkowski wanted a few things in return: Bush's help in boosting the Earned Income Tax Credit; his help in blocking cuts in Medicare payments to inner-city hospitals; his willingness not to push for other revenue-losing tax breaks, such as one to spur development in so-called enterprise zones; and his promise to work for a big deficit-cutting deal for 1991 and beyond that included a sizable tax hike.

Bush never did get his capital gains cut, temporary or otherwise. Other pressures intruded on the secret scheming between these two pals. In the year's most bitter legislative war, Bush won a bruising battle in the House in September against not only the new Democratic leaders who had just replaced Wright and Coelho, but, as it turned out, Rostenkowski as well. Only an all-out effort by Mitchell later that year kept Bush from victory in the Senate. In the process, the White House and Democratic leaders spent much of the good will that each side had carefully cultivated in early 1989. More importantly, the fight virtually ended hopes of constructing a Big Deal on the deficit in late 1989, and it raised doubts whether these players would ever agree on one.

What the fight showed, in essence, was that for all the pledges on all sides to finally solve the deficit problem, America's leaders had more important political matters to attend to. In late 1988 and early 1989, officials, lobbyists, and others who had tired of the annual budget battles hoped that new players, free of the personal animus that those battles engendered, would craft a big deficit-cutting deal. But these observers forgot something. While new players may not carry the scars of past battles, they carry other baggage that makes cooperation difficult. Most important, new players need to fortify their positions as party leaders, as forces to be reckoned with, even if proving the point necessitates that they pick a symbolic fight or two. Bush wanted to fulfill a campaign pledge. He and the new House and Senate Democratic leaders, all rookies in their jobs, hoped to prove their mettle to colleagues and the public at large. If deficit cutting had to take a back seat, then it would.

In 1989, the nation's leaders searched for ways to give new tax benefits to their constituents and, at the same time, find a quick fix to meet Gramm-Rudman's next target. Politically, these goals were far more appealing than doing much about the deficit. And while this push for new tax breaks went for naught, another in 1990 was likely to be more fruitful. For one thing, Bush's setback in the capital gains fight seemed temporary. After whipping him in 1989, Mitchell admitted he would be hard-pressed to do so again a year later. The majority leader even said that under certain conditions he himself could support a capital gains cut. For another thing, Democrats would probably bring back their idea, first proposed as an alternative to the capital gains cut, of broadening eligibility for individual retirement accounts (IRAs). In Bush's second year, Washington seemed likely to reinstall a lower tax rate on capital gains and to expand IRA benefits.

■   ■   ■   ■

That tax cutting is more politically tempting than tax raising should surprise no one. Pity the poor elected official who brings only bad news to the folks back home; he'll be looking for another job before long. Nor is this a strictly American phenomenon. Jean-Baptiste Colbert, the 17th-century

French finance minister, supposedly described the art of taxation as "plucking the goose so as to obtain the largest amount of feathers with the least possible amount of hissing." But Americans have long displayed an unusually ferocious anti-tax attitude, and it only intensified under Reagan. Much of it is rooted in peculiar aspects of the nation's development; a good chunk is tied to a more recent public dismay with Washington's performance in solving problems. Together, these factors shaped a populace that, by the late 1980s, displayed an almost irrational antipathy toward suggestions that it merely pay for the amount of government it had collectively chosen. George F. Will lamented "a nation that seems to believe that taxation, with or without representation, is tyranny."[1] Republicans, controlling the White House through their antitax agenda, would not abandon it. Democrats, cowed by recent blowouts in presidential races, were less willing to argue that more taxes were needed.

Americans' disdain for taxation is part of a larger historical tradition—their distrust of central government. Fearing an omnipotent government, the American answer has been to keep it lean by not sending too many dollars to Washington. For this is a nation born of revolution against central government, against that of King George III. It is also an individualistic nation, one whose culture was shaped, according to an influential theory, by a western frontier that Americans conquered through courage and grit. "The frontier is productive of individualism," historian Frederick Jackson Turner wrote in 1893. "Complex society is precipitated by the wilderness into a kind of primitive organization based on the family. The tendency is antisocial. It produces antipathy to control, and particularly to any direct control. The tax-gatherer is viewed as a representative of oppression."[2] Turner's theory is questionable. The individualism of which he wrote is less so. Central government is less imposing in the United States than in Western Europe. Its social insurance system is leaner. The taxes supporting it represent a smaller share of the economy.

Nor have America's leaders had to be habitual tax raisers, at least at the federal level. Not only did Keynes reduce the tax-raising imperative by providing an intellectual justification for deficits. Also, as we have said, before Washington "indexed" the tax code in the 1980s, inflation pushed taxpayers into higher tax brackets. Thus, the nation's leaders received more money from their constituents each year without voting to take it from them. And when inflation was not high enough to feed government, Washington took advantage of peace, such as after Korea and Vietnam, to shift Pentagon funds to new domestic programs. Only on very rare occasions, at least until the deficit-riddled 1980s, have federal officials had to vote for income tax hikes.

In recent decades, Americans have found more reasons to oppose tax hikes. By 1980, they had tired of the dreams of social engineers. Johnson's Great Society, however much it helped ameliorate poverty, surely had not fulfilled its maker's lofty promises. The public was sick of watching its hard-earned dollars poured down Washington's rat hole of "waste, fraud, and abuse." With living standards stagnant, or worse, for many in the economically sluggish 1970s, Americans were less willing to part with the pretax dollars they brought home. And with Social Security payroll taxes rising to support that program, Americans wanted relief from other taxes to soften their overall tax burdens. Enough, they said. No more big government in Washington, except to beef up the nation's defense. And no more big government in the states, they said, as they launched "tax revolt" initiatives from California to Massachusetts to cut taxes or limit their growth from year to year.

Before and after he took office, Reagan fanned the antitax flames. Not even a rather noteworthy inconvenience like the deficit prompted him to moderation. As Stockman wrote later,

> By means of flagrant agitation and excitement of a democratic electorate's most singular vulnerability—resentment of the taxation its collective demands for public expenditures compel—Ronald Reagan has transformed the nation's institutionalized budgetary process into an extraordinary *fiscal plebiscite*... he has deployed his vast popularity and communications skills toward a single end: arousing, mobilizing, and concentrating the ordinary citizenry into an overpowering block vote against necessary taxation.[3]

As Reagan departed, Americans expressed more willingness to pay higher taxes for such domestic needs as child care and education but only if assured that the money went just for these purposes. Despite their growing support for more government, Americans told the pollsters that for every dollar it gets, Washington wastes 50 cents.

Bush's no-tax pledge of 1988 was designed to assure the Reagan voters that, on the tax issue, Bush was trustworthy. "He's saying to everyone who voted for Ronald Reagan, 'read my lips,'" Vincent J. Breglio, director of polling for Bush's campaign, told me in early 1989. "It was the symbolic connection to Ronald Reagan. This guy will continue to do what Ronald Reagan started to do." Bush's pledge did not bode well for deficit cutting. Rostenkowski recognized the problem immediately. Upon hearing the "read my lips" line, he called James A. Baker III, Bush's campaign chairman and the former Treasury secretary with whom he worked closely on tax reform. "I said, 'What are you doing? He's repeating it,'" Rostenkowski recalled. Baker's reply? "We're going to elect a president of the United States. We'll talk about *that* after he's elected."

Baker was not around for such chitchat in early 1989; the new secretary of state was keeping his eye on international affairs, not fiscal policy. He did not miss much. Everybody— Republicans and Democrats, the White House and Congress— understood the political realities. To win an election, Bush had planted himself in linguistic concrete, at least as far as Darman's "duck test" was concerned. Anything that smacked of new taxes was off the table for the early part of Bush's tenure, if not longer. To help reach Gramm-Rudman's 1990 target, Bush could cut spending or close a few tax loopholes that the public would not miss. Or, better yet, he could raise the money by *cutting* a tax.

■   ■   ■   ■

How you view a capital gains "differential"—that is, a lower rate on gains from the sale of stocks, bonds, real estate, and other assets than on ordinary income—has much to do with how you view the tax code. For many who see it as an instrument of social policy, a differential is fine. From their standpoint, the code should encourage whatever the country needs: housing construction, research and development, or, as in the case of capital gains, job-creating ventures. For others who subscribe to the theory of tax reform, the code should be a "level playing field," in which individuals and businesses invest as wisely as possible, unswayed by considerations of how the code treats each investment. This debate has no right or wrong answers, though advocates and critics of a capital gains cut tried to provide some in 1989. The advocates pointed to indications that the economy was slowing, and argued that a capital gains cut could provide a boost to avoid recession. Armed with an October 1989 study by Citizens for Tax Justice, the critics said that not only had business investment risen since the code was overhauled in 1986, but that tax reform forced former corporate tax escapees to pay their fair share.

Bush's support for a differential fit nicely into his philosophy, based on his days as a Texas oil man, that the tax code should encourage the entrepreneurial spirit of Americans seeking a better life. That Bush was a close friend of William A. Steiger, the House Republican from Wisconsin who successfully pushed for a capital gains cut in 1978, also may have helped hook him. Bush is the godfather of Steiger's son, William, and he remains close to Steiger's widow, Janet. Ten days before his inauguration, Bush told a group of business leaders that he was "committed" to a capital gains cut. He had, he said, raised the issue in the campaign against the advice of his political aides—aides who surely foresaw that it would open him to the attacks against his "rich man's tax cut" that Dukakis leveled. Now that he had won, the capital gains cut was a pledge he hoped to fulfill.

Bush was hardly the first officeholder to support a lower rate. Even as top personal income tax rates have fluctuated between 94 percent and 33 percent since World War II, the top capital gains tax for individuals has ranged between 25 and 35 percent. On the corporate side as well, while top income tax rates fluctuated between 52 percent and 34 percent, top capital gains rates stayed at a steadier level of 25 to 34 percent. Low capital gains rates are supposed to spur investment in business start-ups and expansions, which in turn would generate economic growth and create more jobs. The lower the rates at which investors have to pay tax on their gains, the theory goes, the more attractive are investments that carry those rates.

For a notion that is so widely accepted, evidence suggesting that a capital gains cut actually provides the economic boost that advocates contend is surprisingly thin. In 1985, the Treasury Department argued in a report that the capital gains cut enacted in 1978 would boost economic growth by 0.24 percent over 50 years. Democratic opponents, such as Rep. Sander Levin of Michigan, gleefully calculated that such growth would increase incomes by just one dollar per person per year. Some boost! When Levin in early 1989 sent an aide to find evidence that supports the arguments behind a capital gains cut—whether compiled at a federal agency, a Washington think tank, or elsewhere—he returned with just the Treasury report. "I can't believe that's all there is," Levin told the aide.

Even advocates seemed to rely more on faith or, as they might say, common sense than on evidence. When asked in August about complaints that a rate cut would cost Washington billions in lost taxes over the long run, Darman told a TV interviewer, "You can't prove it.... But I think one should look to intuition here, rather than to economists. If you encourage more longer-term risk-taking investment— more sweat-equity investment, more pioneering investment— ultimately, the society is bound to be more productive. And if it's more productive, that means greater economic growth and greater revenues." When I asked Mark A. Bloomfield, president of the American Council for Capital Formation and a leading capital gains lobbyist, whether he agreed with Darman's assessment, he modified it slightly. Rather than intuition, he said, "It's judgment." As for congressional advocates, former House GOP aide Steven I. Hofman said, "They really believe in the spreading effects of economic incentives. And the fact of the matter is, most of them were not strong supporters of tax reform."

Whatever else it did, a capital gains differential let people avoid taxation by converting ordinary income to capital gains. In eliminating the differential as part of tax reform, policy makers hoped to close down such income-shifting schemes, which helped the rich and angered others without the means to do likewise. And because tax reform lowered personal and corporate income rates dramatically, many policy makers felt they no longer had to offer a still lower rate on capital gains to encourage investment in new businesses. To many, this was an explicit deal: Conservatives got low income tax rates; liberals got the steps to ensure that the wealthy paid a fair share. To some, the capital gains change was the glue that solidified this deal, if not tax reform itself.

"If capital gains gets put back in the [tax] code, it's a knife in the back of tax reform," Sen. Bill Bradley, a New Jersey Democrat and Congress's strongest proponent of tax reform, said at one point. When a proposal to cut the capital gains tax hit the House floor in late September, Rep. Donald J. Pease, an Ohio Democrat, declared, "The ink will not be dry on this bill, if capital gains is included, before smart lawyers and smart CPAs are figuring out a way to reinstitute tax shelters." Not even the "smart lawyers" disagreed. In mid-October, Theodore P. Seto, a partner with Drinker, Biddle & Reath in Philadelphia, wrote in the *New York Times*, "I'm one of those fancy, high-priced tax lawyers whose job is to help the wealthy keep their taxes down. I'm very good at it, and ordinarily I enjoy it. But I come from a family of modest means, and my politics reflect that fact. When the country is not paying attention, Congress inevitably gives away the store to people with enough money to lobby effectively. And that burns me up." Predicting the likely return of tax shelters, Seto went on, "It starts with allowing taxpayers to exclude a percentage of capital gains from taxation. This will open the door for promoters to structure shelters that let the very wealthy avoid paying taxes on all sorts of income, not just capital gains.

It will be possible to generate phony (but legal) tax losses of any size, provided that the taxpayer has enough money to take advantage of the loopholes the preference permits."[4]

After their 1986 triumph, tax reform's biggest supporters realized that their handiwork faced an uncertain future because it represented such a sharp break with tradition. For decades, a key difference between Democrats and Republicans was that, while the former sent goodies to the folks back home by spending, the latter gave out tax breaks. As Hofman remarked, many Republicans were hostile to tax reform because it curtailed their opportunities to do so. Some Democrats, too, were hostile. As the deficit closed the spending spigot in the 1980s, they had also turned to the tax code to allocate targeted benefits. Under tax reform, the code was a less useful tool. Soon after the law was enacted, lawmakers of each party wondered whether they had gone too far in curtailing tax breaks, such as for constructing low-income housing. In 1989, in fact, Washington expanded a low-income housing credit.

The capital gains change was also the subject of early debate. In 1987, Bloomfield's council of Fortune 500 and other companies drafted the "15 percent solution," the basis for Bush's plan to cut the top capital gains tax rate to 15 percent. Ways and Means Republicans, with some of the panel's conservative Democrats, latched on to the "15 percent solution" and expressed interest in restoring the differential that year. But they faced two problems: Congress's Joint Tax Committee estimated that a cut to 15 percent would immediately cost the government tax revenues. And Reagan was devoted to tax reform and unwilling to do anything that might jeopardize the low personal and corporate income rates it brought. Bush's election dramatically changed the dynamics of this debate, for now the nation's most powerful leader had a capital gains cut atop his list of promises.

■   ■   ■   ■

How April's budget agreement fit into the capital gains debate was unclear. Democrats claimed that by pushing a rate cut against their wishes, Bush violated the spirit, if not the letter, of that agreement. The idea behind the deal, they said, was for the president and Congress to work together, rather than for one side to ram an unwanted series of tax changes down the throat of the other. "The agreement, sort of spoken and unspoken, was that we would cooperate with the administration in trying to take the path of least resistance in 1990, and establish an era of good feeling, and go through sort of a confidence-building time," Sasser recalled. Because Ways and Means, by mid-1989, had found a way to raise $5.3 billion before any capital gains amendment was offered, Sasser and others argued, Bush should have pulled back.

"That is unmitigated balderdash," Frenzel told me later. April's agreement implied nothing about capital gains, he said. More specifically, it declared only one thing: that a tax bill would not move forward until the president signaled his support for it. The Democrats, Frenzel said, insisted on that language because they were confident about stopping a capital gains cut and replacing it with tax changes of their own. They were free to try, he said, just as Bush was free to do his thing. The White House surely thought so. Within days of April's deal, Sununu, Brady, and Darman talked up the idea of a capital gains cut on TV news shows. Several months later, as the House prepared to vote on a rate cut, Frenzel said on the floor, "It is time for those Democratic leaders to utter the politician's prayer: 'O Lord, make my words both tender and sweet for tomorrow I may have to eat them.'"

But this was more than a simple misunderstanding. Some Democrats admitted to a broader agenda. To get the Big Deal that many wanted, they needed to get Bush to the bargaining table. Well, what did Bush want? He wanted a capital gains cut. If he got one before the Big Deal, they said, he might have little incentive to accept the tax hike that the Big Deal entailed. He should get his capital gains cut as part of that deal, not separate from it. But Bush's allies thought the Democrats had it backwards. A capital gains cut, they said, was the path towards the Big Deal, not an obstacle to it. By getting his rate cut, Bush's standing would be stronger with the political right, which supported the cut and feared that Bush was not one of them. With his enhanced standing, he would have more freedom to accept a tax increase down the road. And with a win under his belt, he might have the self-confidence to take the political risks that a Big Deal would generate. Speaking to the latter point, Domenici told me after the capital gains battle ended, "I think it would have had a little ameliorating effect."

Either way, when the battle heated up in midyear, Bush was advised to fight it vigorously. For one thing, the White House could not abandon the key House Democrats who had bucked their party leaders to support a capital gains cut; if it did, nobody would help the White House in future battles, for fear of similar treatment. For another, this was now an issue of governance, of whether Bush could push a priority through a Democrat-run Congress. It was a battle over perception as much as reality. Darman worried about such things. As a top aide in Reagan's White House, he had written memos in 1981 to Baker, the chief of staff, and to Reagan, advising that early legislative victories over the Democrats could set the tone for White House-congressional relations. Nor had his views changed since then. In his confirmation hearings in early 1989, Darman said with reference to the early Reagan battles, "The presidency is a much, much weaker institution than I think most people assume it is, and I think if you start an administration with a highly visible, highly advertised loss, you permanently weaken that presidency for whatever else it might do." Had capital gains not become a "highly visible" issue in 1989, the stakes would not have been so high.

That Bush's relations with Democrats might suffer was a price he seemed willing to pay. With the battle raging by summer, Rostenkowski privately cautioned Bush that "you're a president for four years," and that he needed good relations with Congress. When the president persisted, Democrats complained openly. Within hours after the House vote in September, a Ways and Means Democrat told me, "You don't go in a ring and kick a guy in the balls and then say, 'Oh, Jesus, I knocked this guy out. Well, hey, we're buddies yet, though, right?'" As Mitchell fought a rate cut a month later, he said in a fiery floor speech, "The capital gains tax cut has become the Holy Grail of this administration. It has cast aside any concern for the deficit. It has cast aside any concern for the budget process. It has now cast aside any concern for fairness. And it has now cast aside any concern for relations with the Congress in pursuit of this Holy Grail."

Bush and his aides took a less apocalyptic view of things. Sure, tension was running high. But administration officials seemed to think they could fight this one with both barrels— and repair the damage later. Bush made that point to Panetta at a social event in late July while the House was embroiled in conflict. Panetta had approached him to advise that the capital gains fight was damaging executive-legislative rela- tions. Asked about Bush's reaction, Panetta said it was "kind of typical George Bush: 'Gosh, if we have the votes, we win. We could kind of go on. If you had won, we'd go on, too. That's kind of the process.' " Similarly, Darman told reporters in late September:

> The reality is that, whatever people say ... most of these people in a political system, Congress especially, are people who have battles every day, every week. They win some and they lose some and they keep on. If they don't have the kind of personality that can do that, they, generally speaking, aren't comfortable in the political process and they sort of drop out, or they certainly don't rise to leadership positions.... Sure, there'll be a little bit of ill will that carries over, but that happens all the time. And mature parties just rise above it and keep going.

If not for the revenue effects of a rate cut, Bush might not have come so close to winning. In the long term, most experts thought that a rate cut would cost Washington money (al- though some conservatives insisted otherwise). On the other hand, experts of all stripes agreed that, in the short run, a rate cut would raise revenues as investors rushed to sell assets. For officials focused on next year's Gramm-Rudman target—and not on the deficit's future path—a cut like that was appealing. If you, as the Ways and Means chairman, were worried that a permanent rate cut would create tax shelters and thus jeopardize tax reform, then you might find a temporary cut more attractive. And if you happened to be pals with the president of the United States, who needed a way to raise money without breaking his no-tax pledge, you might have concluded that a one-year cut was your answer.

■   ■   ■   ■

"I love George Bush," Rostenkowski told me in mid-1989. "I think he's one of the greatest guys I've ever met in my life. I talk to him very frankly. And I think, as I never thought he was a wimp, I think he can be a great president because I honestly believe that George Bush will, when the time comes, make the right decision." I was not alone in hearing such talk. Some Ways and Means Democrats felt uncomfortable at the committee's 200th anniversary celebration when the Democratic chairman told the Republican president that he came within "one step" of endorsing him in 1988. A capital gains cut had been the subject of kidding between the two at least since Bush made his campaign proposal. Bush knew Rostenkowski hated the idea. "Every time he'd see me in an audience or something, he'd throw one of those snide remarks about capital gains," Rostenkowski said. In Bush's February 9 budget speech, "when he talked about capital gains, he gave me one of these," the chairman said, raising an eyebrow. "It's always been a controversial link in our friendship."

It was not only his friendship with Bush that ultimately drove Rostenkowski, however. The chairman is a pragmatist, not an ideologue. While others try to score political points by confrontation, by drawing distinctions with their opponents, Rostenkowski cannot be bothered. "I don't think that we accomplish anything by just throwing bricks at each other on the floor of the House of Representatives and calling Republicans Republicans and Democrats Democrats, conservative or liberal," he told me. "I think we're going to be judged pretty much by not what we promise, but what we accomplish." While loyal to Democratic values, Rostenkowski has generally worked to create a bipartisan consensus that would not only bring legislation out of his committee, but also ensure passage in the House. Thus, Republican presidents can be more of a help than a hindrance. As he put it, "It's always been my philosophy that I can govern better with Republicans in the White House because I can deal with them."

Until the capital gains fiasco tarnished his reputation, the chairman was viewed as perhaps Congress's best legislative poker player. Maybe he still is. "He's Lyndon Johnson without any of the venalities," one admirer said of him. A big, back-slapping, gravelly-voiced pol, schooled in the backrooms of Chicago Mayor Richard Daley's famed urban machine, Rostenkowski puts a premium on such old-school values as loyalty, trust, and candor. Those who act accordingly generally get on well with him. Those who do not are often ignored, if not ostracized. When Ways and Means Democrat Kent Hance of Texas worked against Rostenkowski in 1981 to push Reagan's big tax cuts through the House, the chairman responded by, among other things, removing the wheels from Hance's committee chair. When he needed to choose Ways and Means Democrats for the House-Senate conference on tax reform in 1986, Rostenkowski took the unusual step of bypassing several senior members in favor of those who displayed the most loyalty to the chairman's tax reform ideas. When he and I discussed his goals for 1989, he said, "My responsibility is to give the president of the United States, as long as he has this silly whim about 'read my lips,' something that he could sign." If the only way to do so was with a capital gains cut, then so be it.

Rostenkowski's offer to Bush of mid-April could not be kept quiet forever. In the first half of 1989, many lawmakers received signals from lobbyists as far away as California that something was up. "It wasn't just my district," recalled Rep. Robert T. Matsui, a Ways and Means Democrat from Sacramento. "It was Los Angeles. A lot of people there were piped into the White House, financial people, and they would be saying things like, 'Well, it may be put together.'" Then came more tangible evidence. A May 26 story in the *Los Angeles Times* that said Rostenkowski was considering a plan to cut the top capital gains rate to 20 percent "for at least one year" did not get much attention.[5] But the tax community buzzed in early June when Peter J. Davis, Jr., vice president in Washington for Prudential-Bache Securities, wrote in his newsletter that Bush and Rostenkowski had hatched such a deal and that investors should wait until later that year before selling assets.[6]

With facts trickling out and rumors swirling, the chairman figured it was time to set the record straight. Yes, he was open to the idea of a capital gains cut. In June 7 interviews with the *Wall Street Journal* and *New York Times*, the latter of which put the story on its front page, Rostenkowski suggested that critics of Bush's plan would have to show him how to raise the $5.3 billion required by April's budget deal without relying on a capital gains cut. "If my Democrats or my Republicans can offer me a way to raise revenue without a capital gains cut, I'll jump at it," the *Times* quoted him as saying. "But so far, I haven't seen a way."[7] Committee members replied, but not as he had hoped.

In a caucus of Ways and Means Democrats, one after another lambasted the idea. Some worried about tax reform, others about a tax scheme that disproportionately helped the well-to-do, and still others about whether Rostenkowski should be working so closely with Bush. Nor did the Democrats feel better when Rostenkowski told a story. At a recent White House meeting, the chairman said, he urged Bush to get serious about a big deficit-cutting deal for 1991 that included tax hikes. According to Rostenkowski, Bush reacted coolly. Well, the Democrats said, if Bush would not agree to that, Rostenkowski should not help him get a capital gains cut. From other House Democrats, Rostenkowski heard the same message. On the House floor, at a meeting of the Democratic Study Group's executive committee, and elsewhere, opposition to a capital gains cut was strong. Rostenkowski told others he had gotten a "verbal hazing."

So he backed off. In a June 28 interview with the *Wall Street Journal*, Rostenkowski said that he would raise $5.3 billion without a capital gains cut. His announcement was designed for two audiences: Ways and Means' liberal Democrats who were his close allies, and the White House. Unfortunately, only the former seemed to get the message. Brady came to see Rostenkowski later and talked up a rate cut. He apparently thought the administration had struck a deal with Rostenkowski months earlier and was implementing its part of it. As the chairman had asked, the White House was not pushing for Medicare cuts that would hurt inner-city hospitals. And, as Rostenkowski had wanted, Bush said publicly that he would be willing to consider an increase in the Earned Income Tax Credit. Rostenkowski thought that he had *not* struck a deal and that he could not turn his back on his Democratic allies at Ways and Means.

But not even a chairman as powerful as Rostenkowski has total control over his troops. With his June 7 interviews, Rostenkowski let the capital gains genie out of the bottle. In indicating that he would support a rate cut, Rostenkowski gave the very idea a new aura of respectability. Now his committee's conservative Democrats could pursue it without fear of raising his ire. His June 28 reversal came too late. By then, Democrat Ed Jenkins of Georgia, a longtime advocate of a differential, was crafting his own plan and trying to gather support for it. When I spoke with Rostenkowski later, he denied widespread speculation that, while remaining publicly opposed, he had privately encouraged Jenkins to plow ahead. Nevertheless, by late July, Jenkins and Bill Archer, the committee's senior Republican, had all 13 Republicans and the "gang of six" conservative Democrats (Jenkins and five others) ready to push the proposal. These 19 formed a bare majority on the 36-member committee.

The Jenkins-Archer plan was less than ideal, as even staunch advocates of a capital gains cut agreed. It called for a two-year rate cut, after which the rate would have gone back up; at that point, gains would have been "indexed" so that investors paid taxes only on real gains, not on the inflation-based run-up in profits. Shaped as much by Gramm-Rudman's short-term focus as anything else, Jenkins-Archer probably would have distorted investment decisions and provided little incentive for the long-term, high-risk ventures that a differential is supposed to encourage. Even after counting its burst of quick revenues, it would have cost the Treasury an estimated $21 billion over 10 years, adding that much more to Washington's deficit troubles.

"An across-the-board, temporary tax cut, by encouraging the churning of assets, would worsen the shortsightedness that plagues the U.S. investment horizon," five leading economists wrote about Jenkins-Archer in an open letter on September 11. "To call the Jenkins proposal a capital gains proposal in the truest sense of the word, which means to me long-term productive investment, is in my judgment an abuse of a brand name," AuCoin, a longtime supporter of a capital gains differential, said two weeks later on the House floor. "It is an invitation to sell off assets." Because of the two-year window of low rates, Rostenkowski said, "The stock market, real estate market, and the timber market will be flooded over the next two years, thus depressing prices and values."

Even capital gains advocates acknowledged the problems. For some, Jenkins-Archer was a means to an end, not the end itself. Plenty of economists who opposed a rate cut viewed indexing as a good idea. Besides, if the advocates' only option was Jenkins-Archer, they would pass it now and improve it later. Were it not for Jenkins, Archer, and a few other key members, a capital gains cut proposal would not have moved this far. Advocates felt they had to support it to the end. Quoting an old political maxim, H. L. "Sonny" Callahan, an Alabama Republican, told the House, "In the South, we have an old saying, that if you go to a dance with a lady, you dance with her, and ... I encourage you to 'dance with the one who brung you,' and Jenkins-Archer has brought us to this point." As for possible changes, Darman and others talked openly about converting the two-year rate cut into a permanent one, either while the bill moved through Congress or once the two-year cut was enacted.

The $9.4 billion revenue boost that Jenkins-Archer would have produced in a little over two years was seductively appealing. With Washington focused on Gramm-Rudman's target for the next year, those revenues could be used to off-set spending for a new program. When the revenue surge stopped, of course, Washington would face two new deficit-swelling headaches: the revenue loss from Jenkins-Archer and the costs of whatever new program was created. But if some lawmakers talked about such problems, plenty of others did not. If advocates of a rate cut had to set up a new program or two to attract enough votes for Jenkins-Archer, they would.

"In the 27 months the capital gains cut will be effective under my proposal, it's estimated [that] asset sales will raise $9.4 billion in new revenues that may be applied to deficit reduction as well as to financing other pressing concerns such as child care or the war on drugs," Jenkins wrote in a September 22 op-ed piece in *USA Today*.[8] A few days later, Ronnie G. Flippo of Alabama, one of the "gang of six" members, defended Jenkins-Archer on the House floor as a useful tool for financing other tax credits that were due to expire as well as new child care provisions. Similarly, Guy Vander Jagt, a GOP House member from Michigan, told his colleagues that because Jenkins-Archer would help Washington meet its Gramm-Rudman responsibilities for the next year, Congress should grab it. He did not mention anything about the long-term effects.

■   ■   ■   ■

The House's new Democratic leaders chose to make the Jenkins-Archer plan the first big test of their power. It was easy to see why. In 1981, Reagan plowed over an earlier group of House leaders by pushing his tax and spending cuts through with a coalition of Republicans and conservative Democrats. Only after Democrats picked up 26 seats in 1982 could Speaker O'Neill, along with Majority Leader Wright and Majority Whip Foley, control enough votes to effectively combat Reagan. O'Neill and Wright were now gone. But Foley surely recalled the unpleasantness. Some Democrats feared that in 1989 history would repeat itself, though Bush had fewer Republicans to work with than Reagan had had in 1981. Because a permanent coalition seemed out of reach, Bush's aides talked about creating shifting coalitions through which to win from time to time.

But if the House leaders' decision to fight made sense, their strategy may not have. In contrast to Mitchell, who rallied his troops with a tough partisan appeal, House leaders relied on philosophical points that are not easily understood and that do not pack much political punch. Besides, to be successful, the leaders needed a party unity that was probably beyond reach. For one thing, lots of Democrats had supported a capital gains differential in the past, and they saw no reason not to do so again. For another, even the leaders sent mixed signals. While he opposed a rate cut, Foley said he could support a proposal built around "indexing." And until late September, Rostenkowski tried to craft a compromise with the White House to avoid the all-out war that others advocated.

Maybe their biggest problem, though, was timing. Democratic leaders came into the battle late. Wright's problems, prompting his departure in early June, left a policy void. He was too consumed with his own troubles to provide direction on how the party should approach capital gains. When he left, Foley and the others took time to get settled in their new jobs. While this was occurring, rank-and-file Democrats positioned themselves on one side of the issue or the other. By the time Foley and Gephardt launched their broadside against Jenkins-Archer in July, many Democrats had committed themselves to support it. Foley received that message clearly when he met with Ways and Means Democrats in July. J. J. Pickle of Texas, a "gang of six" member, told him, "I feel like I'm in the delivery room, and now my mama's telling me I shouldn't have kissed the girl."

Lacking the votes to block Jenkins-Archer, but pressured by the party's leaders to try, Rostenkowski delayed committee action until after the August recess. By then, he hoped to have all sides on board for a compromise. The challenge seemed daunting, since Bush and Foley had drawn separate lines in the sand. Bush was determined to get a rate cut. Foley said he would only accept indexing. Rostenkowski did his best, unveiling a proposal just before the recess that centered on indexing but that also offered lower capital gains rates for profitable ventures in which investments were held for at least five years. If the assets were held for 10 years, they would be eligible for even lower capital gains rates. Over the recess, he continued working with Darman and other administration officials, sharpening his proposal to attract support.

But he fell short. In a last-ditch effort on the morning of September 14, the day on which he had scheduled Ways and Means to decide the issue, Rostenkowski tried to convince his Democratic allies to accept his compromise plan. The "gang of six," which was excluded from the meeting, had signed on. So had Ways and Means' Republicans. So had the White House, which thought that, down the road, Senate Democrats would more likely support a compromise plan than one that House leaders had contested. In fact, Bentsen privately told Bush's aides that he could support a compromise; it would give him "political cover" from Democratic attacks. But the liberals would not budge. They did not like the plan or the idea of compromising on such an important issue. Rostenkowski backed off, preferring to stick with his close allies.

Although they hoped to win on the House floor, Democratic leaders were clearly more anxious to lose than to compromise. This was a fight they had to wage, according to their pollsters. Democrats had all sorts of problems as a national party. Republicans had effectively tarred them as the party of "tax and spend." With nearly seven years of economic growth under their belt, Republicans in mid-1989 held a remarkable 21-point advantage over Democrats in opinion surveys that asked which party could better handle the economy. Republicans also had sizable leads when Americans were asked which party could better maintain peace and handle the nation's biggest problems. "Good feelings about the state of the U.S. economy and the international situation have helped lift the image of the Republican party to a postwar high," the Gallup News Service wrote in late July.[9]

And yet, all was not lost. Democrats were still viewed as the party of fairness. At stake was one of the party's remaining strongholds with the public. To compromise on a capital gains cut, whose tax benefits would flow overwhelmingly to the wealthy, would put Democrats behind an approach that is identified with Republicans. According to another maxim, when voters are faced with an original and an imitation, they opt for the original. Rather than imitate the GOP, Democrats needed to remind voters who they were, what they stood for, and why the nation had entrusted them with the mantle of leadership in the recent past. Making the case, Democrat Robert G. Torricelli of New Jersey told the House in September, "Rarely in this institution does a single vote define us as members. Rarely can one issue provide a real view of the differences between our political parties and our philosophies."

Voters seemed responsive to such appeals, despite having put Republicans in the White House so often of late. Dukakis's attack on Bush's capital gains proposal was the most effective part of his "on your side" message, according to pollsters. With Bush having vetoed legislation in June to raise the minimum wage higher than he wanted, Democrats thought they had an even more compelling, class-based message. The GOP was not insensitive to such attacks. When I asked Roger B. Porter, Bush's assistant for economic and domestic policy, about Democratic complaints that a capital gains cut would mainly help the rich, he pointed to a provision in Bush's plan that was designed, in part, to counter them. Bush had proposed that those making less than $20,000 a year not pay *any* capital gains taxes. Other administration officials argued that a capital gains cut should not be evaluated in terms of the distribution of tax benefits. "There can be no reasonable doubt, in my opinion," Darman told reporters in June, "that if you get the greater growth that is presumed ... the greater tilting toward productive investment ... you will ultimately, by definition, get more jobs and a higher standard of living by which *everybody* benefits."

Democratic strategy was designed not for immediate political payoffs, but for the long run. If, for instance, the economy slipped into recession, throwing millions out of work and raising fears among millions more, voters would more likely focus on what they had, what others had, and whether the distribution was fair. Added to the growing "signs of resentment against the wealthy and upper-bracket tax favoritism," conservative commentator Kevin Phillips wrote in his newsletter, the *American Political Report*, in September, Democrats might have a winning combination in the near future. Under the heading "Class Warfare and Democratic Historical Precedents," Phillips wrote, "Candid discussion goes against the 1980s grain, but it's these issues more than anything else that have enabled opponents to break up prior periods of national conservative or Republican dominance."[10]

In the short run, however, a lawmaker's smartest move was to support a rate cut. "It's a free ride," Matsui said. In good times, few are bothered by a tax cut that favors the rich. Beneficiaries are pleased. And those who might get hurt later probably do not realize it. Democrats argued that because a cut would cost money over the long run, Washington would have to find it somewhere else. Having given the rich a break, Democrats said, Bush would try to cut social programs or raise taxes that disproportionately burden those of modest income. Gephardt distributed buttons that read "Bush tax plan/you're gonna pay." As Pease told me, when deficit cutting gets hard, "As sure as you're sitting there, there are going to be people saying, 'We don't want to do it, but we'll have to raise excise taxes on beer, wine, tobacco.'"

But Democrats had no proof, so Americans had little reason to worry. Sure, the tax benefits of a rate cut would flow more to the wealthy, for they had the income to invest. Bush's Treasury Department estimated that, under his plan, more than 60 percent of the gains would be claimed by those making at least $100,000 a year; more than 46 percent would go to those making at least $200,000. But everyone was eligible for a break. Even a struggling worker who scraped together enough to buy a few shares of stock could benefit if the rate were cut. Plenty had done so. In a figure that advocates of a rate cut liked to quote, three quarters of Americans who claimed *any* gains on their tax returns made less than $50,000 a year. How much *each* of them claimed was not the point. If the average guy had a choice between getting a $10 tax cut while Donald Trump got $10 million, or getting nothing while Trump got nothing, he would likely choose the former. Dole told his GOP colleagues in late 1989 that when he attended a political fundraiser in New York, none of the wealthy individuals on hand asked him about prospects for a capital gains cut. But as he was leaving, a waiter stopped him with a question.

Nor did the advocates let anyone forget about hardworking Americans who had one big asset to sell, and had counted on a low rate. "You try to tell that person with a farm who has farmed for 40 years, and that is their only asset, they are ready to sell it and to use that profit, inflation-driven, whether it be $100,000 or $200,000, and you tell these people that have no government pension, that have no fancy retirement plans, that they are the rich, that they ought to pay 40 percent—the federal plus the state, capital gains tax," Jenkins told the House in September. That some Americans fit this description was undeniable. But their numbers were probably not as large as advocates suggested. According to the advocates, figures showing how benefits of a rate cut would be distributed across classes were tilted unfairly. They included the many Americans who took a big, onetime gain. If, say, a businessman earning $40,000 a year sold his firm for $200,000, he was included that year in the category of those making over $200,000. But as it turned out, even with these onetime takers ignored, CBO found that the wealthy would still enjoy the vast share of benefits of a rate cut.

Just how the tax benefits accrued to different classes was not necessarily the point. As Archer told me before the August recess, "I don't think there is a great deal of political mileage in this for those who want to use the rhetoric that this helps the rich, because it in no way increases the taxes on those of the middle- and lower-income classes. It's very hard to activate lower-income people, to use this as an issue to get their vote, because it does not punish them. And they may see the benefits of increased job opportunities." Moreover, a "soak-the-rich" appeal may not strike chords among those who still hope to hit it big someday. Were they to get rich, they would benefit from a lower capital gains rate. "People who might not have a lot aspire to have a lot," Archer said. "So the great secret to this country is that people recognize that they have the opportunity to help themselves. And if they've done that, they don't want it taken away from them."

As the debate heated up in the House, the public did not seem particularly excited. The number of letters and calls on this issue that arrived at congressional offices was light. Those that did tended to express support for a rate cut. A letter to Rostenkowski from a constituent of Rep. Michael Andrews, a "gang of six" member from Texas, pointed up the problems faced by Democrats who tried to exploit class-based arguments. "My wife and I were born to working parents in rural East Texas," the one-page letter began. A World War II veteran with three children, the writer described how he worked his way through college rather than ask for assistance under the G.I. bill. After working 15 years in private industry, he put in 23 more for the National Aeronautics and Space Administration before finishing his career as a civil engineer. Since inheriting a small piece of land 20 years earlier, he enjoyed some financial return. But because capital gains rates rose in 1986 and the economy slowed in that region, the land's value had fallen. He wrote,

> The reduction in capital gains to the previous level would promote an equitable and deserving incentive for middle-class America. It would reinvigorate a nearly lost hope of rural farmers and wage earners to overcome the break-even struggle to achieve a better standard of living, and provide some real inheritance for their children. We are not rich and do not perceive the reduction in capital gains tax as a means for the rich to become richer. I urge your support in reducing capital gains tax to its previous rate.

■   ■   ■   ■

Another political maxim is "You can't beat something with nothing." Hoping to beat Jenkins-Archer on the floor, House leaders thought they needed a proposal of their own.

Gephardt took over, consulting with the rank and file before crafting a plan in September that he cosponsored with Rostenkowski, who was now openly warring with the administration. Rhetorically, it played to class-based appeals against the "rich man's tax cut." But it was far less of a populist plan than its principal backers let on. Besides, it brought a load of its own political baggage. Most troubling was a provision to raise income tax rates for the nation's wealthiest taxpayers. Though defensible as a matter of equity, it let Republicans revive the "tax and spend" chant.

About two weeks earlier, Bentsen had unveiled a plan to expand IRA benefits. The popular IRA program, designed to encourage savings, was set up in 1974 on a limited basis but expanded a bit in 1976 and then greatly in the big tax cuts of 1981. Washington, however, reversed course in tax reform, limiting deductible contributions to those without pension protection or with limited incomes. Bentsen proposed that everyone be able to make deductible contributions and to make withdrawals without penalty to buy a first home or pay for college. Buttressed by polls showing that IRAs were more popular than low capital gains rates, House leaders essentially adopted Bentsen's plan as their own.

To hear the Democrats, theirs was a battle between rich and poor. "While some of the president's wealthy contributors are rewarded with ambassadorships," Gephardt said at one point, "the rest are being taken care of by this capital gains proposal."[11] On the House floor, Rep. Marty A. Russo of Illinois huffed, "This is a question of outright greed. We have people starving in the streets. We have a problem in our school systems. We have the scourge of drugs going through this country. We have an infrastructure that is decaying. We have a national debt that is choking our country. What is our response? What is this administration's response? Give the wealthiest people in this country a $25,000 tax cut.... This is outright disgusting greed." As for the Democratic alternative, Ways and Means Democrat Thomas J. Downey of New York said of the IRA portion, "It will be paid for by the rich, and it will help the middle class to realize the American dream of a new home or a college education."

Reality suggested otherwise, as even some Democrats supporting their leaders conceded. "George Bush wants to give big tax breaks to the rich, and we want to give big tax breaks to the near-rich," Rep. Byron L. Dorgan, a Ways and Means Democrat from North Dakota, said of the battle.[12] A study by Ways and Means' Republican staff showed that 84 percent of those who would benefit from the IRA plan earned more than $50,000 a year. Even the administration tried to turn class-based arguments against the Democrats. At a Senate Finance Committee hearing on Bentsen's IRA, a day after the House voted for Jenkins-Archer and against Gephardt's alternative, Brady cited figures similar to the Ways and Means GOP estimates. He said such a plan could not substitute for a capital gains rate cut that would produce new businesses and jobs for everyone's benefit.

Because their IRA plan would cost billions, House leaders proposed to raise that money by eliminating the infamous "bubble" of tax reform and boosting income rates on the nation's wealthiest 600,000 individuals. Here's how: Tax reform set up marginal income tax rates of 15 and 28 percent. Individuals paid at the 15 percent rate on their income up to a certain level, and at 28 percent on income above that. For those of fairly high income, policy makers chose to phase out the initial 15 percent rate and the personal exemptions. To do so, they imposed a 5 percent surcharge on each dollar of additional income. As a result, those at the phase-out levels paid a 33 percent tax rate (28 plus 5) on each dollar of additional income. Those of even higher income, however, paid only 28 percent on each dollar. The 33 per cent "bubble" was widely viewed as unfair, and House leaders proposed to eliminate it by extending the 33 percent rate to the wealthiest Americans.

Republicans could hardly contain their glee. Forget questions about equity or fairness. The Democrats, they said, were up to their old tricks—proposing tax hikes. Bush threatened to veto any such bill. Gingrich framed the issue for the House as "a capital gains tax cut versus the Son of Mondale tax increase," and he added, "... just as McGovern and Mondale and Dukakis campaigned on the premise that Americans should pay more, the liberal Democratic leadership is proposing that Americans should pay more." In a short floor speech that rankled some Democrats, Republican Paul B. Henry of Michigan had this to say before criticizing the Democrats' plan in more common prose: "Tax, tax, tax, tax, tax, tax, tax, tax, tax, tax, tax, tax, tax, tax, tax, tax, tax, tax, tax, tax, tax, tax, tax, tax, tax, tax, tax, tax, tax, tax, tax, tax, tax, tax, tax, tax, tax, tax, tax, tax, tax, tax, tax, tax, tax, tax, tax, tax, tax, tax, tax, tax, tax, tax, tax, tax ... "

Whether fears about such attacks swayed Democrats from their leaders' plan is unclear. Months earlier, Darman had told others privately that Bush could get his rate cut through the House with the votes of Republicans and timber-state Democrats (presuming timber profits were eligible for some preferential treatment). While Bush lobbied scores of wavering Democrats in White House meetings and phone calls, the "gang of six" and the House's timber caucus, known as Forestry 2000, did their share. A private capital gains coalition that included venture capitalists, the securities industry, small business interests, and others also worked the lawmakers. Democratic leaders tried "sweet persuasion," as Foley put it. It was not enough. The size of their 239–190 defeat on September 28 surprised pundits who called it a serious loss for the new team.

Personal wounds seemed deep. In a call to Archer after the House vote—a call that he did not realize was piped into a room of reporters—Bush said he was "displeased with Gephardt, the way he made it so personal." Rostenkowski had a lot more to be unhappy about. He had been frustrated by White House insistence on pushing the issue after he and other Democratic leaders warned that it would affect interbranch relations. He was the subject of a biting, *Wall Street Journal* story September 19 that said "the usually shrewd Chicago pol acted like a puppy dog to Mr. Bush, weakening when his pride and vanity were stroked by the President."[13]

A month later, he told a group of insurance company executives, "If I sound bitter, it's because I feel that way."[14] When I asked Rostenkowski at year-end whether he still thought, as he said at midyear, that "when the time comes," Bush will "make the right decision," he replied, "I'm starting to have my doubts."

■   ■   ■   ■

Looking on from across the Capitol was another rookie Democratic leader. Mitchell had witnessed the indignities suffered by House leaders. He had seen the *Democrats in Disarray* banner that splashed across *Congressional Quarterly Weekly Report*'s September 30 cover or equally biting headlines after the House vote.[15] He surely had heard the whispered doubts about whether House leaders had what it takes. (Almost everyone in Washington was voicing them.) Mitchell had already faced pressure in his own ranks to more aggressively confront Bush, and he had been doing some of that. But when the capital gains issue hit the Senate, this former federal judge had a wonderful issue on which to show he could be more than cerebral. He could be plenty tough as well.

The Senate debate turned philosophy, or at least consistency, on its head. Mitchell had long supported the idea of a differential, and he even offered an amendment to the Senate's 1986 tax reform bill that, while designed mostly to change the tax rates, would have restored a differential, too. Throughout 1989, he expressed continued support, although he said such a change would have to come in the context of other provisions that would make the code more progressive and not swell the deficit. Packwood was even more awkwardly situated. As Mitchell reminded everyone, it was Packwood's tax reform bill that eliminated the differential in 1986, and Packwood had rough things to say back then about Mitchell's amendment to restore it. "So we have brought the capital gains differential back," Packwood said in that floor debate. "It is the biggest single loophole for the income class above $200,000." More harshly, Republican John H. Chafee of Rhode Island said of Mitchell that "by restoring the differential between capital gains and ordinary income, the senator from Maine is leading us into that old quagmire from which we are trying to extricate ourselves. Much of the artful dodging that now takes place under our code will once again be encouraged. Deal after deal will be structured to be a capital gain."

Of the 53 voting, 49 Republicans opposed Mitchell in 1986. But now, a new Republican president was engaged in bitter battle with a new Democratic leader, each hoping to emerge stronger. Bush needed GOP help. At least publicly, Senate Republicans stood firmly behind him. Now arguing that the capital gains change of 1986 was *not* the key element of tax reform that he once suggested, Packwood said in October as he unveiled his own capital gains cut, "The president campaigned on capital gains. He won an election in which capital gains was a major issue. And I think he's entitled to have that bill put before the Congress."

By then, Bentsen and Mitchell (a Finance Committee member) had kept an earlier capital gains proposal from Packwood out of Finance's tax bill on a 10–10 vote. That gave Mitchell a big victory. Rather than needing to strip a capital gains cut out, as the House leaders had to do, Mitchell just had to keep the pending bill intact. But along with GOP support, a capital gains differential had much Democratic backing. Majority Whip Cranston was a longtime supporter, as were numerous southern and midwestern conservatives. David L. Boren of Oklahoma, the lone Democratic vote for Packwood's cut in the Finance Committee, made it clear that he wanted to pursue the issue on the floor. Boren and Graham spearheaded an effort among a dozen or so colleagues to draft a Democratic plan.

In moving to quash such activity, Mitchell's tack was far different than that of the House Democrats. Whereas Foley and Gephardt had appealed to class-based arguments, concerns about revenue losses and the long-range path of the deficit, Mitchell left those philosophical arguments for his floor speeches. In the privacy of Senate offices, Mitchell asked Democrats to protect his emerging stature as a Senate leader, particularly as he confronted a first-year president. In mid-October, on the night before Boren, Graham, Cranston, Bryan, Lieberman, and Dennis DeConcini of Arizona were expected to unveil a Democratic capital gains plan, Mitchell talked them out of it. Then, and at other times, he asked a simple question: "Do you want to give George Bush a win?"

By all accounts, Mitchell's was a sterling performance. "He was very, very effective," Bloomfield, who was working with the dissident Democrats before Mitchell reined them in, said in early November when Mitchell seemed assured of victory. "I mean, this is worse than LBJ." Most Democrats would not budge, although the White House had calculated that 22—more than a third—had expressed support for a capital gains differential at one time or another. No, they would not desert their rookie leader. There was something in it for them as well. As Sasser told me later, "I think it indicates to the administration that they can't work their will over here in the Senate. They're going to have to work *with* us and deal *with* us."

Nor would Republicans carry the fight as far as the White House wanted. Packwood tried to make the case and attract Democratic votes. Along the way, he gave deficit concerns the same short shrift as had Jenkins and Archer. To pay for the permanent capital gains cut that he proposed, he joined with Sen. William V. Roth, a Delaware Republican, to offer a "back-loaded" IRA: Instead of getting a tax deduction for contributions, individuals would pay no tax when they withdrew money at retirement. The new IRA would raise money in the short run as holders of current IRAs transferred their money into the new ones and paid taxes on it at that time. But, according to a CBO staff memo, the plan would eventually cost about $10 billion more (in inflation-adjusted dollars) than it took in. Even Brady, at Finance's hearing in late September, expressed concern about long-term losses with this approach. But that was before Packwood hooked it to his capital gains plan.

Republicans, however, would not jeopardize their relations with Democrats or challenge Senate procedures, no mat-

ter how badly the White House wanted a capital gains win.
When Democratic leaders in early October offered to strip the
reconciliation bill of items with no connection to deficit cutting, Republicans latched on to the idea. True, the Democrats
obviously would use this procedure to rule out attempts to cut
the capital gains rate. But Mitchell had already made it clear
that he planned to force Republicans to find 60 votes for capital gains, not just a majority of 51. To do so, Mitchell could
use Gramm-Rudman's technical rules or mount a filibuster.
Republicans, with 45 votes, knew they could not find 60 to
stop a filibuster—not with Mitchell holding most Democrats
in line. So, they thought, why not use the Democratic offer to
strip out items that they themselves did not like? When White
House officials, not prepared to give up on reconciliation as a
vehicle for capital gains, resisted, several Republicans reacted
angrily. A capital gains cut, they said, was not worth the legislative junk that would come with it. The White House "got
plenty of guff on that," Domenici told me later.

Nor did Republicans follow through on threats to offer a
capital gains amendment to each bill that came to a floor vote.
That strategy, Darman said in October, was supposed to make
some Democrats face the prospect of voting repeatedly against
something they had previously and publicly supported. About
to force the issue on a few occasions, Republicans found themselves in embarrassing postures. When Packwood offered an
amendment to an Eastern European aid bill, Democrats accused him of blocking American efforts to spur democracy
behind the Iron Curtain. When Steve Symms of Idaho expressed interest in delaying votes on a Bush-Democrat minimum wage hike unless he could offer a capital gains cut,
Democrats roared. Howard Metzenbaum, an Ohio Democrat,
responded:

> I have seen a Republican party that day in and day out
> stands up and fights for the rich of the country and is totally in-
> different to the problems of those who earn far less, those who
> earn $3.35 an hour. What kind of a party is it that sits across
> the aisle and is concerned only about those who make the most
> money in this country and does not have enough compassion

to concern itself about the people working for the lowest wages in this country?

Republicans even threatened to offer an amendment to the must-pass debt limit bill. Packwood expressed confidence in breaking Democratic unity behind a filibuster if, to support one, Democrats raised the odds of a default.

To avert such a high-risk showdown, Democratic and Republican leaders reached a backroom deal to give the White House two floor votes on a capital gains cut, both of which would need 60 votes to carry. In mid-November, a week before Congress adjourned for the year, Republicans could muster just 51. Mitchell claimed victory. So, too, did the White House, which noted that a Senate majority had voted for a differential. And yet, the whole experience had a surreal aspect to it. During debate on the first vote, several Democrats said they were reluctant to vote against Packwood's plan, for they liked the idea of a capital gains cut. Mitchell began his speech against the proposal by reminding everyone that he likes the concept of a differential. Weeks later, he acknowledged that for all his success in 1989, he probably could not block Bush's efforts again in 1990. Bentsen said he would be interested in cutting the rate. Rostenkowski said he would not stand in the way.

■   ■   ■   ■

On the Senate floor before the first of the two votes, Dole said, "This is not a contest between the president of the United States and the majority leader of the U.S. Senate." But, of course, he knew better. It was a contest—a war, really—between two powerful men who were trying not only to secure their roles as national leaders with whom to be reckoned, but to set the tone for future clashes. The Senate leader had won, as the House leaders had lost less than two months earlier. That other, perhaps more important, substantive issues took a back seat in Washington while the battles in both chambers raged was unfortunate, but it was probably unavoidable. Not only was the goal of deficit cutting almost perverted, as it would have been if either Jenkins-Archer or the Packwood plan had made its way into the law. But the months of fierce combat left enough personal scars to raise questions about whether the White House and Congress would ever get to the Big Deal.

At about the same time, legislation to help American families cope with social change fell victim to different pressures. Child care, the subject of heated debate between the parties, nevertheless died more because of a split within Democratic ranks. The Earned Income Tax Credit, a favorite of both parties, was left untouched in 1989 because Washington could not find the money needed to finance the expansion that many wanted. Whereas the capital gains fight helped block efforts to cut the deficit, battles over child care and related issues showed how hard it would be to create or expand programs while the deficit remained large. It is to the yearlong debate over "family issues," and why so little was accomplished in 1989, that we now turn.

CHAPTER EIGHT

MARIAN'S MEMO

It was a most unusual letter. "This memo is for the record," Marian Wright Edelman, president of the Children's Defense Fund (CDF), wrote November 14, 1989, to House Democrats Thomas J. Downey and George Miller.

> Without doubt, it is the saddest memo I have written in 20 years of lobbying on behalf of children. Its purpose is to let thousands and thousands of child care and Head Start advocates, women, and working parents all around the country—who have worked unceasingly for years to push child care to the top of the national agenda and to establish a safe, affordable child care system—know that if child care legislation is not enacted this year, the two of you will deserve the full blame for this tragic and unnecessary outcome.

Nearly a year earlier, Edelman's group had honored Miller, who chairs the House Select Committee on Children, Youth and Families, at CDF's 15th anniversary dinner. But in late 1989, she was hopping mad. In a string of bitter denunciations unleashed on her estranged allies, Edelman complained that Downey and Miller had privately plotted to kill the Act for Better Child Care (ABC), a Democrat-backed, $1.75 billion child care measure that passed both houses and for which she had long worked. Dismissing a Downey-Miller al-

ternative as inadequate, she asked, "Is having it all your way
or nothing" worth killing all child care legislation, throwing
away the work of many other lawmakers, and alienating the
nation's huge child care constituency that had once trusted
them? "The power you have used to impede and destroy rather
than affirm the hopes and work of countless children and parents and child care workers, and the trust and respect with
which they once held you, is a costly temporary 'victory' for
you at the expense of children and the country," she wrote at
the end of three pages.

So harsh was the letter that Rostenkowski joined Democratic and Republican members of Ways and Means's human
resources subcommittee, on which Downey served as the acting chairman, three days later in responding. "We were dis-
turbed by the personal nature of the memo's attack," they
wrote, "and the fact that the apparent purpose of it was to
bully two members of Congress into supporting a policy with
which they don't agree. Tom Downey and George Miller are
no enemies of children or child care; you know that as well as
we." When I visited Edelman a month later, after other child
care activists had privately fretted that her memo would come
back to haunt them, she showed no remorse. Yes, she said, she
would do it again. If quieter lobbying would not succeed, she
would go public. As for the letter she got back, she laughed
and said, "I loved the idea that poor old children are bullying
Mr. Rostenkowski and the Ways and Means subcommittee. I
mean, can you imagine? If it weren't so funny—these folks
who deal with corporate interests, and these people who deal
with elderly needs, and these folks who deal with really high,
upper [income] groups, they have to yell about our bullying
them. You know, I must say, the reaction I get back from the
field is, everybody said, 'Oh, you bully, you!' "

Humorous or not, Edelman's exchange with Rostenkowski & Co. brought a bitter end to a child care battle in
1989 that no one would have predicted. Many policy makers
had expected Washington to turn the nation's growing interest
in "family issues" into a new child care initiative and maybe
legislation on related issues. By 1989, liberals and conserva-

tives had achieved what had become rare in modern American politics: a consensus. They focused on the same problems and often on the same tools to solve them, such as the Earned Income Tax Credit (EITC). Asked to delineate the issues of concern, Robert Greenstein, director of the Center on Budget and Policy Priorities, said:

> That there are a lot of poor children; that there are a lot of poor children who grow up without good education, good skills, good health care, and maybe more likely as a result both to be poor and to be less productive members of the work force; and also that there are a lot of working families with children that are not on welfare, that are doing what we say we want them to do—they're working—but they're still poor; and that, in addition, there are families of moderate income as well as families that are poor that are working, and that are hard-pressed, and that are incurring a lot of child care costs; finally, that there are a growing number of working families without health care coverage.

Edelman had high hopes for 1989. She had attended the Democratic and Republican conventions a year earlier, the first time she was at either in a quarter-century. The Reagan era was over, she explained later, no matter which presidential candidate won. With half of the nation's most important leaders in Atlanta and the other half later in New Orleans, she hoped to spread her message about children to as many as possible. If, as seemed likely, the nation turned again to Washington to solve its social problems, she did not want children left out. Nor, it seemed, did anyone else. Just a few months after the Senate, in late 1988, deadlocked over child care and other family-related proposals, the White House and Congress moved in early 1989 to face child care again. But the key players had different ideas about what to do. Republicans clashed with Democrats, Democrats with each other. While Senate Democrats overcame their differences and pushed through a measure to expand child care services and help the working poor, their House counterparts could not do so. A dispute between two powerful committees, which House leaders failed to resolve, as to who would control the flow of funds to these programs prevented Congress from sending a bill to Bush (much less getting his approval).

But Washington's failure on the child care front did not result merely from a clash of big egos, although that played a role. In a broader sense, child care fell victim to competing visions of how activists can squeeze money out of Washington in an age of huge deficits. It was the kind of fight likely to be repeated, as long as the deficit hovered over policy making. Nor was this the only item under the rubric of "family issues" that, while backed by most sides of the political spectrum, fell victim to Washington's deficit troubles. Yes, Bush and Congress raised the minimum wage after nearly a year of wrangling. But that was largely because the costs would fall on the private sector. More notably, they could not find the money to expand the more popular, and probably more effective, EITC for working families with children. Although they expressed hopes of moving a child care bill to fruition in early 1990, the nation's leaders would likely continue to have problems in reconciling their inability to eliminate the deficit with their desire to allocate more benefits to Americans.

■   ■   ■   ■

Children have long held a special place in American politics, normally because candidates have picked them up to kiss their cheeks, hoping to delight their voting parents. But in 1988, kids moved from the fringes of American politics to the core at the national, state, and local levels. They were no longer just the cute, cuddly things whose tummies you pinched, whose sides you tickled. They were "capital," as one writer put it, youngsters in whom America needed to invest today so they would become productive members of society tomorrow.[1] Facing demographic change at home and economic competition from abroad, the nation could ill afford to treat its kids the way it had been.

Asked why children's issues received such attention in the late 1980s, Greenstein talked about the years of public education performed by Edelman's CDF and other groups, about the growing interest in these issues by newspaper reporters and editorial writers, and about the slew of reports from business groups worried about tomorrow's work force. All told, he said:

> Part of what's . . . being reflected here is sort of some basic economic pressures that then get manifested in various ways and through various kinds of institutions—those simply being that economically, the country increasingly cannot afford the degree of child poverty that it might have been able to afford in the seventies, when you had lots more people looking for jobs and there were jobs going around and employers could be more choosy, and the work force didn't require quite as high a degree of education and skills.

Added Edelman:

> The business community woke up and discovered that, my goodness, we have a shrinking pool of kids and not enough folk coming into the labor force, and more and more of those folk are minority and women. And so, these demographics of children and families began to affect the bottom line of powerful segments. And so, *who* says something makes a difference. So it wasn't just these child care advocates out there talking. College presidents, along with the business community, began to understand that they had a shrinking pool of good kids coming to the universities and, my goodness, there's a connection between what's in the pipeline and what ends up here. So you had powerful new voices who raised these demographics in a new term, in a new way.

Maybe the best example of these "powerful new voices" was the Committee for Economic Development, a respected organization of business executives and educators, which issued *Children in Need* in 1987. The report stated:

> This nation cannot continue to compete and prosper in the global arena when more than one fifth of our children live in poverty and a third grow up in ignorance. . . . If present trends continue without corrective action, American business will confront a severe employment crisis. This scarcity of well-educated and well-qualified people in the work force will seriously damage this country's competitive position in an increasingly challenging global market.[2]

Similarly, for Ford and Carter's *American Agenda,* such domestic policy experts as former Sen. Edmund S. Muskie, a
Maine Democrat, wrote:

> We recommend a national campaign to assure a world-class
> work force in the year 2000. We can make a high-yield invest-
> ment in America's human capital by improving our education
> and job training. Shortcomings in those areas will jeopardize
> America's future living standard and competitive position in
> the world economy.[3]

The growing labor shortage, of which Edelman and
Greenstein spoke, was already affecting corporate decision
making in the late 1980s. To attract workers, firms across the
nation began to build homes on the land they owned, guarantee mortgage loans to help workers get them more cheaply,
and lend money for down payments (sometimes forgiving the
debt later). Hospitals, facing a severe shortage of nurses, re-
cruited from overseas; companies involved in computer science and electrical engineering were expected to do the same.
The nation's leaders considered changes in immigration policies that would rank prospective immigrants on the basis of
their job qualifications. For those unwilling to look abroad,
more companies tapped into the disabled population, which
welcomed the labor shortage as a godsend. Companies also
began to look more favorably at hiring the young. More hired
teen-agers, especially for part-time jobs that adults did not
want. Companies and trade groups lobbied the federal and
state governments to loosen child labor laws. Violations of
those laws rose sharply in the 1980s.

In the Washington, D.C. area, where the shortage grew
increasingly severe, some companies provided their own
transport services to bring workers to and from home, even
from as far away as Pennsylvania. Others hired the hardcore
unemployed: the homeless, the mentally ill, recovering ad-
dicts, former prison inmates, and so on. To assimilate them
into their work forces, the companies provided housing and
counseling, job training, and other services. Still other companies that could not find enough jobtakers used unusual

recruiting techniques. Giant Foods inserted job applications in its customers' grocery bags, Domino's Pizza advertised for drivers on its pizza boxes, and McDonald's put job applications on its counters, with the benefits of working at a fast-food chain explained on the other side.

Unfortunately, just when they had grown increasingly important to the nation's future, more and more children were being reared in poverty and ill health, without the necessities to guarantee their development. In his Index of Social Health of Children and Youth, Marc Miringoff, director of the Fordham Institute for Innovation in Social Policy, reported that 1987, the last year for which figures were available, was "the worst year for children in two decades."[4] His index, comparing data back to 1970, included such variables as infant mortality, child abuse, children living in poverty, teen-age suicide, teenage drug abuse, and high-school dropouts. More specifically, poverty among children under 18, which had dipped from 27 to 14 percent between 1959 and 1969, rose after that and hovered around 20 percent throughout the 1980s; for kids under 6, the rate was about 22 percent. For children under 14, poverty was higher in America than in Australia, Canada, and the United Kingdom, and more than twice the level in West Germany, Norway, Sweden, and Switzerland. This nation also ranked ahead of the others in the percentages of children living way below the poverty line and of families with kids living way below it. As researchers Timothy Smeeding, Barbara Boyle Torrey, and Martin Rein, who compiled these figures, put it, "American children are not only at a disadvantage relative to American elderly; they are at a disadvantage relative to their peers in all of the other countries examined here, except Australia."[5]

Along with their life of poverty, or indeed because of it, came a host of other problems. The National Association of Children's Hospitals and Related Institutions, representing 100 children's hospitals in this nation and Canada, warned in late 1989 that more poor children were at risk because, with the rise in their numbers, only about half were covered by Medicaid. The number of children without health insurance had risen, as had the numbers of abused kids. Suicide among children was rising. Vaccination rates for young children against several major diseases leveled off or fell, and incidents of whooping cough and other ailments rose. The number of babies born to unmarried teens grew as a share of all births. Perhaps most appalling of all, the nation ranked 18th in the world in infant mortality in 1986, behind such nations as Spain, Singapore, and Hong Kong. If only figures for infant mortality among American blacks were used, the nation would have ranked 28th, behind Cuba and Bulgaria. Those not victimized by health problems faced high odds of a violent death. In 1989, the Health and Human Services Department reported that of children at least one year of age who died in 1987, an astonishing 10 percent died of gunshot wounds.

In study after study, analysts had identified several cost-effective federal programs for disadvantaged children. Child immunization saved $10 for every $1 spent to combat rubella, measles, mumps, polio, and other diseases, according to Miller's committee. For every $1 invested in preschool education, such as through Head Start, the nation saved $6 later in costs associated with special education, public assistance, and crime. The WIC program saved up to $3 in short-term hospital costs for every $1 invested in prenatal care. Prenatal care through Medicaid saved $2 in health costs for children for every $1 invested. Unfortunately, these and other programs were not reaching nearly all needy children in the 1980s. Less than 20 percent of eligible children participated in Head Start. Only 44 percent were receiving WIC. Just half of the needy received compensatory education through Chapter I. Less than half of all disabled children were in early intervention programs. The share of children from ages 1 to 4 who were immunized against major diseases ranged from 74 to 87 percent, depending on the disease.

Even the healthy faced serious obstacles to prosperity, the most notorious of which was the nation's education system. Test scores of American students lagged behind those of other nations. Compared to students in 12 other nations, American students finished last in biology, 11th in chemistry, and 9th in physics from 1983 to 1986. Lab work, which could have improved the science knowledge of students, was less available. Student scores on standardized math and English tests also fell in the post–World War II period before picking up slightly in recent years. Students did not know much about economics, either. A 1988 survey by the Joint Council on Economic Education found that students could correctly answer only 40 percent of multiple-choice questions about such basic economic concepts as inflation, profits, and the GNP.

By 1989, the ignorance of American youth had assumed an almost comic quality. "When some of our students actually have trouble locating America on a map of the world," Bush said in his February 9 budget speech, "it is time for us to map a new approach to education." Only half of Americans, aged 18 or older, knew the Sandinistas and Contras were fighting in Nicaragua. Just over half could locate England on a map or knew that Joseph Stalin ruled the Soviet Union during World War II. American high school and college students scored at least as dismally on surveys to test cultural knowledge. The effects of such ignorance were no laughing matter, however. The 700,000 youths who dropped out of high school each year cost the nation an estimated $240 billion in lost earnings and taxes over their lifetimes. An equal number, as *Fortune* magazine said in late 1988, "could not read their high school diplomas."[6] At the National Economic Commission, Brock called public education "the most dangerous of all the threats facing the United States," and added, "If we solve all other problems and fail to deal with this one, all will come to naught. This nation cannot survive if it doesn't care enough about its children to prepare them better than we're preparing ours."

■   ■   ■   ■

Activists spread the message: Children were "in trouble." Public awareness grew. Issues once reserved for social scientists assumed a new political importance. Examples abounded. Take, for instance, the Democratic National Convention. As the *New York Times* wrote at the time, "Michael Dukakis's speech accepting the Democratic nomination ... conveyed no strong organizing theme—yet the whole convention did and it was a startling theme indeed: children."[7] The first day brought storyteller Garrison Keillor and 35 kids to lead in the Pledge of Allegiance, and Texas Treasurer Ann Richards' speech in which she mentioned her "nearly perfect granddaughter, named Lily"; the second brought a now-grown "John-John" Kennedy to introduce his uncle, the Massachusetts senator, as well as Jesse Jackson's five children to introduce their father; the third brought a nominating speech from Arkansas Gov. Bill Clinton that, although best remembered for its unbearable length, discussed such themes as teen-age pregnancy, infant mortality, and education for the poor; the fourth brought Dukakis's speech, which included references to his own son and daughter-in-law—then expecting their first child—and to the need for a federal child care program so young parents no longer have to choose "between the jobs they need and the children they love."

Not to be outdone, Bush issued an "Invest in Children" campaign paper, calling for measures to cut infant mortality, enhance child nutrition, strengthen immunization and health services, extend child care tax credits, expand the Head Start program, and better protect the rights of children victimized by crime. "Our children are our future," the paper said. "The way we treat our children reflects our values as a nation and as a people. ... George Bush believes that our national character can be measured by how we care for our children—all of the nation's children—how we invest in them, how they grow, and what we convey to them. ... George Bush believes our children—especially those at risk—require a more intensely focused effort, by all of us."

Yet, it was not so much what Bush and Dukakis said that was striking, but where they chose to talk. Day-care centers were a common stop on the campaign trail in 1988, so much so that Edelman later joked, "those poor old kids ... must have gotten awfully tired of cameras." In a two-day period in July, for instance, Bush visited a day-care center in Tysons

Corner, in a Virginia suburb of Washington; Dukakis went to one in Secaucus, New Jersey; and Bentsen pulled into one at the University of California at Los Angeles. As the *Washington Post* wrote later, "In the realm of political imagery, the 1988 presidential campaign will be remembered as the election when day-care centers replaced factories as the backdrop and battleground of choice."[8]

Meanwhile, by the late 1980s, at least 34 governors had outlined children's initiatives in their State-of-the-State messages. More specifically, New York's Cuomo declared in 1988 that the next 10 years should comprise a "decade of the child," and he began to propose a series of programs. In early 1989, Virginia Gov. Gerald I. Baliles pushed through his legislation to set up a Council on Child Day Care and Early Childhood Development to provide child care for disadvantaged four-year-olds. Around that time, Pennsylvania's Gov. Robert P. Casey was pushing for stiffer penalties for child abuse, while governors and legislators in other states debated whether to offer tax credits to encourage private day care and boost local taxes to bolster education. In California later in 1989, prominent citizens issued a "children's report card," giving the most populous state an overall grade of "D" for the conditions in which its 7.6 million children lived. In Fairfax County, Virginia, the school system decided to stop its long-standing practice of closing elementary schools early on Mondays—done to give teachers time to plan—because of complaints from working women who had trouble finding baby-sitters and did not want their kids to be home alone.

Fairfax County's decision pointed to the new demographic facts of life in the United States. No longer did the average American family follow the "Ozzie and Harriet" model: dad at work, mom at home with the kids. Fewer than 10 percent of them now fit that model, according to the Labor Department. "I regret that we have reached the situation where only 1 in 10 American families have a parent at home," Democrat Christopher J. Dodd of Connecticut, the Senate's prime force behind its ABC legislation, told the Senate during its June debate:

I did not grow up that way. I never remember a single day
that I ever came home from school and my mother was not
there. I never remember a day, and I wish every American
child could have that blessing, could have a parent at home....
That is not the issue. The question is not what we might like
or wish or hope for or regret. What we have to deal with are
facts and trends. And the facts are the people are working,
single mothers or both spouses, because they have to.

By 1988, women comprised 45 percent of the labor force.
Just over half of the mothers with kids of age 2 or younger
were working, as were 57 percent of those with preschool children and 65 percent of those with kids under age 18. Looked
at another way, about half of the 22 million kids under age
6 had mothers who worked, as did more than half of the 27
million between ages 6 and 13. Many working mothers were
inspired by sheer need. Almost two thirds of them were single, widowed, divorced, or separated, or had husbands earning
less than $15,000 a year. Working wives contributed an aver-
age of 30 percent of their family's income, although the figure
was higher for low-income families. Indeed, about a quarter
of working mothers provided the only support for their children. In a 1983 *New York Times* poll, 71 percent of mothers
who worked said they did so primarily out of need, not because they wanted to. Nor were the trends expected to sub-
side. By the year 2000, 61.5 percent of women were expected
to be working, according to the Labor Department. Between
1986 and the next century, an estimated three fifths of new
entrants into the work force would be women. By 1995, an
estimated two thirds of the preschool kids and four fifths of
the school-age kids would have working mothers.

Work and family, once the distinct phases of a man's day,
were now the confused, overlapping parts of a woman's. An estimated 1.6 million unemployed mothers with preschool age
children would have looked for work had they found adequate
child care. "It is well documented that every day, 5,000 mothers turn down paid jobs because of a lack of adequate, affordable child care," Rep. Nick Joe Rahall, a West Virginia
Democrat, told the House in October. Rather than reject job
offers, others had to leave their kids alone. The figures were

staggering: more than 2 million "latchkey" kids left alone for part of each day; 1.8 million children between 5 and 13 left unsupervised by an adult; and, according to Sen. Orrin G. Hatch, a Utah Republican who worked closely with Dodd on the Senate's ABC bill, "20,000 children less than 4 years of age with no adult supervision during daylight hours."

While liberals and conservatives debated how best to provide child care, few doubted that those without any suffered the most. In telling the Senate how his amendment to the ABC bill would encourage schools to set up day care, Missouri's Bond said of the "latchkey" kids: "These children have been the focus of much concern, stemming from the fact that these children may be exposed to a variety of dangers and are at risk for school absenteeism and other school-related problems as well as for emotional problems caused by loneliness, fear, and lack of opportunity to interact with peers." In a Louis Harris survey of 1,000 teachers in 1987, most said that a major reason why some children had trouble in school was that they lacked adult supervision after school. In a reader survey by *Sprint*, a magazine for fourth- to sixth-graders, kids were asked to write about "a situation that is very scary to you." A large majority wrote about being home alone.

■   ■   ■   ■

Just what all of the figures indicated was unclear. To the Labor Department and others, they were nothing about which to be alarmed. "This report finds no evidence in support of the contention that there is a general, national shortage of available child care," the department wrote in 1988. When such providers as day-care centers, nurseries and preschools, relatives, and nonrelatives were taken into account, just 3.9 percent of all children up to age 14 were caring for themselves. And yet, the department wrote,"it does appear that certain types of day care may be in short supply in some communities," including "infant care, sick child care, and after school care."[9]

ABC's proponents painted a gloomier picture. Space shortages and long waiting lists showed up in surveys of centers in various states. In New York, 135,000 licensed day-care placements were available in 1987 for an estimated 830,000 to 1.2 million preschool or school-age kids in need. That year, 136,254 families in California were waiting for child care openings. Public housing projects had a combined waiting list of about 96,000. More recently, according to lawmakers who described their states' situations during the 1989 debate, Maryland offered only 90,000 child care slots for 588,000 children who needed them, while Connecticut offered 90,000 for 280,000 waiting youngsters.

Cities faced similar problems. New York City, for instance, reported that 250,000 kids under age 5 were competing for 44,000 licensed day-care slots. In a 1989 survey by the National League of Cities, child care was listed as one of the two most urgent needs of dwellers in the nation's 278 largest urban centers. Nor did the wait tend to be short. In a 52-city survey a year earlier, the United States Conference of Mayors found that the average wait for subsidized day care was 38 weeks. In the following cities and counties, the average wait exceeded a year: Cambridge, Massachusetts; Evanston, Illinois; Hartford, Connecticut; Dade County, Florida; Irvine, San Diego, Santa Barbara, and Santa Monica, all in California; Somerville, Massachusetts; Trenton, New Jersey; and Washington, D.C. An estimated 45 percent of the need for licensed child care in the 52 cities went unmet, with unmet needs reaching 80 percent or more in Oakland, California and Lincoln, Nebraska.

When available, child care was often too expensive for parents who, in turn, were forced to stay home with their children rather than work. By the late 1980s, child care was the fourth largest family expense, behind housing, food, and taxes, according to the National Commission on Working Women. Average yearly costs for day care were estimated to be $3,000. As Moynihan noted in introducing a child care bill with Packwood in early 1989, such costs alone would consume 40 percent of the salary of minimum wage workers. After studying data for 1986, the Census Bureau announced that while working mothers paid 6 percent of their income on child care, poor women paid 22 percent of theirs.

Child care problems were particularly unsettling to employers, for these problems could affect the productivity of workers. If, during working hours, parents were thinking about the kids they had left alone, or the day-care center that had them, or the day-care bills coming due, they were *not* thinking about their jobs. The nation could ill afford such worker distractions; it was still suffering from the mysterious drop in productivity growth that had begun in the early 1970s. Prospects of a growing labor shortage also prodded more employer interest in child care. If workers could pick and choose where to work, the highly skilled ones would compare not only salary offers but also compensation plans in which child care might be included. As the Labor Department wrote of management's interest in child care, "Perhaps the key motivator has been the widespread agreement in business, industry and finance that the recruitment of good workers is a real concern. Since child care helps attract and keep employees, management has been prompted to act."[10]

And so the number of corporations offering child care aid grew from about 100 to 3,300 from 1978 to 1988. Offered were on-site or nearby day-care centers; subsidies for child care chosen by employees; and other employer assistance in helping workers find child care, such as sponsored seminars. Washington's largest law firm, Arnold & Porter, opened an emergency child care facility in late 1988, two years after another D.C. firm opened what was apparently the first center in any law firm in America. New York City's police department, hoping to attract women to its force, began work on a day-care center in late 1988. The Pentagon, the world's largest office building, began work on one in early 1989; it already operated more than 600 child development centers at its installations around the world. Also that year, the Air Force Logistics Command offered child care to its 83,000 civilian employees, and the CIA opened its first day-care center.

Child care, in and of itself, had become big business. Kinder-Care, America's largest day-care chain with 17,000 employees in 40 states and Canada, had provided services for more than 1 million children over the last two decades. More developers offered child care facilities to attract businesses to their new buildings. The number of child care consultants, who taught employers how to structure family benefit plans for employees, was growing, as was the number of groups representing nannies. Also growing were the number of centers offering nighttime care to help parents with unusual schedules.

However helpful, Americans viewed the private sector's response to demographic change as inadequate. Three quarters of respondents to a Louis Harris poll in early 1989 expressed support for federal child care legislation. In a *Washington Post*-ABC poll, three fifths said that Washington should spend more on programs that care for the children of working parents who cannot afford to do so themselves. In other surveys, more than half of the respondents consistently supported a greater federal role in providing child care. The politicians heard about it, too. "In town after town," Sen. Thomas A. Daschle, a South Dakota Democrat, told the Senate in June, "I hear families say that they cannot find acceptable child care arrangements. . . . In addition, I have received numerous letters about the lack of financial assistance to help with the burden of child care costs."

Washington had not completely ignored the problem. It had spent sizable, though hardly excessive, amounts on child care over the years. Federal support dated back to 1943, when emergency child care was provided to help mothers working in wartime industries. After the war, such aid was phased out, although an outgrowth of this effort reportedly remains in operation in Santa Monica, California. Nearly 30 years later, Nixon vetoed Congress's attempt to establish a comprehensive, $2.1 billion child development program. Nevertheless, by the late 1980s, the government provided almost $7 billion a year in child care services from a hodgepodge of programs. Nearly $4 billion was distributed under the dependent care tax credit, which helped families offset child care costs if both parents worked. Other programs of child care aid were run by the Departments of Health and Human Services, Agriculture, Defense, Commerce, Education, and Housing and Urban Development.

That Washington would soon provide more was doubted by few. But the question of how to do so opened clear schisms along philosophical lines. With a few exceptions, Democrats and Republicans resumed their long-standing dispute over the proper method of help, with the former pushing for a new or expanded program of grants and the latter looking more toward distributing benefits through the tax code. Only because Hatch worked closely with Dodd on the Senate's 1989 version of ABC did the battle escape the stricter brand of partnership to which it had been subjected during the presidential politics of 1988. With Bush and Dukakis battling across the land, the GOP successfully filibustered an earlier ABC bill on the Senate floor, killing it as the 100th Congress finished its business just before the November elections.

The 101st Congress would be different, if only because of Hatch. The Utah Republican admitted to the resulting discomfort that he felt. Speaking of ABC, he told the Senate in June, "There is a lot of false information, and unfortunately most of it comes from my [GOP] side. Most of it comes from people who in the past have supported me, some of whom have indicated they will never support me again because I have cosponsored the Act for Better Child Care. If that is the case, so be it." Moments later, he returned to his predicament. "To say that this bill has been controversial is probably the understatement of the year. Since I made the decision a year ago to try to work out a compromise with Senator Dodd on this bill, I have been personally likened to Karl Marx, Benedict Arnold, and even Brutus in public print." The bitterness of Hatch's Republican colleagues remained obvious as the debate unfolded. Moments after Hatch thanked several of the Democrats by name for their help, Dole pointedly noted, "I noticed that the senator from Utah praised everybody but the Republicans, and that is his right."

■   ■   ■   ■

As the public clamored for action, Washington put child care and related issues on a legislative fast track. Wright appointed a task force in March 1989 to review children's issues.

Its recommendations were incorporated in the House's fiscal 1990 budget resolution and then, in modified form, in the final resolution after compromises with the Senate. With funds assumed for child care and for increases in Head Start, WIC, Medicaid, children's health, nutrition and immunization, and other programs, CDF's director of government affairs, Mary Bourdette, said of the final resolution, "America's children scored a major victory . . . reflecting a critical shift in national spending priorities" and "the growing national concern about America's children and consensus in support of national action on their behalf."

But whether Washington would actually spend this money or try another approach was the subject of vigorous debate. Disputes broke down mainly along party lines. Democrats unveiled ABC while Republicans, in the White House and Congress, offered tax credit proposals that, they said, would distribute benefits more directly from Washington to America's families. But large segments of each party searched for a combined tax-and-spend approach. Ironically, the Downey-Miller plan—one of two main Democratic plans in the House—was quite similar to a Senate Republican alternative, offered by Dole, that Democrats in that chamber defeated.

At issue was Washington's proper role in expanding child care options for Americans. ABC's backers insisted that only their approach would address what they called the "three pillars" of child care needs: availability, affordability, and quality. ABC would have funneled $1.75 billion to the states, which in turn would have provided direct and indirect aid to 800,000 families. Most of the money was earmarked for direct aid. The rest was set aside to increase the supply and quality of child care. "I believe, as do the sponsors of ABC," Sen. Albert Gore, Jr., a Tennessee Democrat, told the Senate in June, "that the various tax credit proposals will not adequately respond to the pressing child care needs that American families are facing. Tax credits are not child care. Families of low and modest income need safe and affordable child care that can only come about if states have the resources and the incentives to increase the supply of child care providers and improve their child care standards." Gore and Downey, in fact, had drafted a proposal months earlier to expand the EITC. Gore was not backing away from that idea, he explained. He was just stressing that this alone would not address child care's "three pillars."

Republicans countered that they would rely on the free market, not government, to work those problems out. "The way to help working families meet their child care needs is to give them more money and let them use it in the way that best addresses their particular child care needs," Edwards, the House Republican Policy Committee chairman, said in explaining his child care plan of new and expanded tax credits. Similarly, Stenholm, who offered a conservative Democratic alternative, said at a *Washington Times* forum in August, "The ABC bill is a terrible bill and a terrible idea. To think that you can take the federal government, superimpose its will on the local people, the states and the local entities, in providing for child care—a terrible idea." To muster enough votes in Congress, insiders suggested that a final child care bill probably had to include tax as well as spending components.

House and Senate debates provided wonderful rhetorical flourishes, even if truth was often a casualty. *Bureaucracy*— that was a word that arose often. ABC would have required some added child care administration on the federal, state, and local levels. Whether this made the bill excessively bureaucratic was a debatable point. Dole and Dodd had perhaps the best exchange over it. "Let us face it," the minority leader told the Senate in June, "The ABC bill does not stand for Act for Better Child Care; it stands for Act for Bureaucratic Control. And we want to make that case. And we intend to make that case today, tomorrow, next week. This is important." Responding to Dole and others, an angry Dodd shot back moments later, "They know better than that. They know better. Our bill is not perfect at all. Of course, there are ways to improve it. But to suggest somehow that our goals and desires are to create some bureaucracy, some evil-headed monster to deprive people of their choice, that is how weak, that is how shallow, that is how empty their arguments are."

Choice—that was another term that assumed a large role in the debate. What kind of a child care "choice" should Washington offer to Americans? And what could Washington accomplish, in light of overarching demographic trends? Bush and many Republicans said that beneficiaries of federal aid should have the widest range of options: stay at home with the kids, work full-time, work part-time, and so on. Only if Washington gave them money directly, such as with new tax breaks, would their options remain open. If, instead, benefits were funneled through the states to help pay for slots in child care centers, then Washington would be unduly influencing the kind of child care that parents could choose. "At the center of my plan is parental choice," Bush said in March as he proposed new and expanded tax credits and an increased appropriation for Head Start. "The future of this country is in the hands of its families." He urged Congress to "make this burden lighter, and enable them to pursue the path they find best."

What conservatives feared, in essence, was an indirect attack on the "Ozzie and Harriet" model family. If day care provided in a formal center was subsidized, but that provided by a parent was not, Washington would be encouraging the former and discouraging the latter. Rather than staying at home with the kids, women might have more financial incentive to join the work force. That possibility did not sit well with social conservatives and others. "The key contention between us, first of all, is freedom of choice for a parent to choose what is best for his or her child," Rep. Paul B. Henry, a Michigan Republican, told the House in October. "We say that mother knows best, father knows best, not that Uncle Sam knows best in terms of where our children should be placed." At an American Enterprise Institute seminar nearly two years earlier, conservative writer George Gilder spoke in more alarmist terms about a "cult of child sacrifice" in which "the key demand is that the state exalt the full-time working mother above the mother who cares for her children at home; that the state financially punish the virtuous mother in order to make her subsidize the mother who pushes her children aside."

"Choice?" the ABC advocates replied. What kind of choice did low-income Americans have? They were stuck in a cycle of dead-end jobs or worse. Mothers, married or otherwise, had no real choice between working or staying home, unless they opted for welfare. If the nation wanted them to pull their own weight, the advocates said, Washington should help them do so. "What we are about are mothers who have no choice," Sen. Wyche Fowler, Jr., a Georgia Democrat, said in defending ABC to the Senate, "No choice as to whether to stay home or to go into the work force. . . . Why do they have no choice? Well, let us be honest. They have no choice because there are no fathers in the home. They have no choice because they are on welfare. And every year we debate how we can move mothers off welfare into the job market so that they become responsible taxpaying citizens. They cannot do that, they cannot work unless somebody looks after the kids."

Besides, ABC's backers said, conservative complaints that their bill favored the working mother over the one who stayed home were irrelevant. The issue was not whether Washington favored one group over another. Washington practiced discrimination like that in other ways, and nobody objected. It provided loans, for instance, to help students of modest means attend college. Only those who attended got the help. The issue was not whether Washington was discriminating. Rather, the issue was whether the nation supported the goals behind that discrimination. Americans seemed content with the idea of assisting would-be students. But when it came to child care, the president and many conservative allies found this discrimination to be quite obnoxious.

Standards—that was another subject for heated debate. Before compromising in the hope of pushing their bill into law, ABC's advocates hoped to establish federal standards under which day-care centers would operate. Conservatives objected. There goes "Big Brother," they said, imposing its will on local businesses trying to make an honest buck. "OK," said ABC's backers, "no federal standards. We will settle for state standards." After long negotiations, Edelman's CDF and other backers worked out an agreement on state standards with such important groups as the National Governors Association. Rather than impose its rules, Washington would draft model standards but force states only to enforce their own standards in certain broad areas.

Conservatives still did not like the idea. If standards were a state responsibility, then states did not need Washington's encouragement. Besides, the requirement that states impose their own standards was a burden in itself and could prove counterproductive; if day-care facilities could not meet the new standards, they might be forced to close. The supply of day care would shrink. Critics even expressed suspicions that state standards were a stepping-stone to federal ones. "If the standards are not binding on anyone, why are there going to be model standards?" Packwood asked the Senate in June. "Here is the reason: The organizations which are proponents of this bill—in their heart of hearts—wish they were mandated standards. . . . And two, three, four, five years from now when Senator Dodd and I and maybe others may be gone from this Senate, the same people who are lobbying for this bill from the outside will one day try to get federal mandatory standards again."

Nevertheless, supporters of state standards had an interesting point. Government often imposed standards on other kinds of businesses—businesses that handled items far less precious than America's children. "People need a license to cut your hair, but not to care for your child," Daschle told the Senate. "While states require that your car be inspected each year, there is no such requirement for the facility that takes care of your child. Our children deserve better protection." Stories about the problems in some centers were near legendary. Most child-care workers were poorly paid, prompting a large turnover in the staff. Many were poorly trained; some states and localities barely imposed any requirements at all on low-level center employees.

Accidents were rampant, deaths not infrequent. In 1989 alone, two babies died in a Huntington Beach, California, fire at a baby-sitter's house; a small girl was reportedly shaken to death by a baby-sitter in Los Angeles; another young girl died in Hartford, Connecticut, after a day-care operator left her alone in a car on a hot afternoon; an unlicensed day-care provider in Columbia, Maryland, was indicted for child abuse after leaving two toddlers tied up and unattended in her home; operators of an unlicensed center in Hattiesburg, Mississippi, faced murder and felony child abuse charges after one five-month-old died and another was seriously injured; and a Springfield, Virginia, day-care provider was indicted on felony child neglect charges after a 17-month-old boy suffered a skull fracture at her home. In 1987, a 10-month-old Springfield, Virginia, baby died after a day-care provider, convicted 19 years earlier of neglecting her own children, gave the child the drug imipramine to quiet her. A year earlier, two small children died and four others were injured when fire broke out in an unlicensed family day-care home in Brooklyn, New York. In the best-known case of all, little Jessica McClure survived her fall into a well at an unlicensed facility in Texas.

■   ■   ■   ■

The Senate Labor and Human Resources Committee approved its version of ABC on March 15, the day Bush unveiled his child care plan of tax credits. For the floor debate that began in mid-June, Mitchell attached ABC to a child health tax credit that Bentsen had pushed through the Finance Committee a few days earlier. Voting along party lines, the Senate defeated Dole's effort to replace Mitchell's package primarily with new tax benefits, including an expansion of the EITC. Moments later, it passed the package, 63–37. But in the House, the situation was more complicated. The Education and Labor Committee adopted its ABC bill in late June. In July, however, Ways and Means approved the competing Downey-Miller plan to send fewer child care dollars to the states—$350 million in 1991, $400 million a year after that—but to couple them with a big EITC increase. Each committee wanted its child care bill included in the reconciliation bill, which reached the House floor in late September.

ABC fit into the traditional Democratic approach to spending. It would have created a new program, funded in 1 of the 13 annual appropriations bills. Let's say, for instance, that Washington provided $1 billion for the program for 1990. For 1991, Washington would again decide how much money to provide—more, less, even none. The budget's "current services" baseline would have assumed, as a starting point, that the program would get $1 billion plus whatever was needed to offset inflation. But that was not guaranteed, and there was reason to fear it would not happen. The nation's leaders, constrained by Gramm-Rudman's deficit targets, would likely continue to aim their guns at the 13 appropriations bills. After all, these bills had to be voted on, whereas such huge entitlements as Social Security and Medicare continued automatically unless Washington specifically deemed otherwise. Under these conditions, annual child care funds were far from safe.

The other approach, favored by Downey, Miller, and others, would have provided fewer child care funds each year, but it would have done so in a different and perhaps more stable way. Rather than create a new program, the proponents wanted to expand the existing Title XX Social Services Block Grant, an entitlement of state grants, and earmark the new money for child care. Explaining his thinking, Miller told the House in October, "To avoid the vagaries of an annual appropriations process . . . I support a new child care program under Title XX, the Social Service Block Grant, as a substitute funding mechanism [for the ABC measure]. I believe strongly that Title XX, as an entitlement, is the more reliable funding mechanism and that adequate funds are more likely to reach those in need than through an appropriations process where funds have to be fought for every year." Similarly, in defending Downey and Miller from attack, the Ways and Means subcommittee members wrote to Edelman that their Title XX expansion would, among other things, "provide a more dependable stream of funding."

Unable to resolve the dispute between Downey, who was handling the Ways and Means measure, and Rep. August F. Hawkins, the Education and Labor Committee chairman and an old-fashioned liberal from California, Democratic leaders inserted both child care bills in the House reconciliation measure. All sides viewed this as a quick fix and assumed that the matter would be resolved later. At the time, the leaders had bigger child care problems to address. Having lost the capital gains fight, the new leaders needed to reassert their control against attempts by Republicans and conservative Democrats to split their party. Appealing to party unity, they rallied enough Democrats to defeat Edwards' child care substitute by a convincing margin. They had more trouble with Stenholm's, but managed to defeat it as well. But later that fall, Democratic leaders still could not resolve the committee dispute. They chose to put off the issue until early 1990, leaving all sides grumbling about a lack of leadership at the top.

However much this was a dispute about budgetary tactics, it was also one about "turf." Each committee wanted control over whatever child care initiative Washington enacted. Each played hard, and each accused the other of intransigence when meetings that House leaders hoped would foster a compromise in late 1989 did not do so. In one meeting, Downey said to Rep. Dale E. Kildee, an Education and Labor Democrat from Michigan and the House sponsor of ABC: "I'm going to get what I want. I'm going to get it with you or over you. But I'm going to get it." With so few opportunities for advocates to create or expand programs these days, one lobbyist mused, "Maybe it becomes more important to get that money" when an opportunity does come along.

But, for all the hullabaloo, none of the plans would have come close to tackling the nation's child care problems. Estimates on the annual cost of doing so approached $100 billion. Durenberger, the Minnesota Republican, estimated "conservatively" that the cost was $75 billion. In juxtaposing the Senate bill with national need, he compared Congress to a guy with "only one bucket of water to throw on a burning house." Douglas J. Besharov, a resident scholar at the American Enterprise Institute, wrote in a *Washington Post* column in 1988 that subsidizing middle-class child care would cost between $40 and $100 billion.[11] Rita Watson of Yale University's Bush Center in Child Development, put the cost at $90 billion if a network of subsidized centers with quality care included children up to 14 years of age.[12] What Washington debated, at most, was legislation to spend $1.75 billion a year. That, as we have seen, was less than the $2.1 billion child care measure that Nixon vetoed back in 1971—before policy makers fretted over a child care "crisis" and before two decades of inflation made that $2.1 billion of 1971 worth much less in 1989.

Even ABC's proponents acknowledged that theirs was merely a first step in providing the kind of child care that would make a difference. In drafting the ABC bill, CDF had started off with a $5 billion measure—"which is what we really wanted," Edelman recalled. In the deficit-riddled 1980s, realism prompted her to scale it back. Edelman did so, ironically, in consultation with Miller's staff. As for ABC's role, she said, "It's a beginning. If you combine that with full funding for Head Start and if we can combine that with getting people to invest more in preschool, you'll begin to set up a system that begins to respond. . . . You don't do that with a little old token, throw out the door a few pennies. And so, ABC is not the answer, but it is a significant start."

■   ■   ■   ■

In 1990, child care would not likely return to the legislative battlefield alone. The EITC had surfaced frequently throughout the child care debate and was certain to do so again. The popularity of this tax break, evident in both parties by the late 1980s, was a long time in coming. A brainchild of Sen. Russell Long, the Louisiana Democrat who served 15 years as the Finance Committee chairman beginning in the mid-1960s, it was created in 1975 to give tax relief to low-income workers with children and to provide incentives for work. Since then, Washington has occasionally increased the size of the credit and raised the income level at which it was phased out to help offset inflation and increases in Social Security payroll taxes. But despite attention each time that its benefits were expanded, the EITC has received much of its favorable publicity only in the last few years.

"We began working on EITC in 1984," Greenstein told me, "and you could go and tell somebody you were working on the Earned Income Tax Credit then and [the reaction was], 'Who? What do those initials stand for? What are you talking about?' Very few people knew what it was about in 1984." Greenstein himself came to the issue only fortuitously. Ways and Means had asked him to testify at a hearing on the tax burdens of low-income Americans. In preparing for it, he was astonished to discover how combined payroll and income tax burdens had risen for that class. "Once we did that initial piece of testimony," Greenstein recalled, "we said, 'We're going to do a lot of work on this.'" Off he went, pitching the virtues of a higher EITC to groups dedicated to helping the low-income. Reagan had announced in 1985 that he would push for tax reform. Rostenkowski signed onto the idea and pledged cooperation. If an otherwise fanciful idea like overhauling the tax code was backed by Washington's two most important players, Greenstein hoped to capitalize on the opportunity and get an increase in the EITC.

Others were impressed with the EITC's importance. Along with Edelman's CDF, such groups as the Catholic Conference and Bread for the World highlighted the tax break. In the administration and Congress, more and more officials caught on. The so-called Treasury 1 tax reform proposal, the starting point for administration deliberations, called for a sizable EITC increase. Low-income groups pressed for more. When the administration followed Treasury 1 with Treasury 2, the plan that Reagan endorsed, the EITC increase had been enlarged. On Capitol Hill, meanwhile, the credit picked up some key support. Rostenkowski and his staff were supportive, as were some of Ways and Means' liberal Democrats. Rostenkowski's tax reform plan, on which Ways and Means worked in late 1985, called for an even larger increase. As tax reform moved through Congress, the EITC increases continued to swell. On the Finance Committee, Packwood and Bradley were supportive. When a conference committee ironed out the final details of the 1986 Tax Reform Act, it included an EITC increase that dwarfed all of the others.

By the late 1980s, the EITC was the tool of choice for liberals and conservatives alike. It rewarded those in need through no fault of their own—the *working* poor. Distributed as a tax benefit, it did not suffer from the inefficiencies of spending programs. Some conservatives viewed an EITC expansion as an alternative to a minimum wage hike; some liberals sought increases in both. Either way, the EITC was a hard tool to dislike. And so, in 1989, lawmakers worked to expand its benefits again. Dole offered an EITC increase not only as an alternative to Mitchell's package, but as a substitute for Bentsen's child health care credit. Edwards offered an EITC increase in his child care alternative to the House Democrats' proposals. Although Downey's Title XX increase got huge publicity because of his battles with Hawkins and Edelman, the centerpiece of his measure was a proposed increase in the EITC. Unfortunately, a cash-starved Washington could not afford to expand this tax benefit, for that would have put the government deeper into the financial hole. Facing Gramm-Rudman's 1990 deficit target, Washington opted for a lean deficit-cutting bill before lawmakers went home in late November. No child care, no EITC.

■   ■   ■   ■

Under these circumstances, Congress would have adjourned with almost no domestic achievements, if not for a late-year compromise between Bush and Democrats on the minimum wage. Washington's agreement on this, and not on child care or the EITC, was no accident. Whatever they thought of the various child care plans, not many officials favored an increase in the minimum wage more than one in the EITC. Most favored it less. But the minimum wage had an undeniable appeal: raising it would not cost Washington any money. Employers would pay. An EITC expansion, on the other hand, could have proved expensive. Downey and Miller's EITC plan, for instance, would have cost more than $4 billion per year by 1992. For a cash-strapped government, this made all of the difference.

The minimum wage had been a Democratic favorite since 1938, when FDR pushed it through to establish a basic labor standard. So it was no surprise when party leaders placed an increase in it atop their 1989 agenda. Reagan had opposed such increases. But in his campaign, Bush said he was open to the idea. Democrats wanted to exploit that change in the White House. But even some mainstream Democrats expressed doubts that that was a good idea. Some private economists furnished studies to show that a minimum wage hike would fuel inflation and, depending on how big the increase was, cost hundreds of thousands of jobs. Besides, as critics were quick to mention, many minimum wage jobs were performed by members of middle-class families, such as teenagers. Efforts to discredit the minimum wage bore fruit.

At a *Washington Times* forum in August, Rep. Dave McCurdy, an Oklahoma Democrat, said:

> Democrats believe that if a person works full time, trying to support their family, then they shouldn't be in poverty. Now the issue is, how can you best correct that problem? And the minimum wage has been shown, I think, by most economists, not to be the best vehicle because, quite frankly, it affects the middle class more than it does the working poor. The Earned Income Tax Credit gets money into the hands of the working poor, not the person who's just going to draw a welfare check and not work, but the person who's actually striving and trying to support a family, and to go out there and make a difference.

Critiques like that were so common that Greenstein joined Isaac Shapiro, a colleague at his budget center, and David Ellwood, a public affairs professor at Harvard's Kennedy School, to defend the minimum wage in an April 1989 letter to the *New York Times*. Greenstein and Shapiro returned to the *Times* in August with an op-ed piece on the subject. As they noted, critics failed to mention the other side of the coin: Most poor workers were paid hourly, and three fifths of those who were made wages of $4.35 an hour or less; at the time, Democrats had proposed to increase the minimum wage in stages from its existing level of $3.35 to $4.65.

If the nation agreed that all families with a full-time worker should not have to live in poverty, Greenstein and Co. wrote, legislation that would just expand the EITC would not have achieved that goal. A minimum wage hike was needed to supplement it.

But it was politics, much more than substantive issues, that drove the parties toward a minimum wage compromise. After Bush vetoed their minimum wage hike measure in June, Democrats said they would try to embarrass him. What they would do, they said, was repeatedly send him alternative wage hikes that, while lower than their first, were above Bush's $4.25 threshold. By daring him to veto them, they would force him to choose between breaking his word about $4.25 and angering working Americans. But the Democrats changed their minds. Party strategists decided that they could get more political mileage out of compromising and pushing a wage hike into law than by displaying their inability to override Bush's vetoes. Republicans, by contrast, felt vulnerable to other pressures. Asked to support Bush's effort to cut the capital gains rate, they were subjected to criticism about the "rich man's tax cut." Republicans did not want to appear even more elitist and insensitive to average workers by helping to block a minimum wage hike. Some GOP lawmakers encouraged the White House to compromise.

■   ■   ■   ■

The 1989 battle over child care and related issues was a telling one. It pointed up the trouble that Washington would face in finding resources for this or that challenge, as long as its leaders could not solve the all-encompassing deficit problem. In 1989, it was child care and an EITC increase that lost out. Trapped in a deficit-driven milieu, Washington could not respond to the challenges posed by demographic changes at home and economic competition from abroad. In the future, other national priorities would likely go unaddressed. Nor did Washington seem likely to free itself from this milieu any time soon. As Bush's first year drew to a close, the nation's leaders had made little headway on the deficit problem, despite their insistence to the contrary. A year to which the deficit hawks had looked forward ended with no noticeable progress on the interparty dispute over taxes and spending. If anything, the dispute seemed more insoluble than ever.

CHAPTER NINE

"ONE SHOT EVERY FOUR YEARS"

Washington was its normally quiet self between Christmas 1989 and New Year's Day. Congress had adjourned. Bush and various top administration officials were on vacation, as were many Capitol Hill staffers who were still recovering from their bosses' rush to get things done before leaving by Thanksgiving. Only at OMB, where Darman and a staff of about 500 worked to draft Bush's fiscal 1991 budget by late January, were operations in full swing. It was in this slow season, two days before the end of 1989, that Moynihan dropped a fiscal bombshell that disrupted the traditional political ceasefire of the holidays: Moynihan said he would propose legislation to cut the Social Security payroll tax.

Before the inevitable backlash began, you would have thought he had reinvented the wheel. From the Right and the Left, praise poured in. "A blow for candor and equity," George F. Will called it.[1] Added Evans and Novak, "This is a golden opportunity for Democrats to echo John F. Kennedy's call for Americans to keep more of the money they earn."[2] The *Wall Street Journal's* columnist Paul A. Gigot wrote, "This sounds like heresy for spend-happy Democrats, but Mr. Moynihan's proposal makes both political and economic sense."[3] Kate O'Beirne, the Heritage Foundation's director of domestic policy, called the idea "terrific."[4] The Left responded similarly. Robert L. Borosage, Jesse Jackson's senior policy advisor in 1988 and later a senior fellow at the Institute for Policy Studies, called Moynihan's plan "good economics, good public policy and good politics—the first protest of an increasingly hard-pressed middle class."[5] A week before Moynihan's news conference to announce his plans, liberal columnist Michael Kinsley had advocated a payroll tax cut, saying it would be a "supply-side tax cut for working people" to counter Bush's capital gains cut.[6]

And yet, Moynihan's proposal was born more out of frustration than genius, as the senator himself would undoubtedly admit. As a member of the National Economic Commission, he had written in its minority report 10 months earlier that the existing use of Social Security's growing surplus would not go unchallenged. Because the surplus was invested in Treasury securities, it was in essence financing other federal spending. And because it was included in the budget, it helped to "mask" the size of the non–Social Security deficit and reduce the amount Washington had to borrow from the markets. If, for instance, the surplus had not grown by $52 billion in fiscal 1989, that year's deficit would have reached $204 billion—not the $152 billion that was recorded. In fact, if you removed the surplus, which was expected to grow into the next century before being used for the retirement of baby boomers, the deficit was not going down at all. It was still rising.

A surplus of this magnitude did not appear without warning. It arose from changes in Social Security—payroll tax hikes and limits on benefits—enacted in 1977 and 1983 to save the nearly bankrupt program and put it on a sound footing until the middle of the next century. What rankled liberals like Moynihan, among other things, was that with the surplus invested in Treasury securities, a regressive payroll tax, as opposed to the progressive income tax, was supporting more day-to-day spending. He warned in the commission's minority report:

Let no one suppose that a Democratic Congress will much longer allow a *payroll* tax to be used to service a $2 to $3 trillion debt owned in vastly disproportionate amounts by wealthy individuals and institutions.... This is not a threat. It is a political reality and, indeed, an ethical imperative. The nation struggled for a generation to ratify the XVIth Amendment to the Constitution. We are not about to see it effectively repealed by a reform in the financing of Social Security.[7]

His answer: Eliminate the surplus by cutting the payroll tax; return Social Security to the pay-as-you-go approach, in which payroll taxes are raised or lowered on occasion, depending on the program's needs; and force Washington to confront a deficit that grows larger when not "masked" by Social Security.

This was not Moynihan's most favored approach. He understood the potential economic benefits if the surplus, which was expected to reach nearly $12 trillion by the early 21st century, could be used more productively. He was merely worried that it never would be. Nor was this an issue that officials of either party wanted to confront because 1990 was an election year, not an easy time for lawmakers to vote against any tax cut. But by swelling the deficit immediately by an estimated $38 billion in 1991 and more later, Moynihan's proposal would have forced Washington to abandon all pretense of adhering to Gramm-Rudman's schedule of annual targets. If he had to, Moynihan would use such dynamite to shake the nation's leaders out of their complacency. Then maybe he could force Washington to take the kinds of steps contemplated by notions of a Big Deal.

Nothing else seemed to be working. On the deficit-cutting front, Bush's first year was a dismal one. The White House's plan for a two-stage attack died unceremoniously, a victim of huge political battles, soured relations, and—let the truth be known—apathy. In the fall, a private, last-ditch effort by Darman to resurrect interest in the Big Deal was encouraged by the House's Democratic leaders but scoffed at by the Senate's. Thus, April's puny agreement, whose very existence was justified on the grounds that it would lead to a bigger one, was never built upon. Even that deal was not implemented the way Bush and Congress had hoped, leaving the two sides to trade barbs about who had changed the rules of the game. With Washington short on the deficit savings that it had promised in April, officials chose to trigger a slimmed-down version of Gramm-Rudman's across-the-board cuts to pick up some money. Thus, the meat-axe approach to deficit cutting that was supposed to inspire a more rational plan had itself become a legitimate policy tool.

If anything, prospects for the Big Deal in Bush's second year looked dimmer still. Aside from the normal election-related pressures in any even-numbered year, Washington would face a few more. In 1989, senior citizens had mounted a successful, yearlong revolt against a tax imposed on them to finance the new catastrophic health care program. With that reminder of grass-roots strength, the nation's leaders were not likely to confront the elderly again by suggesting that their programs contribute to a Big Deal. And if those programs were protected, advocates for others would argue that theirs, too, should not be cut. Republicans, suddenly vulnerable for their antiabortion views after the Supreme Court gave states greater latitude to regulate abortion, seemed likely to rejuvenate their troops by digging in even harder against a tax hike. Eastern Europe's startling rush toward democracy gave many American leaders the optimistic, but altogether incorrect, hope that budget balancing could be accomplished simply by withholding funds that the Pentagon no longer needed.

■   ■   ■   ■

Darman, as we have seen, had hoped to affix the Big Deal to debt-limit legislation around late October. Also hoping to affix their pet ideas were the usual coterie of lawmakers who wanted to reform the budget process. The annual budget wars had grown predictable. As conflict ensued and hopes for significant deficit cutting sunk, the White House and Congress focused more on the mechanics of budgeting—the rules by which each is supposed to draft budgets, consider spending bills, and so on. Because the players could not solve the underlying problem of the deficit, they hoped that some changes in the rules would prod them along. So they thought about drafting budgets to cover two years instead of one, giving the president more authority to cut spending on his own, altering or eliminating a congressional committee or two, and so on. The more experienced lawmakers, having lived through a few rounds of reform fever, tended to view such efforts with a healthy dose of skepticism; as they knew, no rules change could force Washington to balance its books. Junior members, however, got more excited about reform, as if they hoped to discover something that the old-timers had missed.

In this context, Moynihan first thought about a different kind of Social Security change than the one he later settled on. For some time, he and a few other senators—Democrats Hollings and Terry Sanford of North Carolina, and Republicans Gramm and John Heinz of Pennsylvania—had talked about changing the way Social Security is treated in the budget. As the debt bill drew closer and a debate over Social Security seemed likelier, others chipped in with variations on a theme. Darman outlined one. House and Senate Democratic leaders signed on to Moynihan's earlier plan. House Republicans drafted a proposal as well.

Uniting them all was the goal of "protecting" Social Security, although in reality the existing treatment of the program posed no danger to it. One could be forgiven for thinking otherwise, given the rhetoric of the public debate. Here was the government, taking the unspent portion of payroll taxes and buying Treasury securities. Rather than being "saved," the wide-eyed critics said, the money was being "stolen." On this issue, the public was like a sleeping giant, mostly ignorant but none too happy once it learned the facts. Heinz, whose newsletters to constituents on various subjects usually elicited responses from 2 to 4 percent of them, said he heard from 23 percent after writing about how Social Security's surplus was used. "More important than even the rate," he told me in late 1989, "is kind of the quickness and intensity of the response, which is visceral: 'Keep people's hands off the Social Security system.' "

But, the money was not really being "stolen." After all, what was the alternative? Should Washington have put the surplus dollars under a mattress? That might have kept them safe. But it would have allowed inflation to eat away at their value. In order for the dollars to earn billions of dollars in interest, they had to be invested somewhere. And there was no safer place to invest—your money, mine, or Social Security's—than with the federal government. Referring to complaints that the surplus was being stolen, Penner, the former CBO director, told the House Budget Committee in late 1989, "That is no more true than to say my own private pension system, TIAA, is somehow being exploited because it invests some of its money in Treasury securities."

Nevertheless, all was not well with this approach, as Penner and others recognized. Early in the 21st century, baby boomers would start to retire. The surplus would stop accumulating, and the Social Security system would have to cash in the Treasury securities that it owned. To redeem them, Washington would have to raise taxes, cut spending, or borrow more from the markets. The key questions were these: Would the economy be strong enough that the nonelderly could easily support the baby boomers' retirement? Or would the burden prove so immense that they would balk at financing it? The answer: It depended on how the nation prepared for this eventuality. America's economy had to grow. It needed to raise national savings and to invest in its human and physical capital, so living standards rose fast enough for tomorrow's nonelderly to absorb the burden.

In this regard, the surplus offered a great opportunity. If Washington could balance its non-Social Security books, the surplus could be used to repay the national debt. Private money, no longer needed to refinance that debt, would be available for investment. The economy would burst ahead. Thus, with their payroll taxes generating the surplus, today's workers would provide the funds for an economic boom that would later help to finance their own retirement. The National Economic Commission's majority and minority reports suggested this approach, as did the General Accounting Office and various economists. As Moynihan wrote with characteristic flair for the commission's minority, "To say again, we can slouch into the twenty-first century, or we can march into the twenty-first century. The outcome will turn on whether we get our political arithmetic in order in the next five years."[8] But, as Moynihan knew, Washington was doing more slouching than marching. The non-Social Security books were nowhere near balance. Rather than repaying the debt, the surplus was being used to support a federal budget that was, by most accounts, heavy on consumption and light on investment. For this reason, one could justifiably argue that the surplus was being "wasted."

Unfortunately, most proposals that were bandied about would not have corrected this situation. In fact, they might have made it worse. To "protect" Social Security, many lawmakers wanted to separate it as much as possible from the rest of the budget. One popular proposal was to remove the surplus from Gramm-Rudman's calculations. If this occurred, the federal ledger would have two distinct parts. On one side would stand Social Security. On the other would be a non-Social Security budget with a deficit that was now larger because the surplus did not "mask" any of it. Having made the recorded deficit larger, many lawmakers in turn wanted to adjust Gramm-Rudman's annual targets. Instead of balancing the budget in 1993, as the current schedule requires, they wanted to delay that goal until, say, the year 2000.

The desire to "protect" Social Security's surplus may have been laudable, but this approach seemed naive. If Social Security was kept to one side, the surplus would have been a tempting pot for would-be spenders. Rather than using the surplus to repay the debt, Congress might have tried to curry favor with the elderly by raising Social Security benefits or creating new programs, such as long-term health coverage. To do so would not affect Washington's effort to reach Gramm-Rudman's targets; Social Security no longer would be involved in that. Speaking to this threat, Darman said in late October, "All you do is open up the possibility that the surplus that's being accumulated on paper can be spent for anything and everything that man could invent without being subject to any fiscal discipline." That would be worse than the existing situation. Not only would the surplus not contribute to national savings, but the nation would face the future burden of new spending commitments. Even a requirement (as some sought) that a "super-majority"—say, 60 percent of Congress—vote to spend part of the surplus seemed like a minor obstacle.

With trillions in excess payroll taxes arriving in the coming decades, could Washington be trusted with the money? Not everyone thought so. In a 1989 paper for the Committee for Economic Development, Penner suggested that Washington should return Social Security to a pay-as-you-go system. "Because of the danger that politicians will not be able to resist spending the . . . surplus," he wrote, "a radically different approach to the problem would be to prevent the surplus from burgeoning in the first place."[9] In other words, as Moynihan suggested at his December 29 news conference, cut the payroll tax. Penner foresaw other benefits from this change. If Social Security were returned to pay-as-you-go and kept in Gramm-Rudman's calculations, the nation's leaders might be more inclined to examine it, as they did other programs, for deficit cutting. Rather than enjoy a special status that kept their benefits unchallenged, the elderly would face the same deficit pressures faced by others. Otherwise, fueled by Social Security (and Medicare), spending on the elderly would continue to rise at a fast enough pace to squeeze out spending on other groups. The losers, once again, would be children, the poor, the homeless, and others whose programs did not enjoy Social Security's privileged position.

In late 1989, however, the Social Security debate was expected to involve how Gramm-Rudman treated the surplus, not whether it should accumulate in the first place. But when the Senate debated the debt bill, most of those pushing to take the surplus out of Gramm-Rudman's calculations held off; under a complex deal, Democratic and Republican leaders decided to keep the debt bill fairly free of amendments. Almost everyone went along. Heinz would not. A day before a potential national default, he refused to let the Senate raise the debt limit unless he could offer his Social Security measure. He and Mitchell had an unusually testy floor exchange. Only after Mitchell's repeated assurances that the Senate would consider Heinz's or similar legislation in 1990 did Heinz relent. All of that, though, was nearly two months before Moynihan announced plans to take a different approach. How Moynihan's push to cut the payroll tax would affect the whole debate was unclear.

■　　　　■　　　　■　　　　■

Darman was no happier than Heinz about the Democratic-Republican deals by which Congress pushed ahead on its legislative necessities. The more that Congress concentrated on the few things that it *had to do*—like raising the debt limit— so that it could adjourn by Thanksgiving, the less time Darman would have to pull a rabbit out of his hat. By autumn, nobody was talking publicly anymore about crafting the Big Deal before adjournment. Even Darman expressed pessimism about the chances for one. Time was short and, more importantly, relations had soured. With the capital gains fight raging in the Senate, and memories of the House war still fresh, only a miracle could raise the prospects.

But despite the huge obstacles, Darman made a private, last-ditch effort to revive interest. After the House passed its reconciliation bill, with the Jenkins-Archer plan tucked inside, Darman paid a call on Panetta. Although he came to discuss how to finish the pending business for 1990, Darman mentioned that he still had hopes of a Big Deal before Congress adjourned. Perhaps, he suggested, it could be wrapped around a capital gains cut, maybe as the reconciliation bill was completed. If Bush got his capital gains cut, maybe he would be willing to attach a tax increase to it to bring the deficit down. Darman and Panetta tossed around the idea of raising the gas tax.

"I, at that time, said I was very discouraged about that possibility," Panetta recalled, "because there had been, obviously, these clear lines drawn on capital gains. And I said, 'Members' feelings are kind of stretched to the raw, in terms of suddenly coming back and doing any kind of bigger package.' It would be very difficult to do a tax package. I just could not see the dynamics, at least the political dynamics, of how you could do that at that stage." But the Big Deal was what Panetta had wanted, so he did not discourage the OMB director. "I said, 'I'm certainly not going to tell you not to explore it. I certainly would want to do it.'" Warning him about the obvious political hurdles, he suggested that Darman speak to Foley. A few days later, the OMB director did. With Panetta on hand, Foley gave him the same message as had the budget chairman: it would be tough, but give it a try.

Their Democratic counterparts in the Senate were far less accommodating, however. Darman, this time with Brady, went to see Mitchell and Sasser. With the four in Mitchell's office, discussion revolved around the steps needed to wrap up action on fiscal 1990 measures. Brady brought up the question of fiscal 1991, reminding the Democrats that the administration still wanted to craft that Big Deal. As Sasser recalled with a smile, "Mitchell... sort of snorted and he said, 'Look, I don't know how we can talk about '91 when we can't even carry out what we agreed to in '90.' That was the end of that discussion."

That the House leaders were more receptive to Darman's effort was predictable. His relations with Foley and Panetta, the two key congressional players probably most predisposed toward negotiations, were much better than those with Mitchell and Sasser. Darman had angered Mitchell early in the year when, in negotiating with Congress on a supplemental spending bill, he had cut a deal with Byrd, the Senate Appropriations Committee chairman, to which Mitchell was not a party. Asked at year-end by *U.S. News & World Report* whether Democrats resented Darman, Mitchell shot back, "You're damn right."[10]

An equally telling remark came in my discussion with Sasser in December. When I asked about the status of relations between the White House and congressional negotiators from April, he said:

> I have a very high regard for Nick Brady and personally am very fond of him and have a great deal of respect for him, and like him a lot, and enjoy being with Nick...and he's a first-rate guy. With Darman, you know, it's a little different. I think Darman's a very intelligent person and charming and a pleasure to be with on social occasions. But getting into some of these—I felt like they, kind of, didn't carry through with the original promise of the negotiations. And that is "Let's get through this and then we're going to work together, and together we're going to solve this fiscal problem."

Sasser and I digressed for a moment to talk about the capital gains fight and how that had soured relations. When I pressed him about Darman, asking whether he trusted the OMB director, Sasser hesitated and then said, "Well, that's a pretty tough question, you know. And nobody wants to—but I would just say that he's got his own agenda, and that agenda, I think, changes to suit circumstances on occasion."

The Darman-Sasser relationship had become an increasingly uncomfortable one, although it did not seem rooted in deep personal dislike. The two had joked with one another occasionally during the negotiations that lead to April's agreement. Distrust was perhaps a better word. Towards the end of an October briefing with reporters, Darman alluded to the May 31 breakfast in Foley's office and said, "Senator Sasser said he couldn't come to any more meetings." When I later asked Sasser about that, he denied making such a statement and said, "Darman somehow got it in his head, and I don't know who planted that, that I didn't want to meet or something. That's not the case at all."

Just why the group never met again remains unclear. Sasser was so unsure that he asked me whether, from my contacts, I had any insight. Clearly, the group was supposed to continue meeting. Frenzel had successfully pushed for a provision in April's written agreement to require that. How soon it was supposed to start was less obvious, however. At the May 31 breakfast, Foley and Panetta made it clear that they would have to hold off for awhile, since rank-and-file House Democrats were still miffed about being shut out of the decision-making process in the spring. Darman and Frenzel were disappointed that talks could not begin immediately. The latter, in particular, complained loudly. "My reaction was that, God dammit, we signed the bipartisan budget agreement [of April], and article whatever-it-was said we were going to go ahead with these discussions," Frenzel told me later.

In the fall, some key lawmakers thought that Sasser did not even want to meet with Darman to settle the remaining issues of fiscal 1990. Sasser denied that. But, he admitted, he wanted to decide some matters with his Democratic and Republican colleagues *before* bringing Darman in. "Darman's got his point of view," Sasser explained. "And sometimes he can confuse things, I think, intentionally. And I just want to sort of define the issues among ourselves. It doesn't mean we have to agree. Just define the issues. And be working off the same baselines." Darman was, in fact, barred from some of these sessions and had to be briefed later on what the parties agreed to. About a day before Congress adjourned, he insisted that the congressional staff walk him through the material, top to bottom, before he would sign off on it. As the staff did so for about two hours, he tabulated the items with a calculator.

It had been a rough autumn for the budget director. The more he pressed for capital gains, viewing the issue as a key test for the Bush presidency, the more he ran headfirst into his philosophical musings in July about "now-now-ism." Darman, said his critics, was the one acting like "the spoiled fifties child in the recently revived commercial." Like the little boy who wanted his Maypo "*nowwwwww,*" Darman wanted his capital gains cut. Contradicting his wish to steer public policy toward the future, critics said, he pushed for a tax cut that would increase the deficit (although Darman had not accepted those projections). Nor did Darman's words haunt only him. Critics directed them at the administration's allies in

Congress. When Packwood proposed his capital gains amendment to the Eastern European aid bill, Bradley called it the "ultimate now-nowism. The proponents of this amendment cannot wait until there is a tax bill, a second tax bill; they cannot wait until there is a tariff or other revenue measure; and most assuredly they seem unable to wait until next year. They have to get it now-now."

Darman, meanwhile, seemed increasingly frustrated by what he felt was a double standard in how the media reported the issues of fiscal 1990. Democrats were given free rein to rail against a capital gains cut, saying it would increase the deficit in the long run. But when it came to new spending that Democrats tucked into reconciliation, particularly in the House bill, reporters were mum. Darman's anger boiled over in late October when reporters asked him to justify the "backloaded" IRA that Packwood had attached to his capital gains cut. Citing other deficit-raising items in the reconciliation bills, he mocked the Democrats by saying:

> Those don't count. "We are for fiscal discipline," somebody says. Those don't count. Those are irrelevant. That's not the real issue. But if capital gains, estimated by the Joint [Tax] Committee, loses a fraction of a billion in any one year of five years, that is disqualifying. That's disqualifying. Now, are you going to tell me that that's a fair standard that's being applied? If ever there were a gross double standard that is being applied, it is right there. And I really don't think you all should let them get away with it.

Double standard or not, Mitchell proved strong enough to block a capital gains cut. As his success grew likelier through the fall, the White House decided to turn the Democrats' arguments against them. So the Democrats say that a capital gains cut will increase the deficit, eh? Well, what about all of their new spending programs in the reconciliation bills? And what about those gimmicks that do not save money in the long run, but are merely designed to help reach Gramm-Rudman's next target? In a November 2 message that Darman drafted, Bush announced that he would not accept a reconciliation bill that included less than $14 billion in "real" savings—that is, no gimmicks. Gramm-Rudman's across-the-board spending cuts had taken effect in mid-October. When that occurred, lawmakers of both parties assumed that they would be rolled back and replaced by whatever reconciliation bill of small tax hikes and spending cuts was enacted. But the president now said that without the kind of reconciliation bill that he wanted, he was ready to leave the cuts in place. "I will not accept a reconciliation bill that fails to do the job that should be done," Bush said in his four-page statement.

By that point, fiscal policy had hit rock bottom. Under Gramm-Rudman, the threat of across-the-board cuts was supposed to spur a more rational deficit-cutting approach. Those cuts were everyone's favorite metaphor for impending, unacceptable doom: a gun to the head of lawmakers, a train wreck around the corner, or, as Stockman put it in his memoirs, a fiscal "two-by-four."[11] Few expected Washington to ever live with those cuts, to accept them as the deficit-cutting tool of choice. But the longer conflict ensued, and the more intransigent both sides grew, the more appealing was the mechanized irrationality of Gramm-Rudman. By the time Bush issued his statement, plenty of Republican lawmakers were suggesting that the across-the-board cuts be used for the full year. Rather than make choices, rather than protect high-priority programs and cut others that had grown less useful, Washington found it easier to apply a formula for deficit reduction that was last examined in 1987. That was good enough for many of America's leaders.

Not that everyone was happy about this. As a full year of cuts grew more imminent, warnings about how they would affect various programs came from lawmakers, federal agencies, and private interest groups. The House Appropriations Committee's Republican staff, in a break from the stern GOP posture favoring the cuts, issued a report a day after Bush's statement, detailing the effects if across-the-board cuts stayed in place: 170,000 fewer active personnel and 131,000 fewer reservists at the Pentagon; reduced loans and payments to 2 million farmers; problems in adequately conducting the 1990

Census; education cuts affecting hundreds of thousands of disadvantaged children, college students, and illiterate adults; job cuts at Social Security offices; reductions in low-income and job-training programs; job cuts affecting air traffic controllers and others who ensure transportation safety; cuts affecting the war on drugs, and so on. The Budget Committees distributed their own studies. The Health and Human Services Department, in a report to Congress, warned that across-the-board cuts could have a severe impact on services provided for Social Security recipients. Families U.S.A., a Washington group that lobbies for the elderly poor, complained that a full year of cuts would, in the words of executive director Ronald F. Pollack, "gut the war on drugs, exclude tens of thousands of children from Head Start, reduce low-income housing funds below last year's level, deprive 300,000 children of vaccines against measles, mumps, polio, and other diseases, and push funds for the disabled down below last year's level."

Clearly, across-the board cuts remained a political liability for whoever was blamed for them. In a statement issued in late October, House Republicans blamed the cuts that were already in effect on Democratic inability to finish Congress's budget work on time. "This failure by the Democratic leadership will mean, among other things, disruption of programs that affect students, farmers, and the war on drugs," they said. Not to be undone, Democrats shot back. Soon after Bush's November 2 statement, House members and senators tried to shift the blame. "It's going to be embarrassing to everyone in government, but the one people hold responsible is the president," Rep. Henry A. Waxman of California told the *Washington Post*.[12] Speculating that Bush might veto legislation that, while fulfilling the requirements of April's deal, did not meet his November 2 demands, Foley said that, "he would have to assume the responsibility for the many unfortunate consequences of that."[13]

Despite the political pitfalls, across-the-board cuts looked more appealing to the White House and some lawmakers as the year progressed. With dramatic change occurring in Eastern Europe, officials in both parties predicted that defense spending, which had not kept pace with inflation since 1985, would come down in inflation-adjusted dollars even faster. Armed conflict with the Soviet Union had never seemed less likely since World War II. Prospects for U.S.-Soviet arms agreements began to brighten, and the $150 billion or so that America was spending each year to defend Western Europe looked quite excessive. All of this put conservatives in the driver's seat when it came to Gramm-Rudman. If defense was likely to get slashed anyway, there was less reason to worry about the impact of across-the-board cuts on it. And by allowing those cuts to take effect, conservatives could obtain some reductions in domestic programs that they otherwise were not likely to get, while also avoiding a tax increase. For 1990, there was hardly a downside.

Across-the-board cuts had another appeal. Because they would replace some of the one-shot gimmicks to which Bush and Congress had agreed in April, the cuts would produce more long-term savings. Thus, by leaving them in place, the White House would have less trouble finding the requisite savings to hit Gramm-Rudman's target for 1991. By mid-autumn, Sununu and Fitzwater had talked up the idea of across-the-board cuts for a full year (although Fitzwater admitted that some Cabinet secretaries were not happy about what that would do to their agencies' budgets). So, too, were Republican lawmakers coming aboard. Packwood called for such cuts in a September 29 column in the *Wall Street Journal*. Later, Republican leaders encouraged Bush to hang tough on his November 2 demands.

Even before change swept through Eastern Europe, raising the prospect of deep Pentagon cuts, Darman warned that he would be willing to live with across-the-board cuts. No, he did not *prefer* the cuts. In his confirmation hearings in early 1989, Darman disparaged the notion of governing under that scenario, saying it was "silly" and, if it occurred, "could have some serious adverse consequences on both the domestic and foreign side." But, he reminded everyone, Gramm-Rudman was the law. Sure, the Pentagon would complain about the cuts, as other agencies presumably would. But a law was not something to take lightly. "And will I suggest that we live by the law if we do not reach a negotiated settlement?" he said in an exchange with Sasser. "Absolutely, unequivocally." By late 1989, however, the White House had decided that not just *any* "negotiated settlement" would do. It had to be one free of gimmicks.

That standard brought the White House face to face with its own deeds. Darman and Bush had both agreed to all of the gimmickry included in the April deal. Now they were trying to excise *all* gimmicks from fiscal 1990 legislation. Their attempt did not sit well with the Democrats. Before long, Darman backed off: Gimmicks approved in April would be OK. Others would not. Even so, Congress had trouble finding $14 billion. Some committees that, under April's deal, were supposed to raise revenues or cut spending had not done so. To make up for that, Washington imposed a mild form of across-the-board cuts. Needing to fill a $4.6 billion gap, it cut all eligible programs under Gramm-Rudman's formula by about 1.5 percent.

So this was it for 1989, a year that so many had hoped would bring a solution to the deficit problem. This was all Washington would do about it—a few spending cuts, a few tax hikes, a few gimmicks, and a mild across-the-board slice to fill in the holes. It was hardly a spirited performance, not a Big Deal by any standard. But you might have thought otherwise from the descriptions that greeted the effort. "An excellent bill," said Fitzwater. Maybe "the best reconciliation bill in years," said Darman, who was citing Panetta's assessment. A day after Congress adjourned, its leaders talked up their performance on the "McNeil-Lehrer Newshour." Dole quoted Darman's comments about reconciliation. Foley, comparing the deficit-cutting effort to those of earlier years, called it "one of the strongest, if not the strongest."

Not that any of this made sense. In the good old days, when Reagan's first few deficits evoked deep concern, Washington undertook some deficit cutting that made 1989's effort seem laughable. In 1982, for instance, Congress passed a tax bill designed to raise $98 billion in its first three years and a reconciliation bill to cut spending by $13 billion. The 1989 effort clearly did not measure up to that. With the tax and spending items taken together, Washington sliced an estimated $17.8 billion off the fiscal 1990 deficit. In January 1989, CBO had projected that the deficit would stay above $120 billion for at least five more years. By January 1990, with Washington's deficit-cutting action of the previous year and new economic assumptions plugged in, CBO's estimates had barely changed.

Whatever their precise size, incremental deficit savings were almost beside the point. Without the Big Deal, and the sustained downward path of the deficit that it would have brought, the problem remained. Fiscal policy was paralyzed. Spending could barely be cut, since most programs had powerful supporters. Taxes could not go up, although Washington could try another round of loophole-closing. Pro-spending activists pushed on anyway in this environment of budgetary gridlock. The children's lobby worked in vain for child care. Housing groups tried for a new financial commitment to their cause. They, too, failed. In fact, the biggest change in the area of new programs was not what Washington set up. It was rather what it shut down. Just a year after the nation's leaders thought they had found a way to create new programs in an era of huge deficits, their handiwork collapsed around them in a hail of public recriminations. The experience left Washington that much leerier about trying to change its fiscal policy to any significant degree. A cautious Washington grew still more gun-shy.

■   ■   ■   ■

Back in 1986, when Reagan announced that he was ordering Health and Human Services Secretary Otis R. Bowen to develop proposals for a catastrophic health insurance program, few experts would have put that issue at the top of national health needs. The elderly, and their lobbyists in Washington, sought a national program for long-term care. More than 60 senior citizens' groups mounted a "long-term care '88" campaign, to focus attention on the issue in the presidential race. In an October 1987 survey by the American Association of Retired Persons (AARP) and the Villers Foundation (later known as Families U.S.A), nearly half of 1,000 registered voters said that they or a family member had needed such care. Six out of seven thought it was time to consider a government program, and five of seven said they would pay an income-based tax to support such care for everyone over 65. But, generally, presidents set national agendas. With Reagan's decision, a debate over how to provide insurance for catastrophic illness jumped to the top of Washington's agenda.

Around that time, policy activists were settling on a new strategy to create programs. Rather than seek money from the Treasury, they tried to tap into new revenue sources that would support trust funds for their new programs. In this way, activists could not be accused of contributing to the deficit. Besides, once the programs were established, they were likelier to escape the deficit cutters for the same reason—with their own revenue sources, nobody could make the case that they were contributing to the deficit. In the late 1980s, Washington had set up a trust fund to pay victims of vaccine-related injuries and considered legislation to create funds for various other purposes: long-term health care, land preservation, nuclear waste cleanup, infrastructure improvements, low-income housing, children's programs, and others.

Along with this new financing strategy came a few demographic and fiscal facts. Although they had once been the poorest group of Americans, the elderly no longer were. Poverty among seniors had dropped from 35 percent in 1959 to 12 percent by 1988. Everyone was happy about that. Indeed, Social Security was considered perhaps the nation's most successful program ever, for all that it had done to lift the incomes of seniors. Medicare also had been considered a huge success since its inception in 1965. But with the improved welfare of senior citizens came more disturbing social news. Children had grown poorer. At the same time, spending on the elderly was consuming a growing share of federal resources. Social Security and Medicare alone comprised 28 percent of the budget, and seniors benefited from a host of other programs. To the extent that Washington could redirect its existing dollars to high-priority areas, children were near the top of many lists. If, then, the elderly were going to get a new program like catastrophic health insurance—the largest expansion of Medicare in a quarter-century—the nation's leaders decided that they alone would have to finance it. That decision represented a break with tradition; Social Security and Medicare are essentially funded by payroll taxes on current workers, although Medicare recipients pay a standard premium to help cover doctor bills.

But health insurance was no cheap item. For years, health care costs had outstripped inflation. To finance the catastrophic program, the White House and Congress chose an income-based tax, with poor seniors not paying at all and the well-to-do paying up to $800 per person in 1989 and more later. The nation's leaders had rejected a flat tax—that is, the same amount from each recipient—because it would have been too high for many struggling seniors. When Reagan turned legislation into law with his signature on July 1, 1988, all sides thought they had found a way to work around Washington's deficit troubles. If they were not going to *solve* the deficit problem, at least it might not hamstring them as much.

The self-congratulatory rhetoric flowed like cheap wine for awhile. Before long, however, Washington faced an avalanche of protest from seniors. America's leaders had erred badly. They had failed to make a good case for the new program they had created. They had failed to understand the deep-seated desires of seniors for long-term care insurance and not for the catastrophic care coverage they were given. They had assumed a level of generosity on behalf of the more well-to-do elderly that was not forthcoming. And, most of all, they had forgotten that the rules of "doing good" within the corridors of Washington are not necessarily those shared by Americans across the land. As Robert D. Reischauer, CBO's director, told me in late 1989, "It may have caused us to create a program for which there wasn't much of a constituency."

The revolt was not surprising, although its intensity may have been. In private conversation, the AARP's incoming president, Robert B. Maxwell, was expressing fears about the program as early as mid-1988. By late 1988, a handful of bills had been introduced in Congress to delay the law or scale it back in some way. But the White House and key lawmakers had decided early on that, as well-to-do seniors reacted angrily when the new tax took effect in 1989, they would stand tough and ride out the storm. Rostenkowski and Bentsen, as chairmen of the committees that created the program, were the most important pillars. Whether they could have withstood the calls for change will never be known. With figures from CBO and the Joint Tax Committee showing that the new tax would produce more revenues than expected, Bentsen said in April that he wanted to cut it. Rostenkowski seethed privately. He and Bush tried a united stand against Bentsen. Four days after Bentsen's announcement, the House chairman released a letter from Bush that said he opposed any change. Rostenkowski concurred. By then, however, Rostenkowski's staff was already expressing doubts that, with Bentsen on record for changing the program, they could withstand the growing calls to repeal the tax or the program itself.

Letters arrived on Capitol Hill by the thousands, a testament not only to the deep public feelings but also to a series of organized campaigns. "A special tax on senior citizens! Have you ever heard of anything so outrageous?"[14] the National Committee to Preserve Social Security and Medicare asked in a mailing to some of its 5 million members. Also distributed by the group were "legislative alerts," which kept its members updated on the issue and asked that they tell their House members and senators on enclosed postcards that a seniors-only tax was "unacceptable."[15] It did not matter that the group, headed by FDR's son, James Roosevelt, a former House member, was suspected of using scare tactics to stir up its members. The letters poured in from every congressional district, and lawmakers would have been hard-pressed to ignore them.

From the senior citizens who wrote, and from others who contacted their elected officials at town meetings or elsewhere, the message was clear: They did not want a tax imposed only on them, and they wanted a program that included coverage for long-term care. When Roosevelt's group surveyed its members in late 1988, 51 percent said that they should not have to pay *anything* for the catastrophic program, while just 5 percent were willing to pay for 75 to 100 percent of it. As for the program's benefits, Rep. Timothy J. Penny, the Minnesota Democrat, told me in late 1989, "I have visited with an awful lot of seniors... and they are not impressed. And that sets aside the discussion of what we are going to charge for them." Added South Dakota's Daschle, cochairman of the Senate Democratic Policy Committee, "The interesting thing is, when I talk to senior citizens, although they are worried about the tax, they care an awful lot about long-term health care. They want that included."

Never mind that even with the new tax, the elderly received a lot more from Medicare than they ever paid into it, according to federal estimates. Senior citizens did not view things that way. All they knew was that Washington had imposed a new tax, and many did not need the program. "So many of these people had the coverage already, and superior to what the government was providing," George F. Hennrikus, cochairman of the Coalition for Affordable Health Care, told me in September. By that time, the public revolt had made change inevitable. Hennrikus's coalition of 44 groups, representing 18 million people, helped ensure that. CBO had estimated that 30 to 40 percent of Medicare enrollees would pay more in taxes than they received under the new program. For those with an employer-paid medigap plan, that figure rose to 40 to 50 percent. So, it was no surprise that in a national poll conducted for the coalition and released in May 1989, seniors who said they were familiar with the new program opposed it, 53 percent to 31 percent.

Those who would benefit—and there were plenty—were not moved to defend the program, for many did not know about the benefits they would get. This was another of Washington's public relations blunders. In a laudable decision to make the program financially sound, the nation's leaders chose to build up a surplus by imposing the tax immediately and phasing in the benefits. Nice job, except from a political standpoint. Those who noticed the program most were those paying for it, not those benefiting. With one group of seniors attacking the program, there were no others defending it. Under the phase-in, only hospital benefits were expanded in 1989. Coming later, had the program survived, were expanded home-health benefits, supplemental medical insurance benefits, and a drug program that included outpatient prescription drugs and insulin.

The program did not survive. Trying to save it, many lawmakers experimented with ways to scale it back. Not only did their efforts not stem the tide, but they also evoked other objections. When Ways and Means passed legislation to lower taxes on the more well-to-do and raise them on others, Families U.S.A. complained that under that approach, almost three fifths of the elderly would pay more, principally those in the lower middle class or just above poverty. "If it is the height of political folly to raise costs for three out of five older Americans," Pollack, the group's executive director, said in a strong statement, "it is the depth of economic injustice to shift the burden of catastrophic health care onto those least able to afford the cost of illness." The House voted to repeal the program, the Senate only to scale it back. Negotiations between the bodies commenced. The House would not budge. As Congress prepared to adjourn, the Senate blinked.

All in all, it was a miserable experience for everyone concerned. It left deep scars on those who were out front when the catastrophic care program was created, and at least surface wounds on everyone who supported it at some point. The nation's leaders were now running scared. How anxious they would be to create another new program in the future was uncertain. Surely, the elderly would have to wait much longer for the long-term care they wanted. Plenty of lawmakers were angry enough about all the guff they took to delay any consideration of new benefits for this politically powerful bloc of voters. A big question was whether *all* other groups would suffer as well. As William A. Galston, issues director for Mondale's 1984 campaign, told me, "Congress is going to think three times before it tries to fund another significant program in a responsible manner. One of two things will happen. Either there won't be a lot of significant new programs, or Congress will try to fund them irresponsibly.... The longer-term question facing the country is whether it's willing to mobilize public resources to carry out tasks that can only be done collectively."

A bigger question still was how all this affected deficit cutting. If Washington could not force the elderly to finance a new program, how could it force their contribution to the nebulous goal of budget balancing? Besides, the same group of senior citizens likely to be affected by a Big Deal—that is, the well-to-do—were those who responded so vigorously to the catastrophic tax. For example, analysts of the Right and Left have suggested that Social Security benefits should be taxed like pension benefits. Rather than the existing practice of taxing just half of the benefits, and only above certain income thresholds, analysts have recommended that 85 percent of the benefits be taxed. Washington could raise $20 billion over five years if it did so with the current income thresholds in place—and a whopping $100 billion without them. But that would force the nation's leaders to confront the very group of middle- and upper-class senior citizens who beat them last time.

■   ■   ■   ■

Where all of this left Washington for fiscal 1991, starting with Bush's budget, was unclear. While the autumn battles raged, Darman suggested that for all of the personal animus that had built up, the deficit problem itself would draw the parties together, even in a highly charged election year. With Washington needing $27 billion in deficit savings—using OMB's optimistic economic assumptions—to avoid Gramm-Rudman's across-the-board cuts, he predicted that Democrats would rather cooperate than propose their own package of tax hikes, spending cuts, or both. Besides, if they used CBO's economic assumptions, the savings required would rise to nearly $65 billion. "Are they going to say at that point, 'We've got a wholly different plan'?" Darman asked in October. "Here's the way we're going to use our accounting, our economic estimates.' And what are they going to say, $50 billion in taxes to start with to meet the targets? What is going to be their proposal?

Mitchell was ready to answer. As House players talked of more negotiating, by early fall Mitchell had ruled out another budget summit. The Senate would use its normal process, with the Budget Committee drafting a resolution that set parameters for appropriations and other bills. After the capital gains battle, he said, he could not trust the White House on another deal. In a typical remark, he told reporters at an October 20 breakfast,

> Here we are, three weeks into the next fiscal year, and we have not been able to implement even that [April] agreement which was universally criticized, and with a good deal of validity in the criticism, as being inadequate. If we are, therefore, unable to implement this modest agreement, because the administration has sought to focus its entire energy and effort on the capital gains cut, with no consideration for any other matter—the heck with the deficit, the heck with the reconciliation process, apparently the heck with relations with Congress—then, in my view, there is no purpose to be served in going through this process again, especially when it will be even more difficult next year.

Personal relations aside, other obstacles to cooperation had arisen. In November, Defense Secretary Cheney made headlines around the world with his pronouncement that he was preparing for deep defense cuts in the coming years. He said he had asked the armed services to find $180 billion in possible cuts over three years. The *New York Times* carried the story in its lead position, the right-hand column on page 1. Other newspapers also played up the news. Cheney's move was a clever one. With his announcement, the secretary put himself out front on an emerging debate over Pentagon spending. No longer would the Pentagon's top dog be left out of the congressional negotiations over spending, as Weinberger was when Reagan's requests for continuing defense increases ran into opposition.

With events unfolding in Eastern Europe with breathtaking speed, lawmakers began to eye the "peace dividend" like kids in a candy store. Liberals, and even some conservatives, talked about spending billions on the social needs that went unmet in the deficit-riddled 1980s. Other conservatives advocated another round of tax cuts. Everyone paid lip service to deficit reduction, although that did not seem to top most people's lists. Newspapers and magazines fueled the hopes, with follow-up stories about how a decline in Pentagon spending would affect not only the budget but the national and regional economies. *Business Week* produced a cover story in December, illustrated with a dove clasping a dollar bill in its mouth and headlined "The Peace Economy."[16] *Newsweek* and other publications chipped in with stories as well. Unfortunately, prospects for a huge pot of money had been severely overstated.

Cheney had been clever, all right. Remember that $180 billion? That was merely the difference between what the Pentagon had assumed in the past that it would get over the three years in question and what Congress now seemed likely to provide. It was no new pot at all. It was the Pentagon's recognition that its internal budget books were out of whack. By asking the services to draft plans for these "cuts," Cheney was merely ordering that they bring the books into line with reality. Consider this: From 1985 to 1989, Pentagon spending was held an average of 2 to 3 percent below inflation each year. If Cheney's "cuts" were implemented, Pentagon spending would continue to be held 2 to 3 percent below inflation for another three years. Some "peace dividend"!

Even if it wished to cut defense spending much faster, Congress would have been hard-pressed to do so. For one thing, Bush seemed likely to object. For another, the Pentagon's spending path is never easy to redirect. Just as Reagan's buildup did not occur overnight, neither would a so-called builddown. Because of decisions made during the buildup, much of the Pentagon budget of later years would be absorbed by spending on expensive weapons that took years to develop. As those weapons moved further along in the development stage, their costs would consume a larger slice of the Pentagon pie. The longer that went on, the more limited would be the options of elected officials who looked for places to cut. As Paul T. Heilig, a former defense analyst at the Senate Budget Committee, told me in late 1989, "You have to view the defense budget as an ocean liner. It just takes a lot of time to turn it around."

Washington could save billions down the road by cutting troops abroad, but it was unlikely to do much without U.S.–Soviet agreements. It could cut spending on operations and maintenance, but that would leave the forces with big weapons but not the means to operate them. Or it could cancel big weapons on which billions had already been spent—a move that would save few dollars in the near term but huge sums as the years went on. But the Pentagon was not alone in liking big weapons. Once a weapons project started, a defense plant that was involved got hooked. Jobs and the local economy thus grew dependent. When Cheney tried to slash a few systems in 1989, he was largely unsuccessful. Lawmakers who were otherwise happy to cut defense spending moved vigorously to protect weapons being built in their districts.

Notions of a "peace dividend" presented a new headache to the budget players. Outside the Pentagon and a few congressional committees, knowledge about defense spending was surprisingly shallow in Washington. What's this—$180 billion? That would eliminate the deficit, many quickly assumed. Speaking of his colleagues, Panetta said in early December, "They're reading the headlines. You know, $180 billion! Jesus. Oh, Christ." Nor did some reporters understand much more. Speaking December 3 on ABC's "This Week with David Brinkley," Mitchell said, "There's been a lot of premature, even wild speculation about the amounts involved, and the pace of it. A reporter asked me two days ago what are we going to do with the $180 billion, as though someone had

handed us a check for $180 billion." Some of the budget play-
ers tried to correct the record. "Defense savings will neither
fund much new domestic programming, nor will it come close
to solving our Gramm-Rudman woes," Frenzel said in December. At a Senate Budget Committee hearing on the issue at
about that time, Domenici explained, "Those who are looking
for an instant pot of gold at the end of the defense rainbow are
going to be disappointed." But with notions of a "peace dividend" running rampant, those working for a Big Deal faced
the new problem of convincing everyone that Washington still
needed to raise taxes and cut entitlements to tackle the deficit
problem.

Also blocking the Big Deal were the higher political
stakes associated with tax hikes. Washington was quite likely
to consider a tax bill in Bush's second year. The president still
wanted to cut the capital gains rate and, as we have said, he
seemed likelier to succeed this time. Besides, in its fiscal 1990
legislation, Washington extended about 10 popular tax breaks
for nine months, starting in January. Included were breaks
for business research and development, employer-paid educational assistance, the hiring of disadvantaged Americans,
the construction of low-income housing, and other pursuits.
A nine-month extension was driven by fiscal considerations,
not by tax policy. Beneficiaries would be far likelier to indulge
in the desired activities if assured that the breaks would last
for awhile. But because tax breaks reduce revenues, a nine-
month extension was all that Washington could afford. And
because these breaks are popular back home, the White House
and its congressional allies saw an advantage in limiting their
life. Recognizing that Congress would probably try to extend
them again, the White House would have a tax bill on which
to affix its capital gains cut.

Along with a capital gains cut and the expiring tax
breaks would probably come another assortment of "cats and
dogs"—$5 billion or so of loophole-closers that could help pay
for various tax benefits that Washington would distribute. But
as for the sizable tax hike that key players believed was central to the Big Deal, that seemed less probable than ever.

Bush showed no sign of bending. When, for instance, Moynihan and Dole said a week apart in October on NBC's "Meet the Press" that each could support a gas tax increase to finance infrastructure improvements, that step was ruled out of bounds by the White House. Nor, at that time, would Transportation Secretary Samuel K. Skinner offer any hint that Bush was flexible, even when pressed hard on CBS's "Face the Nation." Asked whether, in light of the earthquake that rocked northern California in early October, Bush would accept a tax hike to finance repairs, Skinner said, "Well, you know his position, and I know his position."

Panetta feared that for his second year Bush had even more reason to dig in. The Supreme Court's decision in July to give states greater latitude to regulate abortion handed prochoice forces a tool with which to mobilize supporters. No longer were abortion rights covered by the protective umbrella of the 1973 Roe v. Wade decision. Now, such rights could be threatened in 50 state legislatures. The GOP's generally antiabortion stance, extending to the states, represented a new danger on an issue of personal concern to millions of Americans—many of whom were in sync with the GOP on other issues. As a result, prochoice candidates exploited their new advantage in 1989, and antiabortion Republicans were defeated for governor in New Jersey and Virginia, the latter to the first elected black governor since Reconstruction.

The Republican party was wounded, and running scared. Bush complicated matters further. He vetoed three spending bills in late 1989 (one of them twice) because, he said, each contained provisions that conflicted with his antiabortion views. As 1989 drew to a close, Lee Atwater, the party chairman, and other party honchos searched for ways to reconcile the party's far right constituency, which remained adamantly opposed to abortion rights, and its more prochoice supporters. An obvious tactic was to reassure Republican voters who had been drawn to the party for other reasons. The tax issue was one to highlight. Remember, the Republicans could say, this is the party that will *not* raise your taxes. As Panetta put it, "The concern I have is that, with the abortion issue having

hurt them, the tax issue becomes kind of their primary issue.... They might feel like their strongest domestic issue on
a campaign-by-campaign basis is still the tax issue. If they
feel that way, then, you know, that takes care of trying to do
anything on revenues."

■   ■   ■   ■

As we sat in his office in December, Panetta looked tired,
worn out. I suggested that he could not say whether or not
Washington would ever construct a Big Deal. "That's true,"
he replied. I asked whether prospects were growing bleaker.
"I don't want to believe that it takes a crisis of major proportions to force that," he answered, leaning forward, removing
his glasses to rub his eyes. "I mean, deep down, I guess my
underlying fear is that you can't ever put that kind of package together unless we're facing a real economic crisis in this
country." A moment later, he mused, "So the question then
becomes, if you don't want crisis to force it, is the leadership
really there to make it happen? Because you need the leadership there, to provide the cover for the issues that you're
going to take on.... Do you have the leadership to do it?"

The House chairman had returned to one of his fre-
quent refrains about Washington. Action, he often said, comes
through crisis or leadership. "I think the ingredients for the
right political leadership are in place," he went on. "I could
not think of a better group of people to take on this issue than
a George Bush, a Tom Foley, a George Mitchell, a Bob Michel,
and a Bob Dole. That is, there is no one in that group who
I think has an ideological shtick that they're after, or who is
a son of a bitch or somehow is irresponsible. I think the nature of all of those players is to try to do the right thing. The
downside is that because they are so pragmatic, the issue is,
are there some risk-takers there, in terms of their willingness to take on some of these issues?... Is it hot enough, is
it important enough, is it crucial enough to want to get it behind them so they're willing to take some of the heat on some
of the pieces that are going to be involved in this package in
exchange for getting a budget resolution adopted, getting rec-

onciliation adopted, getting it all done in an orderly manner, actually, to some extent, getting this issue behind them?" In other words, getting a Big Deal to solve the problem.

Well, Dole had engineered his own effort some years back. Reagan had just been reelected in the 1984 landslide over Mondale. Maybe in early 1985, with midterm congressional races more than a year away, an immensely popular president and a new Congress could find the courage to solve this problem. As the majority leader, Dole used all the political skills that he had mastered in 25 years of House and Senate service to push a massive package of spending cuts through the Senate on a 50–49 tally. The White House was on board; Vice President Bush, serving as the president of the Senate, cast the deciding vote. But Reagan later backed away. He and Speaker O'Neill agreed to ignore the effort. It collapsed. No comparable one came later in the Reagan years.

Cast your mind forward. It is now September 17, 1989. The House is embroiled in controversy. The Senate is gearing up for the coming battles. Hope for the Big Deal has already evaporated. Dole, now the minority leader, appears on NBC's "Meet the Press." Asked about the prospects for serious deficit cutting in the near or distant future, he says, "It seems to me you have about one shot every four years to deal with the budget deficit. We didn't do it this year; now you almost have to wait until the next—after the next presidential election.... I mean, I think we missed an opportunity this year to make the hard choices."

NOTES

CHAPTER 1

1. Gerald M. Boyd, "Reagan Offers Aquino Wide Support," *New York Times*, Sept. 18, 1986, p. A3.
2. Ernest F. Hollings, "Bush's Real Problem—The Ruins of Reaganism," *Washington Post*, Apr. 30, 1989, p. C1.
3. Paul Volcker, "Who Says We Can't Pay the Costs of Leadership?" *Washington Post*, Dec. 17, 1989, p. B1.
4. Rowland Evans and Robert Novak, "Cuomo: The Hamlet of Albany," *Washington Post*, June 19, 1989, p. A9.
5. Stanley W. Cloud, "The Can't Do Government," *Time*, Oct. 23, 1989, p. 29.
6. David A. Stockman, *The Triumph of Politics* (New York: Avon Books, 1987), p. 442.
7. Theodore J. Lowi, *The End of Liberalism* (New York: W. W. Norton, 1979), pp. 42, 49.
8. Theodore H. White, *America in Search of Itself* (New York: Harper & Row, 1982), pp. 109, 103.
9. William A. Niskanen, *Reaganomics* (New York: Oxford University Press, 1988), p. 280.
10. "Director's Introduction to the New Budget," *Budget of the United States Government, Fiscal Year 1991* (Washington: U. S. Government Printing Office, 1990), p. 15.
11. Jonathan Rauch, "The Fiscal Ice Age," *National Journal*, Jan. 10, 1987, pp. 58–64.
12. Stockman, *Triumph*, p. 165.

13. Tom Kenworthy, "Michel Pulls Out Stops in Rematch of '82 Race," *Washington Post*, Nov. 1, 1988, p. A15.
14. For the changes with regard to congressional committees, staffs, and other related matters, see Norman J. Ornstein, Thomas E. Mann, and Michael J. Malbin, *Vital Statistics on Congress, 1989-1990* (Washington: Congressional Quarterly, 1990); Roger H. Davidson and Carol Hardy, *Indicators of Senate Activity and Workload* (Washington: Congressional Research Service, June 8, 1987); and Roger H. Davidson and Carol Hardy, *Indicators of House of Representatives Activity and Workload* (Washington: Congressional Research Service, June 8, 1987).
15. *Congress Speaks: A Survey of the 100th Congress* (Washington: Center for Responsive Politics, 1988), p. 1.

CHAPTER 2

1. Charles L. Schultze, "Of Wolves, Termites, and Pussycats," *Brookings Review,* Summer 1989, p. 26.
2. Edmund Phelps, "The Golden Rule of Accumulation: A Fable for Growthmen," *American Economic Review*, September 1961, pp. 638–43.
3. Figures in the next several paragraphs come from federal budget documents and from *American Living Standards*, ed. by Robert E. Litan, Robert Z. Lawrence, and Charles L. Schultze (Washington: Brookings Institution, 1988).
4. George Bush, *Building a Better America*, Feb. 19, 1989, p. 18.
5. For a history of the nation's budget balancing fervor, see James D. Savage, *Balanced Budgets and American Politics* (Ithaca: Cornell University Press, 1988).
6. Herbert Stein, *Presidential Economics* (Washington: American Enterprise Institute for Public Policy Research, 1988), p. 135.
7. Robert Kuttner, *The Life of the Party* (New York: Penguin Books, 1988), p. x.
8. Stockman, *Triumph*, p. 44.
9. Robert J. Samuelson, "Deficits: True and False Alarms," *Washington Post*, Oct. 23, 1988, p. C7.
10. Jonathan Rauch, "Is the Deficit Really So Bad," *Atlantic*, February 1989, pp. 36–42.
11. Peter T. Kilborn, "Is the Deficit Still Dangerous? Maybe Not, Some Start to Say," *New York Times*, Jan. 23, 1989, p. A1.

12. Edward M. Gramlich, "How Bad Are the Large Deficits?" *Federal Budget Policy in the 1980S*, ed. Gregory B. Mills and John L. Palmer (Washington: Urban Institute Press, 1984), pp. 43–68.
13. Joseph Grundfest, "Explaining the Events of October 1987," *After The Crash*, ed. Robert J. Mackay (Washington: American Enterprise Institute for Public Policy Research, 1988), pp. 22-23.
14. Karen Pennar, "Did the Crash Make a Dent?" *Business Week*, Oct. 17, 1988, p. 88.
15. "Budget Help for the President-To-Be," *New York Times*, May 21, 1988, p. 30.
16. David Rapp, "Deficit Commission Gets Lesson on the Budget, *Congressional Quarterly Weekly Report*, May 14, 1988, p. 1286.
17. Rowland Evans and Robert Novak, "Higher Taxes: A Time Bomb That's Ticking," *Washington Post*, Feb. 24, 1988, p. A25.

CHAPTER 3

1. Alan Murray and Michel McQueen, "Pinching Pennies: Bush Proposes Array of New Programs, Little Extra Spending," *Wall Street Journal*, Feb. 10, 1989, p. A1.
2. Arthur M. Schlesinger, Jr., *The Cycles of American History* (Boston: Houghton Mifflin, 1986), p. 47.
3. Congressional Budget Office, *Trends in Family Income: 1970–1986* (Washington: U. S. Government Printing Office, February 1988), p. xx.
4. *Americans Talk Security* (Boston: Marttila & Kiley, April 1988), p. 44.
5. Daniel Burstein, "A Yen for New York," *New York*, Jan. 16, 1989, pp. 26–36.
6. *Americans Talk Security* (Boston: Marttila & Kiley, September 1988), p. 14.
7. Paul Kennedy, *The Rise and Fall of the Great Powers* (New York: Random House, 1987), p. 515.
8. Peter Schmeisser, "Taking Stock: Is America in Decline?" *New York Times Magazine*, April 17, 1988, p. 24.
9. David P. Calleo, *Beyond American Hegemony* (New York: Basic Books, 1987).
10. Walter Russell Mead, *Mortal Splendor* (Boston: Houghton Mifflin, 1987), p. 10.

11. George Bush, *Looking Forward* (Toronto: Bantam Books, 1988), p. 25.

12. Ibid. p. 65.

13. "A Talk with Bush: 'People Won't Want to Gamble.' " *Business Week*, Aug. 22, 1988, p. 31.

14. Robin Toner, "Congress Still Purring as Bush Applies the Right Strokes," *New York Times*, Jan. 31, 1989, p. A20.

15. Francis X. Clines, "Reagan's Master of Compromise," *New York Times Magazine*, Feb. 16, 1986, p. 38.

16. Peter T. Kilborn, "Talks by Darman Show Bush's Plan to Handle Budget," *New York Times*, Jan. 5, 1989, p. B10.

17. Susan Irving, "Bushlit," *New Republic*, Aug. 1, 1988, p. 16.

18. Paul Magnusson and Mike McNamee, "How to Balance a Budget, by George Bush," *Business Week*, Aug. 22, 1988, p. 33.

19. Peter T. Kilborn, "Some of Bush's Advisers Challenged Budget Plan," *New York Times*, Dec. 14, 1988, p. B13.

CHAPTER 4

1. Walter Shapiro, "Reaganomics with a Human Face," *Time*, Feb. 20, 1989, p. 34.

2. David Rapp, "New Budget Chairmen: Ready for the Spotlight," *Congressional Quarterly Weekly Report*, Dec. 17, 1988, p. 3534.

3. *Politics in America*, ed. Alan Ehrenhalt (Washington: Congressional Quarterly, 1987), p. 1399.

4. Paul Blustein, "The Charming New Darman," *Washington Post*, May 14, 1989, p. H1.

5. Thomas M. DeFrank and Ann McDaniel, "Say Hello to Charmin' Darman," *Newsweek*, June 5, 1989, p. 24.

6. Clines, "Reagan's Master of Compromise," pp. 36–37.

CHAPTER 5

1. John R. Cranford, "A History of the Thrift Industry.... The 1800s to the Current Crisis," *Congressional Quarterly Weekly Report*, Feb. 18, 1989, pp. 306–10.

2. Jerry Knight, "GAO Raises Estimate of S&L Bailout Cost," *Washington Post*, Sept. 16, 1988, p. C11.
3. House Government Operations Committee, "Combating Fraud, Abuse and Misconduct in the Nation's Financial Institutions: Current Federal Efforts Are Inadequate" (Washington: U. S. Government Printing Office, 1988), pp. 10–11.
4. Paul Duke, Jr., "Easy Money: How Texas S&L Grew into a Lending Giant and Lost $1.4 Billion," *Wall Street Journal*, Apr. 27, 1989, p. 1.
5. Thomas Moore, "The Bust of '89," *U. S. News & World Report*, Jan. 23, 1989, p. 40.
6. David Maraniss and Rick Atkinson, "Hardening the S&L Battle Lines," *Washington Post*, June 14, 1989, p. A1.
7. Jill Abramson, "Revolving Door: S&L Mess Isn't All Bad, at Least for Lawyers Who Were Regulators," *Wall Street Journal*, Jan. 31, 1989, p. 1.
8. Leslie Wayne, "Where Were the Accountants?" *New York Times*, March 12, 1989, Sec. III, p. 1.
9. Richard Morin, "S&L PACs Gave $1.8 Million in '88," *Washington Post*, July 28, 1989, p. A22.
10. Brooks Jackson and Paulette Thomas, "Waning Power: As S&L Crisis Grows, U. S. Savings League Loses Lobbying Clout," *Wall Street Journal*, March 7, 1989, p. 1.
11. Brooks Jackson, *Honest Graft* (New York: Alfred A. Knopf, 1988).
12. Nathaniel C. Nash, "Time of Crisis for Savings League," *New York Times*, Oct. 31, 1988, p. D1.
13. Donald F. Kettl, *Government by Proxy* (Washington: Congressional Quarterly, 1988), p. ix.
14. *Beyond Privatization*, ed. Lester M. Salamon (Washington: Urban Institute Press, 1989), p. 9.
15. Harold Seidman, "The Quasi World of the Federal Government," *Brookings Review*, Summer 1988, pp. 23–24.
16. "The S&L Budget Dodge," *Washington Post*, Apr. 10, 1989, p. A8.
17. "Thriftier Trickery for the Thrifts," *New York Times*, Apr. 5, 1989, p. A28.
18. "We Need You, Toto," *Wall Street Journal*, Apr. 13, 1989, p. A22.

19. Martin Feldstein, "FSLIC Funding Belongs Off-Budget," *Wall Street Journal*, March 1, 1989, p. A14.

20. Paulette Thomas and Alan Murray, "The Lines Are Drawn for a Macho Political Battle on How to Finance the S&L Bailout Package," *Wall Street Journal*, May 12, 1989, p. A16.

21. House Ways and Means Committee, "Financial Institutions Reform, Recovery and Enforcement Act of 1989" (Washington: U. S. Government Printing Office, 1989), p. 53.

22. Paulette Thomas, "Compromise Set on Funding S&L's Rescue," *Wall Street Journal*, Aug. 4, 1989, p. A3.

CHAPTER 6

1. "What's Darman Up to Now?" *Federal Budget Report* (Arlington: Pasha Publications, June 19, 1989), p. 1.

2. Hobart Rowen, "Fraud in Budgeting," *Washington Post*, Apr. 20, 1989, p. A19.

3. "Paper Cuts," *Washington Post*, Apr. 16, 1989, p. B6.

4. "Phantom of the Rose Garden," *New York Times*, Apr. 15, 1989, p. 26.

5. "A Rose Garden Ruse," *Philadelphia Inquirer*, Apr. 16, 1989, p. 6F.

6. "A 'Feel-Good' Budget Agreement," *Chicago Tribune*, Apr. 17, 1989, Sec. 1, p. 16.

7. Walter Shapiro, "Wait Till Next Year," *Time*, Apr. 24, 1989, p. 19.

8. David Pauly, "A Budget Deal in Record Time," *Newsweek*, Apr. 24, 1989, p. 36.

9. "Washington Wire," *Wall Street Journal*, Aug. 25, 1989, p. 1.

10. James A. Barnes, "Partisanship," *National Journal*, Nov. 7, 1987, p. 2825.

11. Richard B. Cheney, "An Unruly House: A Republican View," *Public Opinion*, January-February 1989, p. 41.

12. Janet Hook, "House Outlook for 1989: More Partisan Strife," *Congressional Quarterly Weekly Report*, Dec. 10, 1988, p. 3470.

13. Jonathan Alter, "The World of Congress," *Newsweek*, Apr. 24, 1989, pp. 28–29.

14. Richard Morin and Dan Balz, "Majority in Poll Criticize Congress," *Washington Post*, May 26, 1989, p. A8.

15. Bill Alexander, "My Fellow Democrats: Answer Gingrich or Lose," *New York Times*, Apr. 25, 1989, p. A29.
16. Leon E. Panetta, "Who Will Pay for Bush's 'Vision'?" *Washington Post*, Aug. 3, 1989, p. A27.

CHAPTER 7

1. George F. Will, "Taxation Isn't Tyranny," *Washington Post*, Apr. 13, 1989, p. A31.
2. Frederick Jackson Turner, *The Frontier in American History* (New York: Henry Holt, 1921), p. 30.
3. Stockman, *Triumph*, p. 449.
4. Theodore P. Seto, "Snookered on Taxes," *New York Times*, Oct. 17, 1989, p. A27.
5. Tom Redburn, "Rostenkowski May Be Ready to Deal on Tax Cut for Capital Gains," *Los Angeles Times*, May 28, 1989, Pt. IV, p. 1.
6. Peter J. Davis, Jr., "Bush, Rostenkowski Agree to One-Year Capital Gains Tax Cut," *Potomac Perspective* (Arlington: Prudential-Bache Securities, June 7, 1989), pp. 1–2.
7. Robert D. Hershey, Jr., "Rostenkowski Is Reconsidering Opposition to Capital-Gains Cut," *New York Times*, June 8, 1989, p. A1.
8. Ed Jenkins, "Capital Gains Tax Cut Will Benefit All of Us," *USA Today*, Sept. 22, 1989, p. 6A.
9. "Election Polling," *Gallup Poll* (Princeton: Gallup Organization, July 8–10, 1988).
10. "Class Warfare and Democratic Historical Precedents," *American Political Report* (Bethesda: American Political Research Corp., Sept. 29, 1989), p. 4.
11. Ronald D. Elving, "Capital Gains Cut May Trigger Dismantling of 1986 Bill," *Congressional Quarterly Weekly Report*, Sept. 23, 1989, p. 2448.
12. Rob Bennett, "Don't Do the Right Thing," *Tax Notes*, Oct. 2, 1989, p. 117.
13. Jeffrey H. Birnbaum, "Rostenkowski, Buttered by Bush and Battered by Democrats, Erred Badly on Capital Gains," *Wall Street Journal*, Sept. 19, 1989, p. A32.
14. Susan F. Rasky, "For the Chairman of a Powerful Committee,

the House Is No Longer Home," *New York Times*, Nov. 20, 1989, p. A14.

15. "The Democrats in Disarray," *Congressional Quarterly Weekly Report*, Sept. 30, 1989.

CHAPTER 8

1. Jonathan Rauch, "Kids as Capital," *Atlantic*, August 1989, pp. 56–61.
2. *Children in Need* (New York, Committee for Economic Development, 1987), p. 4.
3. *American Agenda*, p. 4.
4. Daniel Goleman, "New Measure Finds Growing Hardship for Youth," *New York Times*, Oct. 19, 1989, p. B19.
5. Timothy Smeeding, Barbara Boyle Torrey, and Martin Rein, "Patterns of Income and Poverty," in *The Vulnerable*, ed. John L. Palmer, Timothy Smeeding, and Barbara Boyle Torrey (Washington: Urban Institute Press, 1988), pp. 115–16.
6. Nancy J. Perry, "Saving the Schools: How Business Can Help," *Fortune*, Nov. 7, 1988, p. 42.
7. "The Democrats and Grandbaby Lily," *New York Times*, July 24, 1988, p. A24.
8. Barbara Vobejda, "Day-Care Centers Supplant Factories in Campaign Imagery," *Washington Post*, Oct. 12, 1988, p. A12.
9. Report of the Secretary's Task Force, *Child Care: A Workforce Issue* (Washington: U. S. Department of Labor, April 1988), p. 11.
10. Ibid, p. 5.
11. Douglas J. Besharov, "The Politics of Day Care," *Washington Post*, Aug. 21, 1988, p. C5.
12. Paul J. Samuelson, "Government, Child Care Don't Mix," *Washington Post*, June 22, 1988, p. F1.

CHAPTER 9

1. George F. Will, "The Social Security Surplus Scam," *Washington Post*, Jan. 11, 1990, p. A23.
2. Rowland Evans and Robert Novak, "Sen. Moynihan's Social Security Bomb," *Washington Post*, Jan. 10, 1990, p. A19.

3. Paul A. Gigot, "Tax Cut Fever, the Sequel: Coming Soon," *Wall Street Journal*, Jan. 5, 1990, p. A6.

4. Ronald D. Elving, "Moynihan Seeks to Roll Back Social Security Tax Rate," *Congressional Quarterly Weekly Report*, Jan. 6, 1990, p. 32.

5. Ibid.

6. Michael Kinsley, "A Liberal Tax Cut," *Washington Post*, Dec. 21, 1989. p. A29.

7. *Report of the National Economic Commission* (Washington: National Economic Commission, Mar. 1, 1989), pp. 56–57.

8. Ibid., p. 49.

9. Rudolph G. Penner, *Social Security and National Saving* (New York: Committee for Economic Development, 1989), p. 21.

10. Steven V. Roberts, "From Charmin' Darman to Tricky Dick," *U. S. News & World Report*, Jan. 22, 1990, p. 44.

11. Stockman, *Triumph*, p. 457.

12. Helen Dewar and Tom Kenworthy, "Dismissing Veto Threat, Hill Democrats Push Deficit-Cut Package," *Washington Post*, Nov. 4, 1989, p. A8.

13. Jackie Calmes, "Deficit Bill Expected to Count Some Gramm-Rudman Cuts," *Congressional Quarterly Weekly Report*, Nov. 11, 1989, p. 3039.

14. National Committee to Preserve Social Security and Medicare, Washington, letter, 1989.

15. National Committee to Preserve Social Security and Medicare, Washington, legislative alert, 1989.

16. Karen Pennar and Michael J. Mandel, "The Peace Economy," *Business Week*, Dec. 11, 1989, pp. 50–55.

INDEX

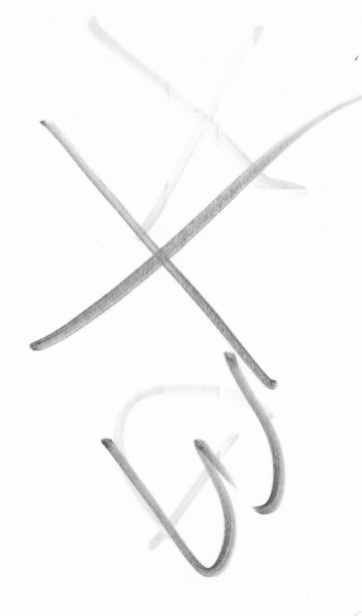